EDWARD BOND

Plays : Four

The Worlds
The Activists Papers
Restoration
Summer

Methuen Drama

Edward Bond
A Chronology

	First performance
The Pope's Wedding	9.12.1962
Saved	3.11.1965
A Chaste Maid in Cheapside (*adaptation*)	13.1.1966
The Three Sisters (*translation*)	18.4.1967
Early Morning	31.3.1968
Narrow Road to the Deep North	24.6.1968
Black Mass (*part of* Sharpeville Sequence)	22.3.1970
Passion	11.4.1971
Lear	29.9.1971
The Sea	22.5.1973
Bingo: Scenes of money and death	14.11.1973
Spring Awakening (*translation*)	28.5.1974
The Fool: Scenes of bread and love	18.11.1975
Stone	8.6.1976
We Come to the River	12.7.1976
The White Devil (*adaptation*)	12.7.1976
Grandma Faust (*part one of* A-A-America!)	25.10.1976
The Swing (*part two of* A-A-America!)	22.11.1976
The Bundle: New Narrow Road to the Deep North	13.1.1978
The Woman	10.8.1978
The Worlds	8.3.1979
Restoration	21.7.1981
Summer	27.1.1982
Derek	18.10.1982
After the Assassinations	1.3.1983
The Cat (*performed as* The English Cat)	2.6.1983
Human Cannon	5.7.1986
The War Plays	
Part I: Red Black and Ignorant	29.5.1985
Part II: The Tin Can People	29.5.1985
Part III: Great Peace	17.7.1985
Jackets	24.1.1989
September	16.9.1989
In the Company of Men	(published 1990)
Olly's Prison (three TV plays)	1992

Edward Bond
Plays: Four

The Worlds, The Activists Papers, Restoration, Summer

The Worlds: 'Mr Bond is at his best in attacking the hypocrisy that condemns one kind of violence while ignoring or justifying another. The play has the customary Bondian values of speed, clarity and economy.'
Robert Cushman, *Observer*

Restoration: 'Mr Bond's great gift as a comic moralist makes Lord Are condemn himself without sacrificing a scintilla of wit. Bond takes the Restoration style, enters it and turns it against itself.'
Robert Cushman, *Observer*

Summer: 'Wonderfully sinewy and vivid.' Francis King, *Sunday Telegraph*

'The plot is revealed slowly and skilfully . . . the writing is as strong and clear as the sunlight.'
Mark Amory, *Spectator*

Also included in this volume are *The Activists Papers* (a commentary on *The Worlds*) as well as Nick Bicât's music to *Restoration*, written for the Royal Court production in 1981 and poems and prose by Edward Bond, written for the Royal Shakespeare Company's Swan Theatre production of the play in 1988.

Edward Bond was born and educated in London. His plays include *The Pope's Wedding* (Royal Court Theatre, 1962), *Saved* (Royal Court, 1965), *Early Morning* (Royal Court, 1968), *Narrow Road to the Deep North* (Belgrade Theatre, Coventry, 1968; Royal Court, 1969), *Black Mass* (Sharpeville Commemoration Evening, Lyceum Theatre, 1970), *Passion* (CND Rally, Alexandra Palace, 1971), *Lear* (Royal Court, 1971), *The Sea* (Royal Court, 1973), *Bingo* (Northcott, Exeter, 1973; Royal Court, 1974), *The Fool* (Royal Court, 1975), *The Bundle* (RSC Warehouse, 1978), *The Woman* (National Theatre, 1978), *The Worlds* (New Half Moon Theatre, London, 1981), *Restoration* (Royal Court, 1981), *Summer* (National Theatre, 1982), *Derek* (RSC Youth Festival, The Other Place, Stratford-upon-Avon, 1982), *The Cat* (produced in Germany as *The English Cat* by the Stuttgart Opera, 1983), *Human Cannon* (Quantum Theatre, Manchester, 1986), *The War Plays (Red Black and Ignorant, The Tin Can People* and *Great Peace*) which were staged as a trilogy by the RSC at the Barbican Pit in 1985, *Jackets* (Leicester Haymarket, 1989), *September* (Canterbury Cathedral, 1989) and *Olly's Prison* (three plays for television, BBC 2 1992). *In the Company of Men* was published in 1990. His *Theatre Poems and Songs* were published in 1978 and *Poems 1978–1985* in 1987.

METHUEN WORLD DRAMATISTS

5 7 9 10 8 6

This edition first published in Great Britain in 1992
by Methuen Drama

Random House UK Limited
20 Vauxhall Bridge Road, London SW1V 2SA
and Australia, New Zealand and South Africa

Distributed in the United States of America by Heinemann, a division of Reed Elsevier,
361 Hanover Street, Portsmouth, New Hampshire NH 03801 3959

The Worlds first published by Eyre Methuen Limited in 1980, revised 1992.
Copyright © 1980, 1992 by Edward Bond.

The Activists Papers first published by Eyre Methuen Limited in 1980, revised 1992.
Copyright © 1980, 1992 by Edward Bond.

Restoration first published by Eyre Methuen in 1981, revised edition published by
Methuen London Limited in 1982 and revised again in 1988 and published by
Methuen Drama in the Swan Theatre Series. Revised for this edition in 1992.
Copyright © 1981, 1982, 1988, 1992 by Edward Bond.

Music for *Restoration* copyright © 1981 by Nick Bicât. The Melodies are included
in this volume after the play; full orchestration can be obtained from London
Management and Representation Ltd., 235–241 Regent Street, London W1R 7AG.

Poems and Stories to *Restoration*: 'A Story' first published by Methuen London
Limited in 1983 in *Derek and Choruses from After the Assassinations*,
copyright © 1983 by Edward Bond. 'Sports Ground Inferno' first published by
Methuen London Limited in 1987 in *Poems 1978–1985*, copyright © 1987
by Edward Bond. 'Water' first published by Methuen London Limited in 1982 in
Summer and Fables, copyright © 1982 by Edward Bond. 'Poets', 'A Hand',
'The Falklands Quotations and Poems', The Lord of the Beasts', 'I Could Not Say',
'The Window', 'You Are the First Generation', 'The Swallows' first published by
Methuen Drama in *Restoration*, the Swan edition, in 1988, copyright © 1988 by
Edward Bond

Summer and *Poems* first published by Methuen London Limited in 1982,
revised edition in 1982. Revised for this edition in 1992.
Copyright © 1982, 1992 by Edward Bond.

ISBN 0–413–46830–3

A CIP catalogue record for this book is available from The British Library.

*The front cover shows 'Death of the Suitors' by Henry Moore/The Trustees,
The Cecil Higgins Art Gallery, Bedford, England.
The photograph of Edward Bond on the back cover is by Charles N White.*

Printed and bound in Great Britain by Cox & Wyman Ltd, Reading, Berkshire

The Worlds

CAST

TRENCH
HUBBARD
KENDAL
HARRIS
TERRY
RAY
JOHN
LORD BIGDYKE
POLICE CHIEF
GATE
BARWAY
MICHAEL
THE PERFECT WAITER
WHITE FIGURE
ANNA
LISA
BERYL
MARIAN
SYLVIA
PRU
LOUISE LINNELL
TWO VOICES (off), one man and one woman

LIST OF SCENES

PART TWO

NOTE

Some of the speeches in this play have titles. The titles are not to be spoken by the actors. They are intended to be a guide to interpretation.

E.B.

The Worlds was first performed by Newcastle University Theatre Society at the Newcastle Playhouse on 8th March 1979 with the following cast:

TRENCH	Graham Blockey
HUBBARD	Andrew O'Hanlon
KENDAL	Ken Price
HARRIS	Steve Bolam
TERRY	Dave Spear
RAY	Tony Dunn
JOHN	Harry Nodwell
LORD BIGDYKE	James Carpmale
POLICE CHIEF	Owen Aaronovitch
GATE	Guy Holmes
BARWAY	Tim Wyatt
MICHAEL	James Nuttgens
THE PERFECT WAITER	Brian Farrell
WHITE FIGURE	Tim Wyatt
ANNA	Louise Kerr
LISA	Alison Southern
BERYL	Nicola Rotsos
MARIAN	Peta Hoult
SYLVIA	Vicki Bennison
PRU	Caroline Hall
LOUISE LINNELL	Debbie Bestwick
JOAN	Sarah Smith

Directed by Edward Bond (*assisted by* Peter Biddle)
Designed by Hayden Griffin and Eamon D'Arcy
Lighting by Andy Phillips (*assisted by* Lolly Schenck)
Scenic artist Dave Lawes; *Production Assistant* Craig Dickson;
Set construction Phillip Bailey; *Properties* Alix Gibson;
Sound Dave Cross; *Wardrobe* Kim Ridley

The Worlds was also presented by The Activists Youth Theatre Club at The Royal Court Theatre Upstairs, London on 21st November 1979 with the following cast:

TRENCH	Geoff Church
HUBBARD	Lindsay Joe Wesker
KENDAL	Mark French
HARRIS	Tom Hodgkins
TERRY	Dan Hildebrand
RAY	Gordon Warren
JOHN	Dave Toneri
LORD BIGDYKE	Bart Peel
POLICE CHIEF	Matthew Purves
GATE	Peter Watson
MICHAEL	Peter Malan
WHITE FIGURE	Patrick Bailey
ANNA	Julie Wallace
LISA	Faith Tingle
BERYL	Belinda Blanchard
MARIAN	Jessica Hawkesly
SYLVIA	Fiona McAlpine
PRU	Diana Judd
LOUISE LINNELL	Caroline Cook

Directed by Edward Bond (*assisted by* Peter Cox)
Designed by Eamon D'arcy
Lighting by Andy Phillips
Sound Peter Deacon
Stage Manager Matthew Richardson (*assisted by* Rebecca Madron, Meganne Hover, Lucy Hornak, Tom Moeschinger)

Two changes in the cast were made for this production. The artist BARWAY was not cast. His 'presence' was created by the reactions of the actors. His line on page 14 was spoken by HUBBARD. His lines on page 16 were cut. THE PERFECT WAITER and MICHAEL were made the same person.

Part One

ONE

Country Hotel

TRENCH *in an armchair*. HUBBARD, KENDAL *and* HARRIS *stand round him*. BARWAY *sketches*.

TRENCH. When the war ended I came out of the army with a scar, a demob suit with a few quid in the pocket and a lot of experience of life and men rammed into six years. I invested that and a lot of hard work and long hours. The result: TCC. It's not all due to me. I know what I owe the team. Some of us have been together for a long time. Some of us are newer comers. But we can all call ourself one of the team.

REST. Here here.

TRENCH (*toast*). To thirty years.

REST. Thirty years.

HUBBARD (*toasting*). And to you JT for the –

KENDAL. Great meal JT.

HARRIS. Well JT at dinner you talked of experience –

KENDAL. Excellent salmon.

HARRIS. – and determination. Right. And I'm not afraid of mentioning a few more old-fashioned virtues. Such as guts. Go out and get it. Self-help. Young people ask for adventure. Well running our organization is adventure!

TRENCH. It is.

HARRIS. Goodlor! Leading four thousand men. Understanding their motivation. Being father. Friend. Disciplinarian when need be. Holding the crew on –

TRENCH. Indeed. We don't often get a chance to talk like this. That's wrong. Job can't be done if you lose the long

view. Now you say the young. What about Kendal's boys?
If I had lads I'd've hoped they turned out like them. If I
have my way they're coming into the team. Mind they'll
have to prove themselves.

KENDAL. They're keen to do it JT.

HARRIS. Yes Ken's lads are turning out just like their father.

TRENCH. Ronnie's right: a changing world. And we're part
of the change. America was there before Columbus discovered it. But we're *making* a new world. Those who have
the stuff of the builder in them.

HUBBARD (*toasting*). And to you JT for the –

KENDAL. Wait a mo Jimmy. I'd like to hear JT on that.

TRENCH. Stuff of the builder?

KENDAL. What is that?

TRENCH (*puffs cheeks, then*): Phoo ... well.

KENDAL. One part intelligence to two parts character and a
squeeze of recklessness shaken up with a lot of experience.

> HUBBARD *retires to one side. The bottle dangles from his
> hand. He tries to stay awake.*

TRENCH. What is character?

HARRIS. Ah there we are.

TRENCH. We can measure intelligence. But how to measure
character? That is the question. Well it's a country
weekend so let's play a game. I ask my think tank: what is
character?

HARRIS (*Looks at* KENDAL). We all know what it is.

KENDAL. But how to define it.

HARRIS. Pon my word yes.

HUBBARD. Ickle more vino? (*He fills his glass.*)

KENDAL. The way a chap looks at you. And the handshake.

TRENCH. Hm. Could be con tricks.

KENDAL. O I don't know JT.

HARRIS. I agree with JT. Sorry.

KENDAL. You can train yourself to spot the creepy-crawlies.

HUBBARD. Do a market survey.

HARRIS. Life. You see if a man fails that.

TRENCH. Mm. Young fella out of college comes in your office. Calls you sir. Looks you in the eye. Why not? – he doesn't know the problem. Firm handshake? – could be brazen. Will it shake when he puts it in the till? And you can't tell if he's failed in life because he hasn't lived it.

HARRIS. Spot on JT.

HUBBARD. Put us out of our misery.

TRENCH. You chaps have all got it. It's the whole man.

HARRIS. Ah now ... that is clever ... the whole man.

TRENCH. He respects and judges you as he does himself. What you invest in a man is what you get out of him. Yes, at times we do harsh things. But we do it cleanly. For the good of the customer. With no malice. No pleasure. We push a man overboard and we sail on. But we throw a lifebelt in the sea behind us. We're all brothers. Big brothers and little brothers. As in every family. At the end of the day we can all offer the next man our hand. Be he from the shop floor or the directors' suite. Couldn't do the job if I didn't believe that.

KENDAL. O it's rewarding to have these talks.

TRENCH. I don't apologize for saying that.

KENDAL. My god what an age when you have to apologize for being profound!

TRENCH. Well now. You may have noticed a little man.

KENDAL. Ha ha.

TRENCH. No doubt you're wondering who he is.

HARRIS. One of JT's little surprises.

HUBBARD. Thought you'd wined us so well I was seeing things.

TRENCH. And what he's scribbling on his pad.

KENDAL. Ha ha. Tax inspector.

TRENCH (*snap*). Artist.

KENDAL (*defensive*). Well they all wear long hair these days.

TRENCH. I'm marking our thirty years with a portrait.

HARRIS. O splendid.

KENDAL. And generous JT. Painter laddies don't come cheap.

TRENCH. Mind not a portrait of me. The team.

HARRIS. Ah now.

TRENCH. Don't want me scowling down at you from the wall as well as from the top of the table.

KENDAL. A handsome gesture.

TRENCH. Thought I'd do it.

BARWAY. Head up a shade.

KENDAL. Sorry old man. My wife's mother paints.

HARRIS. You amaze me JT.

TRENCH. Say why Ronnie.

HARRIS. For two weeks the organization's been paralysed by strike. Thirty per cent demand. No sign of breakthrough. And you invite us away for a pleasant weekend in a fine country hotel in beautiful grounds as your personal guests. You've had a gruelling week and a long drive down. And you sit there and discuss art and life. And you make sense.

TRENCH. We're funny people.

KENDAL. My god I wish there were a few more of us. JT you know me well enough for me to say this and not be misunderstood.

HUBBARD (to himself). Might as well empty the bottle. Insult to waste wine of this calibre. (He pours himself a drink.)

KENDAL. Anyway it ought to be said. Neck out then. If we're being philosophical – and there's no harm in that when it's past midnight as long as you don't make it a habit – then I'll be philosophical. It might not be Spinoza but it's worth a thought. How d'you judge a chap? You said JT: not from the eyes. You're right JT. You're not often not. But I put this question: how does a chap judge himself?

HUBBARD (to himself). First class vino.

TRENCH. Have I got that right?

KENDAL. How d'you look into your own eyes so to speak? (*Shrugs.*) I don't know the answer to that one. But you gave me a clue JT. Let it drop quite casually. Probably didn't even notice the significance it would have for us young ones. Trust. Yes, trust. You threw the word at us: trust. I jumped on that.

HUBBARD. Ready for shut-eye JT?

TRENCH. No this is interesting. Ken?

KENDAL (*panicking*). Well. As I say. I'm no Spinoza.

TRENCH. We're all friends here.

KENDAL (*floundering*). What-say we reformulate it like this: you have to take yourself on trust before you can trust yourself.

HUBBARD. Don't paint me holding the bottle.

KENDAL. How else can those four thousand men trust *you*? They can tell. (*Reassured at suddenly finding safe ground.*) By jimminy yes. You can't lie on the shop floor. That place is sacred.

HUBBARD. I trust you Ken.

KENDAL. Thankyou Hub. And I trust myself when I tell JT – and this is my philosophical remark: JT I'm a better man for knowing you. O there'll be sneerers. And others will say you don't say these things.

HARRIS. Well you've said it.

TRENCH. And I'm grateful.

KENDAL (*quiet malice*). What Ronnie calls the organization's worst moment – it's not for me to second that (who's to know the struggles of your early years?) but let's say: a nasty corner – and you calmly talk such wisdom. My god.

TRENCH. Now now.

KENDAL. I'm glad I said it.

TRENCH. No more thanks. It's past you youngsters' bed-time. Leave us old ones to bore ourselves to sleep.

KENDAL. Night JT. Godbless.

HARRIS. Night JT. And you Jimmy. Sleep well.

HUBBARD. Nighty-o.

> TRENCH *raises a hand in benediction.* KENDAL *and* HARRIS *go.*

TRENCH. Did you get your doodles Mr Barway?

BARWAY. One or two.

TRENCH. Catch their character. That'll prove if you're an artist. They're good lads: I almost look on them as sons. I await the masterpiece. (*He waves* BARWAY *goodnight.*) Goodnight.

BARWAY. Goodnight Mr Trench. Mr Hubbard.

> BARWAY *goes.*

An Advertisement

TRENCH. A running stream. A sky of piercing blue. No cloud. Grass and heather dry in the wind. Crisp. The water. Fish leaping well. It would be nice. To spend the days like that. They get less. (HUBBARD *snorts.*) Despatch box sent down to the lodge. Drop into the office now and then. A day in town. Drop in the club. Give you the benefit of my experience. The hot line always by my hand.

*

HUBBARD. If you don't mind I'll turn in.

A Menu

TRENCH. Fancy a walk in the morning? Come back to bacon, eggs, sausages, mushrooms, toast, rolls, butter, marmalade, fresh orange juice, coffee or tea. They do a first class kedgeree. Early morning walk take years off you. Come back like school boys. The views! Magnificence. You catch your breath.

*

HUBBARD. If I wake up. Shall I order your night cap?

TRENCH. Please. I'll expect you early. I've brought some papers for you to vet. As I'm paying for the weekend.

HUBBARD. Night then.

> HUBBARD *goes.* TRENCH *picks up a book of poems. He reads.* THE PERFECT WAITER *comes in. He carries a whisky and a bottle of soda on a silver tray.*

THE PERFECT WAITER. Goodevening sir.

TRENCH. You didn't know managing directors read poetry.

THE PERFECT WAITER. It's very nice to see sir. Shall I pour the soda sir?

TRENCH (*reading*). If you'd be so kind.

> THE PERFECT WAITER *pours.* Hands the drink to TRENCH. *Picks up the empty wine glass from beside his chair.*

THE PERFECT WAITER. Will that be all sir? (TRENCH *nods.*) Goodnight sir.

> THE PERFECT WAITER *goes.* TRENCH *drinks the whisky in two gulps. Closes the book. Lets it fall to the floor. Collapses.* THE PERFECT WAITER *comes back.*

THE PERFECT WAITER. You called sir?

> THE PERFECT WAITER *goes to* TRENCH, *looks at him and goes out. His face remains set in* THE PERFECT WAITER'*s expression.* LISA *and* MICHAEL *come in. They carry guns. Their faces are hidden under balaclavas.* MICHAEL *gives his gun to* LISA. *He puts* TRENCH *across his shoulder.* LISA *keeps watch. They move towards the door.* THE PERFECT WAITER *comes back.*

THE PERFECT WAITER (*politely*). The service lift.

> THE PERFECT WAITER *goes.* LISA *and* MICHAEL *go out the other way.*

TWO

Boardroom.

HUBBARD, KENDAL, HARRIS, POLICE CHIEF, LORD BIGDYKE.

HARRIS. How long will it take to find him?

POLICE CHIEF. Good question.

KENDAL. Haven't you any idea?

POLICE CHIEF. Always got ideas. How will your strikers react?

HUBBARD. They're meeting tomorrow.

HARRIS. To think we'd been sitting with him then out of the blue . . .

POLICE CHIEF (*smiling*). If we do find him that's the easier part.

HUBBARD. I take over in the chairman's absence. The first question is: do we have any choice?

BIGDYKE. You have the usual obligations of rational people.

HUBBARD. I'm a businessman, I don't know what that means. Look, our concern is the organization. There's money – but we have to invest for expansion. If we cough up our profitability would take a nasty dent. The chairman or the company? What would he want us to do (*To* KENDAL *and* HARRIS:) – provided he was in a position to give an unbiased verdict.

BIGDYKE. It's natural that you see it from a limited horizon. (*He takes a sheet from his briefcase.*) I've had this from the home secretary. (*He gives the sheet to* KENDAL *who reads it.*) Suppose you're lucky. The strikers are appalled and go back on your terms. The terrorists could still hold him for ransom in the so-to-speak normal way. You say you must consider the good of your company. Fine. But there is another good. The good of society. If you give way you set a precedent. What happens at your next strike? The taking

of hostages is a very primitive way of running our affairs.
Everyone ought to agree on that. We're almost hardened to
terrorism by nationalists, for gain by common criminals,
by political groups out to demoralize and weaken government for their minority ends –

KENDAL *passes the sheet to* HUBBARD. HUBBARD *reads.*

BIGDYKE. – but this is new. Terrorists have abducted the
head of a major company while it's on strike. Unless the
striker's demands are met he'll be shot. Where does this
lead? Suppose your football team had to play a vital match.
You kidnap the Chairman of the opponent club or his child
(the imagination runs on) and threaten to kill him if his side
wins. Imagine the spectators at such a game. In one blow
we'd be back in the arena in Rome.

KENDAL *passes the sheet to* HARRIS. HARRIS *reads.*

BIGDYKE. Or you object to the siting of a motorway. A
power station. A factory. A school. A garage. A dog ken-
nel. Civilization is built on the finding of substitutes for
violence in the conduct of human affairs. The shadow of
violence is very dark: it falls and engulfs everything. There
is your obligation: to society.

Unnoticed by the others the POLICE CHIEF *takes the sheet
from* HARRIS. *He reads it.*

BIGDYKE. You tell me that fortunately it is the same as your
obligation to your organization. So be it. Don't give way.
The deadline of three days will be extended. They always
are. We must give the police time to locate them – and then
be firm and adroit enough to free Mr Trench unscathed.
Meanwhile I suggest you meet the strikers and persuade
them that their obligations to the country, their employers
and themselves are also in this matter – fortunately – the
same. You see the Minister's concern. (*He looks for the*

Minister's letter. The POLICE CHIEF *gives it to him.*) We meet here at three tomorrow. Gentlemen.

POLICE CHIEF. I'll keep you posted. Morning.

OTHERS. Goodmorning.

> LORD BIGDYKE *and the* POLICE CHIEF *go.* HUBBARD *pours himself a drink.*

HUBBARD. Anyone?

HARRIS. I will.

> HUBBARD *pours. He and* HARRIS *drink.*

HARRIS. What'll the strike negotiators do?

HUBBARD. Roll like pigs in treacle.

HARRIS. Why us?

KENDAL. For god's sake Harris!

HARRIS. Why us? I can't get over the –

HUBBARD. Stop squabbling the bloody pair of you. Be grateful for the godsend.

HARRIS (*avoiding the subject*). Tomorrow's negotiations. Let's settle our line.

KENDAL. They'll say the kidnapping's irrelevant. That lot'll be sorry it wasn't all of us.

HARRIS. I think we should make a gesture. Seven percent. We'll have to in the end. It's like playing whist at a funeral parlour.

KENDAL. No way! You heard Lord Bigdyke. We stand firm.

HUBBARD. Harris thinks you stop the dog biting your leg by giving it your arm. If no one else is going to talk about it I am.

HARRIS. You want him dead.

HUBBARD (*pleasantly*). I'm not answering that Harris. It happens to be irrelevant. You know what's what. Trench blocked expansion for years. As long as we got a profit he wagged his tail. The *real* fat – he didn't let us go after that. In our business you expand or drop out. We're sitting comfortably on our arses and soon the chair's going to collapse under us. We need major new investment. There's only one answer: we go public. Put the company on the stock exchange.

HARRIS. All right! But there are some decencies! You don't haggle with the undertaker at the graveside. (*Calms down.*) It can be discussed tomorrow.

HARRIS *goes out.*

KENDAL. What's the use of saying all that to Harris? You know he likes to arrive at the accident after the blood's been spilt. The vampire with clean fangs.

HUBBARD. Exploit the situation: that's what it's about. They'll let JT go just to get him off their tits. If we let this slip away we deserve our bloody dicks chopped off. I waited for it. I hope he's shit scared and I'd like the pleasure of smelling his shit.

KENDAL. Hardly generous.

HUBBARD. Shouldn't read poetry.

THREE

Derelict House.
Empty. ANNA, LISA *and* MICHAEL *carry in* TRENCH. *They also bring camping equipment, supplies and arms. Their faces are hidden under balaclavas. They put* TRENCH *on the floor.* LISA *stands guard at the window.* ANNA *unpacks.*

MICHAEL. Is he alive?

ANNA. Tea.

MICHAEL. Price goes down if they're dead.

ANNA. Dying for a cup.

MICHAEL (*going off*). Always wanted to live in the country.

ANNA. Trench.

TRENCH. Are you going to kill me?

ANNA. Not till you've recorded this message. (*Hands him a sheet of paper.*) Are you listening? Read it first.

A Confused Reading of an Ultimatum

TRENCH (*reads*). This is John Trench. I'm being held by RRA. I will be released when the demands of the TCC workers are met in full. If they are not met by 8 a.m. on Thursday I will be executed. Further hostages will be taken from management until the striker's demands are met. If this RRA unit is discovered other units will take hostages a necessary.

MICHAEL *comes in.*

MICHAEL. Kettle's on. Lisa?

LISA. What?

MICHAEL. We made it. We made it.

LISA. We made it. We made it.

MICHAEL *and* LISA *play a game. They hug each other, rock, laugh and repeat 'We made it', 'Lisa', 'Stop it', 'Come on', etc. – at first quietly and then gradually louder.* TRENCH *reads through it.*

ANNA. They'll be coming for the tape. (*To* TRENCH.) Faster.

TRENCH *reads.* MICHAEL *goes out.*

TRENCH. This is why RRA have taken their action. Many of the needs of human beings can now be met industry. And science have made a sane and contented world. Possible yet it becomes increasingly irrational resources are wasted and poorer countries. Plundered while their people starve people. Are forced to seek their own ends. Without regard for the common good human relations. Are destroyed organization breaks down western society no. Longer works as it becomes increasingly irrational so it – (TRENCH *stops*.) The typing. (*Reads*.) – becomes more violent the working class cannot fit into an irrational society nor can it be coerced into fitting into it. By education inducement force. Or fear it is not enough to say this we must. Say why the working class becomes what it is through the very activity of its work that is. How its characteristic behaviour and opinions are formed clearly this cannot be. Changed the alternative is as. Clear society must be changed the working class must. Control not only production and distribution but also information and education only the working class can. Develop our wasting humanity and make society rational it has created. The physical structure of society now it must create. Its culture . . . (*He stops reading*.) The words.

As TRENCH *reads* ANNA *has gone out. She returns before he finishes reading.*

LISA. Go on.

TRENCH (*reads*). We cannot patiently wait. For society to fall apart reaction armed. With modern technology could make the end of this century a graveyard that is why. We have taken this action modern strikes create. Great tensions they are a seedbed. Of revolution we can therefore expect restrictions to be placed on them this will increase. Conflict once again. It will be shown that the relationships between classes are based. On violence therefore we fight. (*He stops reading. Bewildered*.) The words.

ANNA. Go on.

TRENCH (*reads*). I apologize to my workers for the way I have exploited them. It is my wish that as a small compensation their demands be met in full.

*

MICHAEL has come back. He switches on the tape recorder. He gestures to TRENCH to start. Silence.

MICHAEL (*switches off the machine. Repeats the opening of the ultimatum*). This is John Trench. (*He switches on the machine.*)

TRENCH. This is John Trench. I'm being held by hooligans. Don't give way to –

MICHAEL switches off the tape recorder.

ANNA. God you're stupid.
MICHAEL. Try again.

MICHAEL winds the tape back. He starts it again.

TRENCH. This is John Trench. Somewhere in the country. Derelict house.

MICHAEL stops the tape recorder.

ANNA. Take the pictures.

They put TRENCH against a wall. MICHAEL puts a placard round TRENCH's neck. He takes flashlight snaps.

MICHAEL (*snapping*). Wanted to let the workers hear *you* sweat. Give them a treat. Wouldn't expect you to treat them.
TRENCH. I was killing at your age. In the army. I don't know how many. I killed for what I thought was right –
MICHAEL (*kicks TRENCH*). Shut it.
TRENCH. Why d'you do this? You've got everything you want. You don't know what poverty –
ANNA. The last argument of the philistine: I'm all right. D'you measure everything by the trough?

MICHAEL starts to gag TRENCH.

ANNA. No let him go on. The bourgeois whimper as their world ends.

TRENCH. If you use violence others use it. We can't make these decisions. Society decides.

LISA. Fine if you're society.

MICHAEL. Kettle's on!

MICHAEL *goes.*

TRENCH. TCC won't capitulate. I don't want it.

ANNA. Courage is a vice when you use it in the wrong cause. Nothing you do or say has any value now. Go on, try again.

TRENCH (*trying to explain*). You should be helping to run the world. Not pull it apart. You must have reasons for what you do. Then explain them. Make us listen.

ANNA. We just explained. You read it.

TRENCH. But those – words.

ANNA. Meant nothing to you. This society *can't* explain itself to itself. You understand nothing. Yet the public means of explanation – press, television, theatres, courts, schools, universities – almost everywhere ideas are formed or information is collected is owned in one way or another by people like you. Even our language is owned by you. We have to learn a new language. Even our morals. We have to be different people. You think you can live half your life by the laws of banking and the other half by truth. No. Think! – in a scientific age the last thing most people know anything about is their own life.

LISA. Motorbike.

ANNA *and* LISA *remove their safety catches.* MICHAEL *comes on. He brings his automatic. He is taking the film from the camera.*

LISA (*at the window*). Stopped.

ANNA (*counts*). One. Two. Three. Four. Five. Six.

LISA. Started.

ANNA (*to* MICHAEL). Cover from the front porch. I'll do the message.

> MICHAEL *goes out.* ANNA *takes the paper from* TRENCH *and reads it. The motorbike is heard winding up the hill. As she finishes it stops outside.*

A Clear Reading of an Ultimatum

ANNA. This is why RRA have taken their action. Many of the needs of human beings can now be met. Industry and science have made a sane and contented world possible. Yet it becomes increasingly irrational. Resources are wasted and poorer countries plundered while their people starve. People are forced to seek their own ends without regard for the common good. Human relations are destroyed. Organization breaks down. Western society no longer works. As it becomes increasingly irrational so it becomes more violent. The working class cannot fit into an irrational society. Nor can it be coerced into fitting into it by education, inducement, force or fear. It is not enough to say this. We must say why. The working class becomes what it is through the very activity of its work. That is how its characteristic behaviour and opinions are formed. Clearly this cannot be changed. The alternative is as clear. Society must be changed. The working class must control not only production and distribution but also information and education. Only the working class can develop our wasting humanity and make society rational. It has created the physical structure of society. Now it must create its culture.

We cannot patiently wait for society to fall apart. Reaction armed with modern technology could make the end of this century a graveyard. That is why we have taken this action. Modern strikes create great tensions. They are a seedbed of revolution. We can therefore expect restrictions to be placed on them. This will increase conflict. Once again it will be shown that the relationships between classes are based on violence. Therefore we fight.

*

FOUR

Works Entrance.
Large notice on the wall 'No Naked Flames'.
JOHN, TERRY, RAY, BERYL. *They are very cold. One of them has a placard propped against the legs.*

RAY. Worse than bein in the bloody army. Ain this stint over? Phoo. (*He blows into his hands. Pause.*) Stood here bloody hours.

JOHN (*looks off*). Twenty past.

BERYL. Don't read Trench's clock. He'll take it off yer bleedin packet.

JOHN. And it's never bloody right.

RAY. Bugger puts it on for the start of the shift and turns it back for the end. Worked it out in the admin. Had a conference.

BERYL. Hey-up! old age P.

RAY. Don't like the look of that shopping bag.

JOHN. Here it comes.

RAY. They're making Molotov cocktails at the over-sixties.

OAP (*off*). Layabouts.

A stone is thrown onto the stage.

JOHN. Mornin granma.

OAP (*off*). Scroungers.

JOHN. Annual outin is it?

OAP (*off*). Reds. Went through the war for you lot. Day's work'd kill yer.

RAY. What's a nice old dear like you doin on the street corner? Give the flats a bad name.

JOHN. Show us yer nickers darlin. Dead borin here.

OAP (*off*). Won't laugh when they shut down.

BERYL. Why don't you shut down?

OAP (*off*). Lockin your boss up. Don't play the innocent with me. You got him.

BERYL. Go home yer silly old shit bag.

OAP (*off*). Use language.

BERYL (*throws stone back*). I said piss off.

OAP (*off*) *screams.*

BERYL. Next time I won't miss. Piss off.

JOHN. That's right, public relations. Explain your cause politely and simply to the public. Remember your case has been misrepresented. They have a right to know. Listen before replying.

BERYL. Not my fault you ain well off. If it wasn't for us you'd be stuck in some back room with nothin to eat an no fire or light and the water froze except where it comes through the roof.

JOHN (*to himself*). Probably is.

BERYL. So go home you silly old cow. We have to fight for every tanner. Every time. Don't you call me names you silly old windbag.

OAP (*off*). Murderers!

BERYL. Bloody well will be if I catch you.

BERYL *runs off.* OAP (*off*) *screams.*

JOHN (*to himself*). Dear-o-dear-o-lor.

OAP (*further off*). That's a threat. Goin round the law.

RAY. Chuck it in eh? Stuck here in the bloody cold. Off our rockers. The meetin'll send us back anyway.

TERRY. O yeh?

BERYL *walks slowly back.*

RAY. The lads'll vote it won't they.

BERYL. How'm I goin t' vote?

RAY. By bloody computer.

TERRY. You chuck the strike in?

RAY. Weight of public opinion.

BERYL. Not my bloody opinion.

JOHN. Look we got a case – right?

BERYL. Right.

RAY. Did I say we ain? I come out. I'd a stayed out. I've been a paid-up member since you were in short pants Terry. This is somethin else. If they wanna play silly buggers.

BERYL. Trench is pullin a fast one. He's sunnin it out in Monte Carlo. He could pay us with what he picks up in the casino. Took all his loot back the yacht'd sink. It's time somethin changed.

RAY. I'm all for change.

JOHN. He couldn't change his address if his house burned down.

RAY. It's your common humanity.

JOHN. What the hell's that?

RAY. When you don't fight for money while some poor bleeder's fightin for his life. Keep em in the boot an throw food at em like a dog. Tie gelignite round their chest. Human bloody firework.

TERRY. Don't you learn nothin Ray?

RAY. I learn.

TERRY. Listen. We go back to work. They let Trench go?

JOHN. No. That's the nicety of it.

RAY. Now you listen Terry. What is this – Argentina?

BERYL. Not accordin to the weather forecast.

RAY. Since when we run this country with guns? What

good's guns? You got extra money you'd be robbed takin it home. Not my sort of life mate. So? I'm all for solidarity –

BERYL. Between the ears.

RAY. Not a joke girl.

BERYL. Only a laugh.

TERRY. Look. Someone's got a gun. Who else's got a gun?

BERYL. Annie.

RAY. Shut up.

TERRY. The law. Right – let the law fight it out.

RAY. You gotta back em up.

TERRY. Why? Who's law is it anyway? Only time a workin man goes t' court 'e's in the dock. Anyone down your road trainin for the bar?

BERYL. Only bar they train for s'got beer mats on it.

JOHN. An him on the floor.

RAY. O nice. Now we don't want the police. Right I'll come down your's an turn you over.

TERRY. Look. The law's there to see it all stays where it is – in someone else's pocket. It makes the streets safe for me to go to work in and Trench to drive to the bank in. You can't have one law for a millionaire and a man on the dole. It ain on.

RAY. I'm not havin blood on my hands. Not even Trench's. Couldn't look the wife in the face across the table.

BERYL. Wouldn't bother me.

JOHN. You wanna save Trench?

RAY. Don't tempt me.

JOHN. Then what do you want?

RAY. It's a question of standards.

JOHN. Look. (*He tries to make a diagram.*) There's the terrorist. There's the copper. There's the worker.

RAY. Do what?

JOHN. O shit hell. (*He tries another way.*) Look. You're the terrorist. Terry's the copper. I'm the worker. (*He walks a*

few paces away from them. Stops.) Where am I? Here? No.
(*He walks further away. Stops.*) Here? No. (*Walks as far
away as he can. Stops.*) Here!

RAY. Watch that fly bastard. He'll have it off home.

JOHN. On strike. I wait quietly and say: I sweat my balls off
for all the Trenchs and their rich bints, and their rich little
sonnies in their posh schools, and their classy little slags of
a daughter while they go round screwing multinational-
millionaires an havin their pox cured in private clinics on
what I put in their pockets. And I'm saying I want my
money crook. I work. I've got my finger out and if the
Duke of Edinburgh don't believe it he can smell it and ask
that little wanker the Prince of Wales for a second opinion.
That's all. Now if you lot over there are playing gunfights
that's your pleasure. Bang away. I'm over here askin for
what's mine.

RAY. You put a bullet in him?

JOHN. Not the point.

RAY. Answer the question.

JOHN. Yeh. Push to the top of the queue.

BERYL. We pulled it off before. Strike together, stick
together. That's all it needs.

RAY. Then why nab Trench and bring the law into it?

TERRY. Well. I'm the law. (*He walks to* JOHN. *He makes no
attempt to imitate a policeman's movements or the tone of his
voice.*) An what are you doin sittin on the pavement in the
middle of the shift? Who keeps the crooks out your pad?
None of your lip. I'll give the answers. Who stops you bein
run over? Who finds your kid when it's done a bunk?

JOHN. So?

TERRY. So be a good boy and picket for a few days – you look
as if you could use the rest. Then back to work. You've
been comin too much lately. Work. Only this time – at last
– he don't. That's when I jerk him to his feet an wrap my
truncheon round his stupid neck. (*He turns to* RAY *and*

BERYL.) Terrorists didn't bring the law into it. The law's there all the time only it don't show up. Till someone breaks the rules: the terrorists or the workers. Which is fine. Only the rules are bent. They're not meant to find out who wins but to keep *them* on top. They play the match but their goal's boarded up.

RAY. Rot.

> TERRY *walks back to* BERYL *and* RAY.

TERRY. Look. (*A slight pause.*) I'm a thief. I nick Beryl's purse. (*He does this.*)

BERYL. I know what I've got in there.

TERRY. Where's the law now? It nicks me.

RAY. Quite right.

> TERRY *throws the purse back to* BERYL.

BERYL. Next time ask.

TERRY. Now supposin I got (*He takes money from his pocket.*) six quid in my pocket. I work for that in the factory. (*To* JOHN:) You're Trench this time. (JOHN *comes over to him.*) You say: I want three of them. I'm boss and that's my profit. So Trench nicks three quid. (JOHN *takes three notes.*) But no one shouts thief. Where's the law? So today I don't let Trench get away with it. I take one back. But bein law-abidin I don't nick it. I ask. And when he says no I strike.

> TERRY *folds his arms.*

JOHN. Don't worry me sonny. I'm multinational for a start. Doin very well out of the coolies. Mess me about and you won't have a job to come back to. I'll give it to a computer.

TERRY. So I work it out. I say: I'd better make this strike hurt. Fast. I picket other firms. Bring them out. Make threats. Trench threatened me. Anyway he threatens me all the time: his paw on my packet is a paw on my neck. Well the moment I do that the law turns up. To get my money back? O no – to arrest me. Why? Because I used force.

BERYL. And why didn't Trench have to use force when he took your three quid but –

BERYL.
JOHN. } – you had to use it when you want some of it back?

TERRY. Because we do what we're told – like animals. He spends half of what he nicks makin sure we do. The force is always there – only he doesn't have to use it till you play it his way. Then wham! When you come down to it Trench relies on force as much as any terrorist. Only he calls his law and order. So tell me why I should pick him out of the shit when he made it himself?

BERYL. We'd be off our heads.

JOHN. Yeh! The terrorists have caught Trench at his own game!

RAY. . . . I know why. I wasn't taught much but I learned one thing. When they open up we'll get caught in the crossfire. It's us who get it in the neck.

BERYL (*bitterly*). That's right. They've got us where they want us.

JOHN (*angrily*). It's a rotten bad reason when you think of it.

Silence. They start to trudge back to the picket line.

TERRY (*stops*). How well Trench has got us trained.

RAY (*blows on his hands*). What time's Trench's clock?

JOHN. Can't you tell?

RAY. My eyes. Workin in Trench's bloody transit shed.

BERYL. Quarter to, you blind old git.

RAY (*pause. Quietly*). I hate Trench's guts more than you do. I've worked for him longer than you. When you've worked for him that long you'll find out what it's like to hate. You're in for a surprise. When I'm dead there'll still be a little man inside my head sayin: hate Trench.

TERRY. The meetin.

RAY. Take them. Don't want em nicked.

They take the placards and go.

FIVE

Boardroom.

KENDAL *and* HARRIS.

KENDAL. Just be sure what you're doing is right. These things aren't personal.

HARRIS. I'm not a fish.

KENDAL. All right! (*He calms down.*) It's all been a strain. It's good to be challenged, but ...! (*He changes the subject.*) I can't get used to the bodyguard. No privacy. Like taking the waiter home.

HUBBARD *comes in.*

HUBBARD. Taking snaps. Came through the door like a jack-in-the-box.

KENDAL. How is he?

HUBBARD. Same as ever. Whole admin block turned up. Like a cup final. Typing pool. Messengers.

KENDAL. In his element.

HUBBARD. I want this short. And no rowing from our end. Clear?

TRENCH *comes in.*

TRENCH. I could hardly get away. What a crowd! Sorry, sorry. The typing pool gave me roses. And d'you know what the drawing office gave? An illuminated address. Imagine! I've seen another side of people today. All that smiling.

Handshakes.

HARRIS. Congratulations JT. Congratulations.

KENDAL. Well done JT. Good to see you.

HUBBARD. Looks well.

TRENCH. Thankyou. Thankyou.

HARRIS. Sit down JT.

TRENCH. Don't fuss. I've spent enough time on me bum lately. I told them you wouldn't surrender.

HARRIS. To their face? Goodlor!

TRENCH. I should congratulate *you*. Made up my mind when I came to in the boot. I said: don't whine, see it through. I got their respect. It came through in their conduct. How're your good people?

HARRIS. Upset but fine.

KENDAL. The boys were shaken up JT. You think they don't care. Then a thing like this – and they catch you by surprise. Made me feel I'd done right by them as a –

TRENCH. Fine, fine. This place – I missed it!

HARRIS. You must be tired.

TRENCH. Not a bit. It'll catch up on me tomorrow.

HUBBARD. Well you must take a long vacation somewhere that's –

TRENCH. Vacation! In the middle of a strike? Now Jimmy you surprise me. (*He wags a finger at* HARRIS *and* KENDAL.) Hope he hasn't been getting slack while I was away.

HUBBARD. Let's sit.

HUBBARD, KENDAL *and* HARRIS *sit at the boardtable.*

TRENCH. Work is what I *missed*! I want the financial statement and a full briefing on the strike. This will be good for business. O yes! Kendal I want you to –

HUBBARD. I'll run over what's been happening.

TRENCH. Of course. It's good to see you again. Mind you the security will be an erk. But it's better to be looked after by friends than enemies. I'm taking you and your wives out to dinner at –

HUBBARD. JT.

TRENCH. I'm allowed to rattle on today Jimmy without you point-of-ordering me.

KENDAL. We had a meeting while –

HUBBARD. You were away. JT we're very mindful of the services you rendered TCC.

TRENCH. Nonsense.

HUBBARD. You bore it and nurtured it till it grew. Now it wants to go out in the world.

TRENCH (*coldly*). Go public? You know my views.

HUBBARD. This moment – after the last few days – seems opportune all round. We had a meeting and decided – unanimous – that it would be right if you gave up the chairmanship.

HARRIS. We want your blessing JT.

TRENCH. You decided –. (*He stops.*)

HUBBARD. You said you wanted to fish, read your poetry books, travel. And we want to be tested. Of course you'll be hovering over us like the guardian angel. (*He hands minutes to* TRENCH.) There's the minutes JT. I think the vote of thanks will please you. No doubt –

TRENCH (*takes the minutes but doesn't look at them*). Who put this up?

HUBBARD. No inquest JT.

TRENCH. Who had this idea?

HUBBARD. We only reflected the feeling throughout the organization. We took –

TRENCH. Who had this idea?

HUBBARD. I've seen you at your best JT. Don't take the memory away.

TRENCH. What feeling in the organization? Didn't you see those people down there? My god they were crying. Little girls from central filing I didn't know.

KENDAL. JT a show of emotion means nothing.

TRENCH. They hugged me. That was the feeling down there.

HUBBARD (*trying another line*). You're not young JT. You didn't intend to go on forever.

TRENCH (*finality*). *What feeling?* You see! There was no feeling!

HUBBARD. Well the legal situation's clear. A majority of the board can make this decision. You've earned your freedom.

TRENCH. *You're* not young! That's why you – ! (*Stops. Jumps to the next idea.*) The legal situation? When I say you can't do it I don't mean it's against the law but against – (*He stops. Cannot find the words. Jumps back to the earlier idea.*) You're not young! That's why you did it! I sat and ate and slept with a gun turned on me. Those people told the truth: they said they were my enemies! But here! – What's here? (*He finds the words.*) – I say you cannot do it not because it's against the law – I know what the law is! – but because it's against common humanity! You can't! Not if you have one spark of decency! Who had this idea? (*He glances at the minutes.*) I see you gave yourself a rise.

MS LINNELL *comes in. She brings red roses.*

MS LINNELL. I hope you didn't buzz while I was down the corridor. I borrowed a silver vase from the directors' dining room. Our country dancing team won it. You remember? Mr Collins on the banjo. (*Refusing to lower her gaze.*) Roses look so fine in silver. Cut glass is vulgar unless it's very good. The girls in the outer office ask you to join them later. They've got a bottle of bubbly. Champagne.

HUBBARD. Thankyou Louise.

MS LINNELL *goes.*

TRENCH. Is she in this?

HARRIS. You might have asked after her mother. She's ill again.

HUBBARD. The rise JT. You kept us short for years. Well short.

TRENCH. *I've been sacked.* I suppose you were behind this red gang! Had me highjacked! I won't go quietly.

HARRIS. It seemed to be our duty JT.

KENDAL. You name your own handshake.

TRENCH. O I will. I will. (*To* HUBBARD.) Who takes my place?

HUBBARD. I do.

TRENCH. O I watched you. Grab, grab. I said don't judge: envy is human. Now I call my own friend: bastard! Harris, Kendal, Hubbard: you've done this. You provoked this confrontation.

HUBBARD. Only sorry to see you let yourself down.

TRENCH. God in heaven I was *kicked* down! – No. I don't say you panicked. You were under pressure. The decision was wrong. Now we'll put it right. (*He goes to the boardtable.*) As a member of the board I propose a motion: minute number seven of the twenty-ninth be struck from the record. (*He chooses a button-hole from the roses and pins it to his jacket.*) Look at these roses. (*He sits.*) I put the motion. Who will second it?

HUBBARD. You were removed from the board.

TRENCH. You hoped I would be shot. Then this scene would have been avoided. That's why you held out: to get rid of me! That's devilish! Have me shot and take flowers to the funeral! God what people are you?

HUBBARD. Your friends. We acted for the good of TCC. And you call us selfish? I'm not taking this abuse from any –

TRENCH. All right Jimmy . . . (*He walks away. For a moment he seems to be in another world.*) I wanted to come back to the

world. So much. It wasn't easy. Where am I now? All my
life is over. This was my life. You know that. All this while
... behind my back. I was a joke.

KENDAL. JT we're all distressed.

HUBBARD. You have no money problems. The organization's in good hands.

TRENCH. Good hands! Cut throats like you will take over the
world! You stab me in the back and say it's so I don't have
to shoulder the worries. You make black white! Dirt clean!
Evil good! Pervert reason! My god terrorists stand things
on their head. Turn values upside down. But the police go
after them! You do it and vote yourself a rise! You don't
rob a bank you have a cheque book! But no one hunts you,
pillorizes you in the press!

HUBBARD. He's overwrought gentlemen. As far as I'm concerned you've said nothing. Let's leave it at that.

HARRIS. Here here.

TRENCH. Say I was struck dumb? That would be better? *I
have a right to judge!* My god and you had obligations! O
you cowards! Bastards! Behind my back! Why why why
not to my face? No that wouldn't have been mean or low
enough! But this – is monstrous! You act like cowards and
hypocrites because that's the only way you know what
you're doing!

HUBBARD. We couldn't come to you! You weren't here.

TRENCH. I was here thirty years!

HUBBARD. No one was plotting or scheming. Certainly not
thirty years. Only the last few years –

HARRIS. Three.

KENDAL. Five or six at the most. Six years ago. That's when
we first started to notice you'd –

TRENCH. Six years! – you schemed behind my back?

KENDAL. Plotting and scheming! No one schemed! No one
spoke! It was obvious! We kept quiet till we couldn't any
longer. We deserve the rise for waiting! It was obvious to

me seven years ago. At our first interview. Ten years! I've
had enough of this!

TRENCH. Five years! Ten years! A hundred years! Nothing
you say has any meaning!

HUBBARD. This meeting's closed. JT I'm sad you've taken it
like this. Though to be frank you always had to have your
own way –

TRENCH. I will not be insulted in my office!

KENDAL. It's not your office actually!

HUBBARD. Shut up Kendal. Show some sense.

TRENCH. Am I completely out or just demoted?

HUBBARD. Demoted – no. You're not the sort to –

TRENCH. Put me on the broom? Send me out on the road?
Make me the toilet man? I will not stay in a room with you.

   TRENCH *goes*.

KENDAL. Could have been worse.

HUBBARD. I told you to keep quiet Kendal. What's the use
of aggravating the –

KENDAL. He shouted at me! I had to answer or he'd have had
a stroke. (*Turning nasty*.) And anyway I'm not prepared to
be spoken to like that. By him or you Hubbard. You didn't
exactly play it down.

HUBBARD. All right, all right. We've got to stick together.
You'll have to lump it.

HARRIS. Trench'll go to the press.

HUBBARD. Nine days wonder. One day the papers are full of
it. Next day some peer's set fire to his castle and run off
with the au pair. We'll say the ordeal turned his bonce. No
one ever talks sense in a crisis. You can say what you like
and it sounds normal.

HARRIS. Drink?

HUBBARD. Ta. (*He changes his mind*.) No.

HARRIS (*drinks*). Sylvia was pleased with the rise. But what's
left after tax? I ask myself is it worth it? All this fuss. I'm

beginning to be sorry you had the idea. In JT's place I could –

HARRIS. ⎫
KENDAL. ⎬ – easily feel the same.

TRENCH *comes back.*

An Invitation

TRENCH (*quiet*). What you did was wrong. I've met many thieves and I can tell you there's no honour among them. No one of you will trust the others now. I shall be busy. I have a lot to do and think about. I invited you to dinner to celebrate my escape. Now it will be a double celebration. I'll expect you at my house this Friday at seven. Please cancel any other engagements you may have. I intend to go out as if I had been working with gentlemen.

*

TRENCH *goes.*

HUBBARD (*calling after him*). That's fine JT. We put all your private papers in sealed boxes. And the trinkets from your desk.

HARRIS. Are we going?

KENDAL. Why not?

HUBBARD. He wants to go out playing the elder statesman. Mean to deprive him. And he keeps an excellent table.

SIX

TRENCH's *house.*
A large painting draped in velvet.
TRENCH *comes in alone. Everyone in the scene wears formal evening dress.*

TRENCH (*calls*). In here.

MARIAN *comes in*.

MARIAN (*sees picture*). A surprise JT?
TRENCH. Wait for the others.
MARIAN (*calls*). Quickly darlings. One of JT's surprises!

PRU *comes in*.

PRU. Gorgeous fodder JT. Always is. Don't know how you do it without a wife.
MARIAN. If you have a french cook . . .

HUBBARD *enters*.

HUBBARD. Surprise?
TRENCH. Thankyou Pru.
PRU (*takes* TRENCH's *arm and leads him to one side*). I hope this little contretemps in the organization – don't worry, I won't meddle – doesn't mean there's a rift? We're pals for life aren't we JT?

KENDAL, SYLVIA *and* HARRIS *come in. They stand before the picture. Everyone except* TRENCH *carries a glass*.

KENDAL. Course you are.
PRU (*leads* TRENCH *aside*). That's right. I stay well out of anything to do with the company. But that place isn't the world thank god. Even if you boys sometimes behave as if it were. You'll have a lot more free time. I shall see even more of you. Is daddy going to be naughty and take me to a show?
TRENCH. I'm not the one who wanted a change.
PRU (*wags finger*). Naughty.
TRENCH. I'm sorry Pru. I don't respond to being patronized. Please don't. Kendal is as responsible as his colleagues for

kicking me out. Don't try and gloss it over. Did he put you up to it?

PRU (*pout*). JT.

SYLVIA. We had a nice meal. Everyone's behaved themselves. Don't let's spoil it.

HARRIS. Really Pru you might have kept off the subject. I do think it's rather infra to let your –

KENDAL. All Pru said was let's be friends. Damned good advice. Even if it's sometimes difficult to take.

HUBBARD. The subject's closed.

SYLVIA. What's this surprise? (*To the girls:*) Like christmas.

TRENCH (*calmly*). Didn't your men tell you I was sacked behind my back? While I could easily have been killed in –

HARRIS. For god's sake. (*To* PRU:) I hope you're satisfied.

MARIAN. We know JT but it's not our business. I've always cherished our friendship and if there's –

HUBBARD. Fine. Let's leave it there.

TRENCH (*after a silence*). – a ruined hole by a gang of fanatics? They deceived me. Under the circumstances I thought they were deceiving their wives. As you didn't seem disturbed. Not at all. But I see you know. (*A slight bow of the head.*) Excuse me. (*He returns to his subject.*) Still, you don't expect *me* not to care, surely? I was sacked.

KENDAL. JT wasn't sacked. We were in a tight corner. The strike, JT away. He couldn't be consulted. A new initiative was necessary. Let the organization forge ahead. It was the only way to keep our heads above water.

TRENCH. Forging ahead? Dear me. A piece of sophistry not up to your standards. Whenever I looked at you you were going round in circles. I say only that I don't like Pru to talk to me as if I were in rompers or a wheel chair. Such vulgarity should be beneath her. (*Silence. Still calm.*) And that I don't expect to be blamed when I object to being stabbed in the back.

HUBBARD. We're your guests. Drinking your brandy. I

suppose we listen quietly while we're torn to pieces. If that's what you want. The brandy's excellent by the way. It makes it worth it.

KENDAL. JT's wined and dined us handsomely. That's how I'll remember him. A generous colleague. Six months and we'll smile at this.

TRENCH. And so I'm not to be patronized by Pru.

PRU. O dear. Shall I put my head in the oven? I do object to being picked on. I'm not responsible for what happened.

HUBBARD. What'll you call your book JT? Must get a good title. (To HARRIS:) I'm not very literary but if I have to read I go for a good title.

HARRIS (to HUBBARD). Something from a poem.

PRU. Anything I say will mean what he wants it to. If I said sorry that would be patronizing. If I jumped out of a window I'd be doing it to make him feel guilty. (The other women surreptitiously gesture her to be quiet.) I will not be shushed at! (To TRENCH:) If you throw out all this bitterness you cut yourself off from everyone. No matter how forgiving they are.

KENDAL. Pru please.

PRU. I object to being morally blackmailed!

TRENCH. I told you I'd commissioned a painting of our team. As it then was. Now as a parting gift –

KENDAL. O JT that's really something.

TRENCH. Kendal. One advantage of being chucked out of my organization is that I don't have to put up with your innane toadying. Is that what you meant by freedom Hubbard? I've been tactful. The portrait doesn't embarrass you by commemorating me or the standards I stood for. And if I was on it you'd lose it in the basement in a week.

KENDAL. Sorry JT. You may call this toadying. But a portrait of our founder would always be –

TRENCH. Instead it reminds you of yourselves. That's important after all. If we knew what we are the world would change very fast. The little voice of truth. Most of us would have to jump off a bridge.

HUBBARD. You have to be bloody arrogant to think you always know the truth.

TRENCH (*suddenly showing his anger*). You have to be more arrogant to ignore it! You can walk by a heap of bodies and see litter. That's arrogance! Knife someone in the back because you can't look them in the face. Arrogance! Betray your friend for thirty pieces of silver and invest it on the stock exchange. All arrogance! You trip over the truth and get up and brush it off your knees. It stares at you and you smile and turn away and congratulate yourself on turning the other cheek. That's arrogance! Hypocrites wagging their heads till they drop off.

MARIAN. Am I included in that? I'd like to know.

TRENCH. Up to you. Ask Hubbard. He makes up your mind on everything.

SYLVIA. I don't see the point of these recriminations. If JT wants to –

TRENCH. What –? I'm free to speak my mind.

SYLVIA. We mustn't leave the house on its own too long Ronnie.

TRENCH. After all you live on my organization. Eat it. Educate your boys on it. Dress and sleep on it. Have fun on it. You'll be buried out of it.

HUBBARD. You screwed us for everything you could get. He stayed in the office at night pretending to work to make sure we were really working. I've come home past midnight. Marian will tell you. You lived off our fat Trench.

TRENCH (*calmly*). The picture should be unveiled by a lady.

SYLVIA (*disinterest*). So big. You must all be life size.

HUBBARD. Well let's see the –

TRENCH. Do we have a lady?

PRU. Obviously I'm out.

MARIAN. Silly Pru. I'll do it.

> MARIAN *gives* KENDAL *her glass.*

TRENCH. I hope you have all you want – since we all seek the best we can get.
SYLVIA. Say a few words Marian. The men are messing it up.

Speech at an Unveiling

MARIAN. Well. This gesture of JT's is better than any words. What we say sounds clumsy today. We've hurt each other. I don't think we meant to. Giving and receiving – that's what shows true friendship. I believe that's what JT's trying to tell us. He's right and I've taken it to heart. We don't care for each other as we should. I know this: I'm grateful to JT. Unstintedly. We owe him. And we shouldn't forget it.

*

> *A smattering of polite applause: the fingers of the free hand clapped on the palm of the hand holding the glass.*

SYLVIA. For he's a jolly good fellow
ALL EXCEPT TRENCH. He's a jolly good fellow
    He's a jolly good fellow
    And so say all of us
SYLVIA. And so say all of us

> MARIAN *puts her arm around* JT *and kisses his cheek.*

MARIAN. God bless JT.

> MARIAN *and* SYLVIA *drop the sheet from the picture. It is a seaside photographer's prop. It shows a tropical beach. A man flexes the biceps of one arm and holds a cigar in the*

*hand. The other arm is round a girl. She is a blonde. Both
wear bathing costume. Both have a hole on top of the neck.
These are for heads to be pushed through. An ape swings in a
coconut tree. A starfish is stranded on the beach. A battle
cruiser is moored in the bay.*

KENDAL. Pop art.

HARRIS *starts to cry.*

HUBBARD. I call that unnecessary. Confirms the line I took.
HARRIS (*crying*). Tee-hee. Tee-hee-hee-hee. Urghaaah!
(*Gropes.*) Hanky. Tee-hee. Tee-hee. Tee-hee. Er. Er. (*He
doesn't stop crying till he's taken away at the end of the scene.*)
PRU. I was told I was childish.
TRENCH. Put your head in Hubbard.
HUBBARD. Tell Rogers to get our things Marian.
TRENCH. Put your head in. Show us what you are. Kendal –
you? Will it show the truth? Only a game. Afraid of party
games? Little Kenny can't come out and play truth he
doesn't know the rules!

PRU *gives* KENDAL *her glass. She sticks her head through
one of the holes in the painting.*

PRU. Howdee folks! Welcome to the lowdown! What a lovely
party this is an all! (*She puts her hand through one of the holes
and makes an obscene gesture.*) We're havin one hell of a ball!
This here is the greatest strip show on earth! The Trench
festival of striperama! Come and have a peep folks! (*She
starts throwing her clothes over the top of the picture.*) We're
really getting down to the bare facts.
HUBBARD. Get out of the way Trench.
TRENCH. Circus acts! You smashed me! One man? There're
plenty more! You had duties and obligations. You
betrayed all that. Not some little milkman who cheats on
his takings. A few quid a week and he can't sleep at night in

case he's sacked. A child who steals a few coppers and spends its days in terror. You cheat from the top! And sleep well on it! Even when you do good you smash! You're a plague!

PRU. It's strip-strip-stripping time!

KENDAL (*Bored*). Pru shut up.

PRU (*sticks a leg from the side of the canvas*). What the hell they wanna put them holes on different levels for? How's a gal supposed to get her tits through? I'm gonna complain to the manager! They wanna hire a freak!

> SYLVIA *tries to get* PRU *to dress. She chases her round the room, holding out her clothes. She tries to drape her in the sheet.* KENDAL *sits on the empty floor and sips his drink. He has the empty glasses of the three women.*

SYLVIA. Stop it. Pru. Stop it. This is terrible. Look how Ronnie's upset. (*She goes to* KENDAL.) Mr Kendal stop your wife.

> SYLVIA *chases* PRU *round the room.* MARIAN *wanders round the others smiling reassuringly and making calming gestures.* HARRIS *cries.*

PRU. I charge extra for streaking! You wanna stop a strike! Just let me run round the factory and those men'll follow me right in through the main gate.

KENDAL (*calmly*). O my god.

MARIAN. Whatever the other's did you have no right to treat me and Sylvia like this.

HARRIS. Tee-hee. Tee-hee. Hee-hee-hee. Not fair. O tee-hee-hee. Urgh! Urgh! No right to treat me like this. I told them what it would be. They brushed me aside. Tee-hee. Tee-hee. Tee-hee.

SYLVIA (*thumps* HARRIS' *back*). For god's sake Ronnie stop it. You're showing all your teeth. You look ridiculous.

KENDAL (*Bored*). Pru stop it.

SYLVIA *sits on the ground and has hysterics. She throws her shoes at the wall. She drums her heels on the floor. She beats the ground with her fists. She screams.* HUBBARD *throws his cigar on the floor and jumps on it.* MARIAN *wanders round smiling.* PRU *is naked.*

PRU. Let the light in! Hey big spender!

TRENCH. O god o god o god! That there's no justice! People like you – smash smash smash! You smile and read reports and smash!

MARIAN. Let my husband pass!

TRENCH. O are you late for an appointment? Buying up poison? Cornering the market in bones? Paying your hit man? Fixing some little clerk with figures to sell? A secretary in industrial espionage? Selling your family grave for redevelopment?

HARRIS. Tee-hee. Tee-hee. Tee-hee.

SYLVIA. For god's sake cover your face with your hanky.

TRENCH *herds* HUBBARD, MARIAN, SYLVIA *and* HARRIS *out. He goes out with them.*

TRENCH (*as he goes*). Out! (*Off.*) Go and get on with your business! Show us what you are! Then we're warned!

SYLVIA (*off, screams*).

KENDAL. O my god. Showing your tits to JT.

PRU. I'm not having that old bore preach at me. It's the last time I chat up anyone for you.

KENDAL *is collecting her clothes and handing them to her. She dresses.*

PRU. I feel high. Would you take me to a night-club?

KENDAL. Great.

PRU. You'll be managing director soon. There's not much left in Hubbard's cupboard. I shall enjoy your new position. And I'm putting in for a rise. Tonight sweetie.

TRENCH *comes back.*

TRENCH. If you'd like the silver knock the butler on the head. The keys to my safe are in the desk. You'll find some small coins in my overcoat pocket on your way out. If you unscrew the light bulbs be careful.

KENDAL. 'Pacific 203' or 'Silver Orchid'?

PRU. Both.

PRU *and* KENDAL *go. She carries the last of the clothes with her.*

TRENCH. Rid of them.

HARRIS *comes back through another door.*

HARRIS. Tee-hee. O dear look what you've done. No cause to speak to me like that JT. JT tee-hee. Tee-hee. Not spoken to like that since I was a child. Tee-hee. I'm your friend. I knew it was wrong.

SYLVIA *comes on with a handful of tissues.*

SYLVIA. Ronald.

HARRIS. So harsh. So harsh.

SYLVIA. O god you're dribbling. Wipe your chin on these tissues.

HARRIS. Tee-hee.

SYLVIA *and* HARRIS *go.* TRENCH *sits alone on the floor.*

TRENCH. I'm afraid.

Part Two

ONE

Derelict House.
The photographer's prop is in the middle of the room.
Empty. LISA *comes in. She wears everyday clothes. She stares at*
the picture. She looks round. She goes to the window. She gestures
to someone outside. TRENCH *comes in through the side door. He is*
dirty and unshaven. His clothes are of good quality but dirty. He
eats a biscuit.

TRENCH. You're trespassing.

LISA. O.

TRENCH. Heard the car.

LISA. Sorry.

TRENCH. What d'you want?

LISA. Just passing.

TRENCH. No, you stopped.

LISA. Saw this.

TRENCH. Stop at everything you see?

LISA. Looked deserted. I want a place to do up.

TRENCH. Not for sale.

LISA (*picture*). What's that?

TRENCH. Mine.

LISA. O. (*Starts to go.*) Sorry I bashed in. (*Stops.*) You live
  here?

TRENCH. Yes.

LISA. On your own?

TRENCH. My business.

LISA. Why d'you live here?

TRENCH. I bought it.

LISA. Yes. (*She turns to go.*)

TRENCH. Sat by a window for a long time. Then sold up and came here. Was a prisoner here once.

LISA. There are no shops.

TRENCH. Bike to the village.

MICHAEL *comes in. He stands in the doorway behind* LISA.

TRENCH (*points at* MICHAEL). Look.

LISA. My friend.

MICHAEL (*to* LISA). All right?

LISA. Yes. He lives here.

TRENCH. Rut rut rut.

MICHAEL (*picture*). What's that?

TRENCH. Mine. You can have a drink.

MICHAEL. Don't bother.

TRENCH *goes out.* MICHAEL *moves so that he can watch him.*

LISA. He doesn't recognize us.

MICHAEL. What's he doing here?

LISA. He *lives* here. Off his head.

MICHAEL. Must be. Let's go.

LISA. No. I'm enjoying it. It's quite safe.

MICHAEL *stands by the door to watch* TRENCH.

LISA. What's he doing?

MICHAEL. Head in the cupboard. (*He glances round the room.*) Spooky. (*Picture.*) And what the hell's that?

LISA (*looks through the window*). I thought I'd never forget it. I'd even forgot the colour of the walls. (*She puts her hand on the window pane.*) We weren't strong.

MICHAEL. Strong enough.

LISA. No. We should have shot it out.

MICHAEL. Waste. We'd been grassed. If the pigs knew this place they must have known our get-out.

LISA. We could have forced a plane out of them and –

MICHAEL. No. We had to go into hiding on our own. Who'd have given us asylum? Once the pigs were tipped off we didn't stand a chance.

LISA. We should have shot it out. We weren't here to save our necks.

MICHAEL. Don't play the hero. It'll be different next time. Factories strike – you can rely on that.

LISA. What if we still have the grass?

MICHAEL. We weeded. What else can we do?

LISA. I don't trust anyone.

MICHAEL. Not me?

LISA. Nope. If you trust someone it's betraying the rest. (*Staring through the window.*) The heather. I bolted through it and called myself a traitor.

> MICHAEL *gives a warning sound to* LISA.
> TRENCH *comes back with a can of beer.*

TRENCH. You'll have to share.

LISA (*takes the can*). Thanks. (*She drinks.*) Good.

TRENCH (*calmly*). It's strange not meeting people. But then, I'm no longer soiled by them . . . Their horizon is the end of a pig trough. They tear the clothes from the living and the rags from the dead. Till they die and go in a plastic coffin to be burned. They have violence on their faces as if they'd been painted by a savage. Their hands are frayed ends of rope taken from old parcels. Voices like sounds coming out of a wound. I turned away while they spoke. Costs too much to be polite . . . (*He half notices they haven't understood. He tries again.*) Every year the ants came to my garden. A long line going under the fence. A few dragged parts of an insect. There's nothing else. So I left.

> LISA *has given* MICHAEL *the can. He holds it without drinking. He passes it back to* LISA.

MICHAEL. Finish it.

LISA *drinks*.

MICHAEL. Let's go.
LISA. Thanks.
TRENCH. Pleasure.
LISA. Bye.

LISA *and* MICHAEL *go*.

TWO

Derelict House.
Night. Noises off. TRENCH *flat against the wall.*
The door opens. Torches. LISA *runs in. She puts down a bundle.*
She catches TRENCH *in her torch.*

LISA. Stay there. Blow your head off.

ANNA *comes in.* LISA *keeps the torchlight on* TRENCH.

ANNA (*puts blankets on the floor*). Jesus.
LISA. Bloody light?
ANNA. Cover the window.
LISA. Bloody light. Bloody light. (*Searching*.) I thought it
   was here.

ANNA *covers the window.* LISA *finds the light and switches*
it on.

MICHAEL *comes in with a bundle. The terrorists carry guns.*
They wear balaclavas.

ANNA. Get the car away!

ANNA *goes off.*

MICHAEL. Tins.

ANNA (*Off*). Get rid of the car! Everything out?

MICHAEL. All you need. I checked.

ANNA (*Off*). And the boot?

MICHAEL. I checked.

ANNA returns.

ANNA. Hop it!

MICHAEL (*to* LISA). Manage?

ANNA (*moving the photographer's prop to the wall*). Of course.

MICHAEL. Tomorrow.

ANNA. Early! Very early!

MICHAEL. If I can. You may have to be patient.

ANNA. No! Early! Otherwise we've had it!

MICHAEL (*to* LISA *as she stacks things*). I'll give you a hand.

ANNA. No! Go! We can manage!

> MICHAEL *is on his knees. He reaches for* LISA. *He presses his face into her.* ANNA *sorts things. Then she goes out.*

ANNA (*off*). I'll do first watch.

> LISA *gets* MICHAEL *to his feet. They go after* ANNA. TRENCH *stays against the wall.* LISA *and* ANNA *return.* THEY *carry a figure in a white boiler suit, no shoes, white socks and a white hood. The face isn't seen. The legs and hands are tied. It looks like a giant maggot. They lay it on the floor.*

ANNA (*peering through the window*). Move those. All over the place.

> *Off, the sound of a car starting and driving away.* LISA *stacks things.*

LISA. Still got a grass.

ANNA (*to* TRENCH). Do what you're told. You'll be all right. We'll go in the morning.

LISA. Don't like running.

ANNA. No one does. They'll get us a place tomorrow.

LISA. If that's not tipped off. Who is it?

The WHITE FIGURE *pounds its heels on the ground.*

LISA. O god bog time already! (*To* ANNA.) Have I got to be bloody nurse maid again? (*To* WHITE FIGURE.) Get up. Up. D'you want to go or don't you?

LISA *gets the* WHITE FIGURE *to its feet and drags it out.*

TRENCH. I know you. You were here before.

ANNA. Who comes here?

TRENCH. No one.

ANNA. You'd better tell me. You'll get your head shot off if someone comes.

TRENCH. No one.

ANNA (*turning back to the window*). They will after today's fun.

TRENCH. Will you take me with you?

ANNA. I'll see. We were on the way to a hideout. It was crawling with police. We'd been grassed. You can put us up for one night. Do what you're told you'll be all right.

TRENCH. Stay here.

ANNA. Here? They'll come.

TRENCH. I told you –

ANNA. They'll check tomorrow. Another strike at TCC.

TRENCH. O . . . that's Hubbard?

ANNA (*shakes her head*). It went wrong.

TRENCH. Wait in the hills. Come down when they've gone.

ANNA. No. Need somewhere safe. Can't trust you. Can't trust ourselves.

TRENCH. The informer. Always one of your own . . . You left

me tied up like a pig at the butcher's cart. Police cut me free. I went home. My friends killed me. (*His voice has sunk. He's almost talking to himself. He raises his voice.* Could be anyone. That girl. You. Perhaps that man's driven off to the police. Writing your names down now.

LISA *comes back dragging the* WHITE FIGURE. *It falls.*

LISA. Not here! Get up! Over there! Got the runs. Shit scared. I said *down!*

The WHITE FIGURE *lies on the floor.*

LISA. Cock up.
ANNA. We're still in control.

The WHITE FIGURE *pounds its heels on the ground.*

LISA. O god wait. I'm not trotting in and out with you the whole bloody night. Bloody wait.
ANNA. Put that torch out.

LISA *switches off a torch.*

ANNA. D'you want to eat?
LISA. Couldn't keep it down.
ANNA. We take it in turns to sleep. Keep calm and rest.
LISA. I know! – What's the point of holding onto him? Should have dumped him. What's he worth? Get more back on a nonreturnable bottle.
ANNA. A hostage is a hostage. (*Slight pause.*) It'll stink the place out.

LISA *gets the* WHITE FIGURE *to its feet.*

LISA. Up! Drop him on the motorway and clear off.
ANNA. No car.
LISA. In the morning.
ANNA. H.Q. decides.
LISA (*taking the* WHITE FIGURE *out*). Shut up with a loony and a human liability with the runs.

LISA *and the* WHITE FIGURE *go.*

TRENCH. It's safe in the hills.
ANNA (*looks at her watch*). News. (*Radio.*)

THREE

Boardroom.
HUBBARD, KENDAL, HARRIS, LORD BIGDYKE, POLICE
CHIEF. KENDAL's *forehead is plastered.*

BIGDYKE. They hope to weaken you by creating a feeling of
fatalism. We won the first round. Now they show us it was
a pyrrhic victory. The problem comes back unsolved. It
always will. They'll go on harassing your organization
till your spirit breaks and you collapse – or we break
them.
HARRIS. They could have got me this time. Any of us. We
have a right to protection. We pay our taxes. I can't run an
organization in these conditions.
POLICE CHIEF (*smiles*). You could resign.
HUBBARD. Look. You sorted it out last time. What are you
doing now.
POLICE CHIEF. Can't discuss it with you. Can *tell* you
something. In private. (*Smiles.*) A nasty setback. We had
certain information –
KENDAL. You've got a plant?
POLICE CHIEF. We surrounded a certain location. Getting
clever. They didn't turn up. They sent a scout. (*Smiles.*)
Now we don't know where the hell they are.
HARRIS. A never-ending oneway street!
POLICE CHIEF. On the asset side the pressure's off. They
didn't get Mr Kendal.

BIGDYKE. Though we treat all victims the same.

POLICE CHIEF. Yes – but the pressure's off. What can they do? Sheepishly send him back. We should all be feeling very pleased.

BIGDYKE. Let's hope. But it ought never to have happened. From now on whenever there's industrial unrest at TCC precautions must be even more stringent. I hope that is now understood. (*To* POLICE CHIEF.) I thought you were responsible for their safety?

POLICE CHIEF (*smiles*). And your's Lord Bigdyke.

BIGDYKE (*turns away*). This could attract imitators. Terrorism could become as common as street accidents. If it did the country would be turned into a police state. All the advantages our fathers worked for – our science and technology – could be perverted to evil ends.

POLICE CHIEF. Don't worry Lord Bigdyke we don't seek that sort of power. (*To the others*:) But we're ready. O the nature of the beast has changed. Once the ordinary man policed himself. The sight of the uniform was enough. With the odd tap from the truncheon and the occasional hanging. Church and school did their job then. Not now. Press doesn't help: muck. Still, technology's on our side – if that's what you meant Lord Bigdyke? We don't seek it but we're ready.

BIGDYKE. The strike negotiations go on in the usual way. This is an industrial matter not a political one. Terrorism must be seen to be a crime. If ever the public saw it as politics we'd be lost. (*He stands*.) We sit tight till we hear from them. Goodday.

HUBBARD. ⎤
HARRIS. ⎦ Goodbye.

KENDAL. Thankyou Lord Bigdyke. Goodbye.

    LORD BIGDYKE *goes*.

POLICE CHIEF. How d'you feel?

HUBBARD. Shit scared.

POLICE CHIEF (*pleasantly*). Glad to hear it. A proper assessment of the situation. Bye bye.

POLICE CHIEF *goes*.

HARRIS. You know what worries me.

HUBBARD. Don't tell me.

HARRIS. There's no way out. If I left the country, burned my papers, my home, my clothes, changed my sex and divorced the wife, put the dog to sleep, had plastic surgery and closed my bank account I still wouldn't be safe. These louts have diseased imaginations –

HUBBARD. A diseased lack of it.

HARRIS. – In their eyes I'll always be guilty. They'll track me down anywhere.

HUBBARD. No one's changing their sex. We stick together.

MS LINNELL *comes in*.

MS LINNELL. Messers Gate and Lamb.

HUBBARD (*calls*). Come in.

TERRY *and* GATE *come in*.

HUBBARD. What a day.

GATE (*noncommittally*). What a day.

HUBBARD. Take a seat.

GATE, KENDAL *and* HARRIS *sit*. MS LINNELL *shows* TERRY *to his chair*. *She takes shorthand notes*.

HUBBARD. You know the situation. Your claim for twenty per cent has been on the table three weeks. On Monday you took the men out. Yesterday Mr Kendal's car was rammed. Mr Kendal had the foresight to swap hats with his chauffeur.

KENDAL. In this day and age you can't even wear your own hat.

HUBBARD. In the cuffuffle they took the chauffeur in mistake.

TERRY (to GATE). What's the chauffeurs' union say about that?

KENDAL. He wasn't in a union.

TERRY (*To* KENDAL). Makes our point.

A Negotiations Speech

HUBBARD. Four things. First. For the second time an industrial dispute at TCC has resulted in the taking of a hostage. You know what the country thinks.

TERRY. I don't. I know what the papers think.

HUBBARD. They say by staying out you support the terrorists.

KENDAL. Only possible conclusion.

GATE. No. They've got nothing to do with us.

HARRIS. Public opinion! Striking for terrorism!

KENDAL. They've put you on the spot Mr Gate. What comes first: a few quid in your pocket or the security of your families?

GATE. If you're that bothered why don't you give in?

HUBBARD. My god I would to get that man off. But as you'll see that would be doing all of us a disservice.

GATE. How?

HUBBARD. We'll come to it. Secondly. When Mr Trench was taken the hostage was what you'd call a class enemy. A boss. Someone like me – who regrets the passing of rickets. Even a cat that didn't know it had whiskers could tell how you'd react to that. This is different. The chauffeur earns less than you –

TERRY. Shouldn't work for him.

HUBBARD. An elderly man who never harmed anyone. Noted for his kindness. Mr Kendal tells me he didn't like to blow the horn even at lady drivers. Only last summer he rescued a little boy from the boating pond. Shows his medals in a glass case. Old Mr Kendal passed him on to young Mr Kendal with a glowing reference. The wife's poorly. There's a daughter. She came late to bless his grey hairs. And a dog. I'm not trying to get your sympathy for them. They already have it. But this time it's not an exploiter. It's one of your own.

TERRY. Because he pinched his bloody hat.

KENDAL. I don't like your tone. It was his idea. I thought as soon as they got a close look they'd let him go. A routine precaution. I'm not to blame if your pals can't see the difference between an old man and a –

GATE. Our pals?

HUBBARD. Let's say supporters.

HARRIS. My god why don't you condemn them? Bawl them out! Last time not one word! Whatever your grouses you can't say your standard of living justifies that! Four thousand Pontius Pilates washing their hands in their automatic washing machines and drying them in their spin dryers. Mr Trench brutally shot down – well it's only by the grace of god he wasn't! – and it's nothing to do with you? Will you speak up against this outrage?

TERRY (*Quietly*). No. Every penny we get we fight for. You think words come cheap –

GATE. Terry.

TERRY. Yes sir no sir. Well they're not cheap anymore. (*He taps the demand.*) That's the price.

HUBBARD. Please please please. Let's keep to the point.

TERRY. If he talks to me like that I'm leaving.

HUBBARD. Thirdly. We've got to show these fanatics their tactics don't wash. No organization can work under these threats. Can't you see?

GATE. Mr Hubbard the men are asking for a fair return –

HUBBARD. Hold on. Haven't finished. Look. This is an argument to reason – not emotion. Suppose we cave in.

Who did we cave in to? You? Tell that to the terrorists. They'll say they did it. Isn't that right? And it won't end there. These vermin – others are watching from their holes. If they get away with it the rest will move in. You've proved it works –

TERRY. You're enjoying this Hubbard. It's not negotiation it's blackmail.

HUBBARD. Next time a bomb goes off in a shopping precinct and some child loses its eyes or legs or some girl buying her trousseau gets killed – it's happened! – that's part your doing –

TERRY (*stands*). I'm off.

GATE *motions him to stay*. TERRY *stops halfway to the door*.

HUBBARD. Part your doing. Can you deny it? You insist on the full claim – and you're taking money with blood on it. You're not evil men. You didn't make the situation any-more than I did. But the consequences of the situation can't be avoided. You want power? If you have power you have to accept responsibility. Well responsibility means you don't keep saying mine mine mine. You forgo your interest and consider the rest. So last point. They've put you in a position you have to show them where you stand. The only decent thing you can do is take *less* than we offered. The rest is blood money.

*

TERRY (*to* GATE). Come on Joe.

GATE. Mr Hubbard you're not just bosses here. Your class is boss out there. Terror's your responsibility. Don't hang it round our neck.

KENDAL. If Trench had come home in a box at least he could buy the best funeral. What'll you say to the driver's widow?

HUBBARD. Gentlemen. All our hands are tied. What is there

left? Our common humanity. Our decency. I want that man back safe and sound. If you settle for less – as in all conscience I think you must – they can't kill him.

The POLICE CHIEF *comes in.*

POLICE CHIEF (*looks at* TERRY *and* GATE). These ...?
HUBBARD. Union.
POLICE CHIEF. Come outside.

The POLICE CHIEF, KENDAL, HUBBARD, HARRIS *and* MS LINNELL *go out.*

TERRY. What's all that about?
GATE. Must have found him.
TERRY. Was he serious about the cut?
GATE. They try anything.

GATE *stands by the door in a posture of intense listening. He strains to hear what's happening outside.* TERRY *stares at the board table.*

A Public Soliloquy

TERRY. How often do we use a table like that? When we're married? They lay us on something smaller when we're dead. They use it every day. (*He sits in* HUBBARD'*s chair.* GATE *stays at the door in the posture of intense listening.*) If we were here the brotherhood of man would not come overnight. But it would be harder for inhumanity to prosper. Why? Because in everything we did we'd seek only for the welfare of mankind. No-one who's sat in these chairs till now can say that. All their trading was based on competition, aggression and inequality. Under the pressure of daily life these things turn into conflict, violence and injustice. All that comes from their hands. It's more surprising that their world's stayed together for so long than that it now falls apart. One half the effort and struggle needed to hold it together would make a new world. It's far easier to make things better than to keep them as they are. Nor is the cost so great. The world that can't change loses all that it has.

*

MS LINNELL *and* HARRIS *come in.* MS LINNELL *brings a silver tea pot, tea cup and saucer, silver tea spoon, silver milk jug and silver sugar bowl on a silver tea tray.*

MS LINNELL. The typing pool's in tears. (*Looking straight in* TERRY'S *face and giving him the tea things.*) Mr Hubbard, your tea.

MS LINNELL *goes.*

GATE. What's happening?

TERRY *pours tea, adds milk, stirs it and drinks.* HARRIS *sits.*

HARRIS (*calm*). The government will take it out of our hands now. Have I got to be torn apart for the sake of one little chauffeur? Especially Kendal's! I'm out of my depth. You men will ruin everything. (*On the verge of tears.*) It's all right. I'm perfectly in control. (*Outburst.*) Action! Action! Action against anarchy and sabotage! Action!

HUBBARD, KENDAL, POLICE CHIEF *and* MS LINNELL *come in.* MS LINNELL *brings her pad and pencil.*

GATE. What's happening?

HUBBARD. The people holding Mr Kendal's chauffeur have put a price on his head. TCC to pay. One hundred thousand pounds or he's shot in three days. One hundred thousand pounds for a chauffeur.

HARRIS (*outburst*). Ludicrous! Ludicrous! The whole world's laughing at us.

MS LINNELL. You've drunk Mr Hubbard's tea!

TERRY. You gave it to me.

GATE. I must get back to the office. Excuse me. Terry.

GATE *goes*.

KENDAL. On top of the twenty per cent?

POLICE CHIEF. I forgot to ask.

KENDAL. Lord Bigdyke will be finding out.

POLICE CHIEF. I should think he's looking up a suitable quotation. He once quoted Latin at an anarchists' punch-up.

TERRY (*still in* HUBBARD's *chair*). Beautiful.

HUBBARD. He's unwell. Get a nurse.

MS LINNELL. Shock. I've worked in first aid. Glass of water. No not on the top of the tea. Keep them warm. (*She takes off her woolly and holds it out to him.*)

TERRY. Beautiful.

HUBBARD. What's beautiful?

TERRY. Common humanity? Decency? Brotherhood? Well what's he worth? How much? How much? (*A moment's silence. He gives an inarticulate shout. He sits on the back of the chair with his feet on the seat.*) Will you pay?

KENDAL. A hundred thousand pounds?

MS LINNELL (*holding out the woolly*). Get off that chair. It's walnut.

TERRY. Will you pay?

KENDAL.
HARRIS. } Of course not!

TERRY (*violently*). Then where's your common humanity? O more than that's paid for some of them! *They* get off! They've got money in the bank! (*He shouts again.*) Haa! How much? How much? What's he worth?

LORD BIGDYKE *comes in*.

(*Threateningly.*). Hubbard you lectured me! Common humanity? Brothers? So how much? *Nothing!* O you liars! You've got to admire the beauty of the situation.

HUBBARD. The meeting's over. So is the office party. We'll be in touch. Lord Bigdyke please sit down.

> MS LINNELL *follows* TERRY *holding out her woolly.*

MS LINNELL. You must be kept warm.
TERRY. Lord Bigdyke is it?
BIGDYKE. How d'you do?
TERRY. I'll tell you when there'll be common humanity: when the driver's worth as much as the passenger.

> TERRY *goes.*

BIGDYKE. Abiit excessit evasit erupit.
POLICE CHIEF. You see what the force has to contend with in the general public.
HARRIS. I know Kendal likes to play Napoleon. But he's not. Nowhere near. We're all out of our depth. (*To* BIGDYKE:) And you!
BIGDYKE. They do keep one step ahead.
HARRIS (*to* POLICE CHIEF): You must take over.
BIGDYKE. The government has made a law against terrorism and it will do its best to enforce it. But whether you give the money is a moral dilemma. Morality is the responsibility of the individual. The government is not the keeper of your conscience. That would make it totalitarian. In the end the fate of a nation is decided not by its rulers but by those who are ruled. (*Quiet despair.*) I would not hide from you my belief that the times are dark. The Tiber cannot be defended by noble minds and beautiful phrases.
HARRIS. I resign. I'm off to Australia. My brother-in-law has a sheep-farm. I shall lead sheep. Men don't want to be led anymore. They prefer chaos.

> HARRIS *goes.*

KENDAL (*pose*). Lord Bigdyke TCC stands firm. That's still

the tradition of our company. Whoever's taken: me or – as it happens – the driver.

HUBBARD. You forget the sales. All very well Kendal making gestures. Fine if you're in the priesthood or the civil service. (*Smiling.*) I'm sorry, we're business men. We must behave like business men – and carry out our obligation to the business and our workers. If we say no and they dump his corpse on our doorstep sales could drop to nothing. If we fork out they might rise. The mighty giant helping the little man. I know which I'd choose. I know which the chauffeur would choose. And I know what's best for the country. I'm surprised at you jumping in with both feet Kendal.

> HARRIS *comes back with* MS LINNELL. *He's trying to button himself into his overcoat.* MS LINNELL *helps. As he listens to* HUBBARD *he starts to unbutton it.*

HARRIS. I'm prepared to work out a month. On condition I get a bullet proof suit, an armoured car and a –

KENDAL. You can't run a company like that.

HUBBARD. That's the only way you can run a company.

KENDAL. But you don't know sales will rise. (*Grudgingly.*) Probably yes. (*Interested.*) But how much?

HUBBARD. Get a market survey. That's the best bible. With the right publicity. Something beautiful: a bird flying out of a cage. What's a hundred thousand pounds to the future of the company? Just when we're going public. Couldn't have chosen better timing ourselves. Price could have been better. Looks a bit mean. I'd have preferred two hundred thou'. But they've got us by the short and curlies there. We can't fix the figure.

HARRIS (*hands his overcoat to* MS LINNELL). Jimmy's right. A ceremony. Informal – but a large hall. Chauffeur's wife with her arms round Hubbard. Man and wife reunited.

Have you seen the daughter's boobs? Can't remember what your chauffeur looks like.

FOUR

Outside TERRY's *House.*
JOHN *alone.* TERRY *rides on a scooter. He stops and switches off the engine.*

JOHN. Well?
TERRY. Yeh. Misses when you rev.
JOHN. Nothin. Plugs. (*He works on the machine.*) Never let me down.

> TERRY *goes into the house.* RAY *and* BERYL *come on.*

JOHN (*working*). Lo.
RAY AND BERYL. Lo.
RAY. Terry anywhere?
JOHN. Indoors.
RAY. Still floggin that pile of scrap?
JOHN. Yeh. Gotta get the money.
BERYL. Ray wants to go back.
JOHN. That what you come round for?
BERYL. Yeh.
RAY. You with us?
JOHN. He's gonna buy the bike. If we agree the figure.
RAY. He's thick but he's not that thick.

> TERRY *comes out of the house. He brings two small bottles of pop.*

TERRY. O. Want a drink?
BERYL. No thanks.
TERRY (*hands* JOHN *a bottle*). Fix it?
JOHN (*working*). They wanna go back.

TERRY. O yeh.
RAY. You with us?
TERRY. No.
RAY. It's one of our own.
TERRY. Ray they won't kill him.
BERYL. You can't say that Terry.
TERRY. Look. It's a stunt. For publicity. They'll make their point and let him go. Listen.

A Workman's Biography

Hundred thousand pounds? Waitin in drafty corners. Sittin outside nightclubs till three in the morning. Ain done his health no good. Say ninety thousand. Gettin on. Eyesight's goin. Bad hearin. Has to ask 'where to' twice. Say eighty thousand. Wife not too good. Needs nursin. Can't manage the late nights. Seventy thousand. Mrs Kendal wants somethin younger so she can score off the other rich slags. And she'd like to pull into a lay-by on the way home. Which is bad when you're gettin on. Fifty thousand. Votes Tory to please the boss. Thirty thousand. Lives in two pokey rooms cause the rent's controlled. No central heatin. Stairs bad for his heart. Twenty thousand. Reads The Sun. Ten thousand. Never double crossed a customer. Never put one over on the public. Five thousand. Nerves goin. Kendal bawls him out in the hold ups for not drivin out on top of the other traffic. One thousand. On tablets to get himself started in the mornins. Very dodgy. Bloody hell – we owe you!

*

BERYL. You don't know that Ray.
TERRY. What else could it be? Publicity like that's worth more than a hundred thousand! They'll make their point an let him go.

RAY. Great – if they were right in the head. They don't work things out like you an me. They're nutters! I'm goin back. I'd go back if they had you or your kid. You wouldn't for us!

TERRY. If the meetin says no?

RAY. Yeh: back.

JOHN. Okay now. Try it.

TERRY. Not happy if it misses.

JOHN. I fixed it! Try it on the block.

TERRY. Haven't got time.

JOHN. Bloody hell. What I bin fixin it for? *I'll* bloody try it on the block.

> JOHN *starts the motor and drives out.*

TERRY. All right they're nutters. You go back. TCC won't pay that sort of money. So he's killed anyway.

RAY. I don't know about all that. I'm havin nothin t'do with any of it. That's where I stand.

A Speech

TERRY. You don't! Look. They got the money: let *them* give! Yes sir no sir was good enough for our fathers. Well it's not good enough anymore. What good did it do them? We always climb down at the crunch. Where will that get us? Are we suddenly so powerful we can change the world by bein kind? It's been tried. It didn't work. (*Almost hits* RAY.) You *don't* know where you stand! (*Quietens down.*) You fought the war. Did you jack it in when they started bombin back home? They were your own. No. You went on. It's the same now. You're in a fight. So stand there! That's the only way to give anythin any value anymore. You do anythin else and it's wasted. Kindness? Humanity? Decency? They destroyed all that! (RAY *doesn't answer.*) What does it say on this bottle? (*Pop bottle.*) Use contents

and dispose of. They put that on all of us! We're worthless!
Use and destroy! They'll take your bit of kindness and
suck it down into their swamp! We say no – or we're
finished!

*

RAY. An if he gets shot?
TERRY. He's shot.

> *Immediately the sound of the scooter. John rides in on it.*

RAY. Jesuschriss. I never thought I'd hear a mate of mine say
that. I want to puke.
TERRY (*to* JOHN): What about you?
JOHN. Not decided. Look I'll knock ten quid off for a quick
sale.

> TERRY *picks up the two empty bottles and goes.*

JOHN. Thanks! What you wanna upset him for?
BERYL. There are other things apart from your pocket.
JOHN. I can't help it if I need the money. Me maintenance
arrears. You try tellin that to the magistrate. You
could've waited.

> JOHN *drives off on the scooter.*

BERYL. You said you wouldn't shout.

> RAY *and* BERYL *go.*

FIVE

Derelict House.
ANNA, LISA, WHITE FIGURE.
LISA *sits on guard at the window. She is draped in a blanket.*
ANNA *lies in a sleeping bag.*

ANNA. Sleep?

LISA. Hm.

ANNA. Good.

LISA (*pours herself coffee from a flask*). Coffee?

ANNA. No thanks.

LISA. Did you?

ANNA. No. Too peaceful to sleep. The night went so quickly. I've been going over it and asking if we're right. If not I'd give myself up. There's no alternative. It's done. Now we let it take its course.

LISA. Perhaps the grass has done it again.

ANNA. Only Michael knows we're here.

LISA. I can't kill him.

A Poem

ANNA. Last time it was winter. The stream had frozen slowly into strange shapes. I walked up it over the hills. There was a heron wandering about in the sky. A heron is a bird. It flies. But it was lost. When the water froze it had nothing to eat.

LISA. And?

ANNA. It has to come down to live. I have visions – but to change the world you come down. Not because we want to. You only change things on the terms in which they're able to change. Not by the visions. The struggle in the dirt. I don't want to kill him. The world's mad. We're trapped in it. I'd do anything to change it. I'd kill him.

*

TRENCH *has wandered in. He's draped in a blanket.*

TRENCH. Nice. You sit there with your guns and watch your corpse. Arguing about death. It'll come to nothing. The world's already ended except for the crying. One day someone in an office made a decision – probably minor –

and history took a fatal turn. We were condemned. We didn't notice. The day passed and we went on. By the evening it was all over. This generation won't see the century out.

ANNA. You still belong to your business friends.

TRENCH (*calmly*). Not true.

ANNA. You saw through them but you put nothing in their place. They're a civilization without morals. You're a culture of despair. Absurd and empty. You let them think they can still produce a human soul. A hermit to sit on an island and tell them they're nothing. They admire you. You give them the illusion they have a moral sense.

TRENCH (*calmly*). Not true, not true.

LISA. He can't listen anymore.

ANNA. D'you hate us?

TRENCH. No, I see things as they are.

> As TRENCH *talks* ANNA *unpacks a quarter pint plastic bottle. It is transparent and contains blackcurrant juice. A transparent or orange opaque tube leads from its top. She cradles the white figure and pushes the end of the tube through a hole in the hood. It feeds. She nurses it and tidies its clothes.*

A Story

TRENCH. Mankind through the ages. A clown with a gun. An idiot with a stick. Little men plotting in tiny corners. Hunting for a uniform to cover themselves in. Or a mob to hang on to. The human species. Homo mob. Have you seen it? I saw it once. Screaming. One of the sounds it makes. The others are loud laughter and a muffled gibbering. I was abroad on a trade mission. I watched from the Hilton. They filled the square. There was a pedestal with a man on a horse on it. He was a general: he had a better uniform. The head was three feet across. It was smiling.

The mob threw ropes over it. Some of them climbed up and tied them on. An old man with a beard fell off. They dragged him away. Then the herd began to pull. 'Heave'. In their lingo but the meaning was clear. Heaving together. As if the sea was vomiting. Till it toppled and fell on them. There was blood. They broke it up with hammers and stones. They almost became quiet. The head came off. It was still smiling. They sawed off the horses legs. They pulled the man apart. The head rolled away into a corner of the square and smiled at them. When I came back a few years later there was a new statue on the pedestal. Of someone else. The new government was short of money. They had to use as much of the old statue as they could. Only the head was left. So they took it out of the corner of the square and stuck it on top of a new uniform. It was still smiling. Now you're here to change the world. Once upon a time. I don't hate you. One thing: your voice. The human voice still gives me pain. That's all. One day the world will be silent. Peace after the last shot.

*

ANNA *has finished feeding the* WHITE FIGURE *and put away the bottle.*

A Lecture

ANNA. Listen. There are two worlds. Most people think they live in one but they live in two. First there's the daily world in which we live. The world of appearance. There's law and order, right and wrong, good manners. How else could we live and work together? But there's also the *real* world. The world of power, machines, buying, selling, working. That world depends on capital: money! Money can do anything. It gives you the power of giants. The real world obeys the law of money. And there's a paradox about this law: whoever owns money is owned by it. A man buys a house. Does he own it? No, because to keep it he must get more money. He must obey the laws of money. And so the house owns him. The same is true of the clothes on your back and the food on your plate. Our lives, our minds, what we are, the way we see the world, are not shaped by human law but by the law of money. Behind our apparent freedom there's this real slavery. In the apparent world anyone can choose to be moral. But morality never touches the real world. Nothing is changed by the apparent 'good'. The real world follows its iron law. You understand? Let's see.

*

The Examination

We get rid of plagues and sickness, eat more, live in better houses, often we're less cruel, there are no executions. But at the same time things get worse. Vandalism, violence, fascism, weapons. Men run camps of mass murder and sing carols. So why is this paradox? Why is morality weak?

*

TRENCH *doesn't answer.* LISA *repeats the lecture.*

A Lecture Repeated

LISA. We live in two worlds. The real world of money controls the whole of the apparent world. Everything. Science, technology, work, education, law, morality, the press. Even us – our minds, our behaviour, the way we see the world: we're slaves unless we resist. That's why the world isn't human.

ANNA. As to the 'human mob'. We're not violent because

we're born with the need to hate. It's because instead of changing the real world we merely do good in this one. The earth can't hold two worlds anymore. It's too small. So we make the two worlds one. That's all revolution is: making the two worlds one. Making morality strong so that the real world will be changed. The morality of the world of appearance is too weak to do that. It's a matter of weapons. Using them causes suffering. But when appearance and reality are one there'll be less suffering. Men will know themselves – and the world will last in peace and prosperity.

*

LISA. Understand?

TRENCH. I didn't listen. I've heard it before. Better said. There *are* two worlds: your's and mine. We're in mine.

ANNA. There are the tools of the twentieth century: the machines, computers and bombs. Where are the ideas of the twentieth century? You can live – you can get fame and power – with the ideas of a stone-age hunter or a medieval fanatic. The ideas of the twentieth century are still not learnt!

TRENCH (*quietly. In his own world*). I try to stay awake. I don't want to sleep when the world ends. I want to see it end. The sky will turn bright. There'll be a roar. A great wind will blow open the windows and doors. Dust will come down on everything like a white sheet. It will blot out the horizon. I shall go blind. The world will begin to shrivel. A great noise will come from under the sheet. Then it will be silent.

A Confession

LISA (*staring through the window with binoculars*). I wish Michael was here. I want to get in the car and go. What will become of us? We'll always be hunted. In the end they'll get us.

ANNA. No. It will change.

LISA (*still staring through the binoculars*). Yes Anna. But after us. We have to pay. I'd've liked to have been an ordinary woman. Lived in a simple world. Loved Michael. Worked at what I wanted. Talked to the neighbours and children. The world isn't like that. It will be for our children. But I've only begun to live and now I could die.

*

ANNA. Well we chose.

A Fantasy

TRENCH. That white worm. Crawling along the floor. Food shoved up its hood. Led out to shit. Covered with a gun. What keeps it alive? A little thread of hope or cunning or hate or malice. It doesn't know the difference under the hood. Not that it matters. As long as it can dangle on it for a little time before it drops into the hole. If you took off its hood it would hang itself. That white corpse. That –

LISA (*at the window*). Car. (*She looks through binoculars.*) Michael.

ANNA (*collecting* LISA's *blanket*). That blanket.

LISA. Anna?

ANNA. What?

> ANNA *goes to the window. She takes* LISA's *binoculars. She looks through them.*

ANNA. He's driving too fast. Why's he driving so fast? (*Turns back to the room.*) Check his straps.

> LISA *checks the straps on the* WHITE FIGURE. ANNA *looks through the binoculars. The car is heard.*

ANNA (*binoculars*). He's alone.

LISA (*to* TRENCH *and the* WHITE FIGURE): One sound and I shoot.

ANNA (*binoculars. Under breath*). Don't hurry. Don't hurry. Don't hurry.

LISA. He's being chased.

ANNA (*binoculars*). The road's empty.

The car stops outside. ANNA *still looks from the window.*

MICHAEL (*off*). Anna! Anna!

ANNA (*to* LISA): Out of sight. It may be a trap.

LISA. But not if he –

ANNA. It may be a trap!

ANNA *and* LISA *hide.*

MICHAEL (*off*). Lisa!

ANNA. The bloody fool shouting our names!

MICHAEL *bursts into the room.*

MICHAEL. Lisa! Anna!

ANNA (*hidden*). Michael!

MICHAEL. HQ's busted. They must know this place. We've got to run. Quickly. (*Looks from the window.*) Quickly.

ANNA *and* LISA *come out of hiding.* ANNA *starts to pull the* WHITE FIGURE *to the door.*

ANNA. Help me.

MICHAEL (*looking through the window*). Leave that!

ANNA. We must –

MICHAEL (*looking through the window*). Leave it! No time! The car!

ANNA. What about the –

MICHAEL (*looking through the window*). We must move!

ANNA. A hostage is our only chance if we –

MICHAEL (*turns to* ANNA). Anna! No time!

LISA (*aims gun at* MICHAEL). It's a trap. Don't trust him.

MICHAEL. Please! Please!

> *They stare at each other.*

ANNA. No Lisa. Go with him. I'll shoot it out. I'll cover you from the porch.

> LISA *hesitates. Then lowers the gun. Goes out.* MICHAEL *follows her.*

MICHAEL (*off*). The hills.

> ANNA *picks up more ammunition. She goes out to the porch.* TRENCH *and the* WHITE FIGURE *are alone.* TRENCH *goes to it. Stoops. Undoes the straps on the legs. Goes to the picture. Hides behind it.*
>
> *The* WHITE FIGURE *staggers to its feet. It writhes to free its hands. It can't.*
>
> *Off, the sound of a helicopter.*
>
> *The* WHITE FIGURE *is terrified. It moves round the room to find a way out. It gets into the corridor.*
>
> *Off, the helicopter passes low overhead.*
>
> *The* WHITE FIGURE *panics. Tugs at the hood. It won't come off. Confuses the direction and returns to the room. Feels along the walls.*

HELICOPTER (*off*). Drop your arms. Face down on ground. Arms stretched out. Hands flat to ground.

> *The* WHITE FIGURE *writhes. Frees one hand. Tugs at the hood. It won't come off. It flays round with its free hand. Tugs at hood again. It comes off. The chauffeur is blinded by the light. Peers. Staggers. Sees picture.* TRENCH's *head is in the hole. Chauffeur tries to speak. No sound.* TRENCH *pushes his hand through the canvas. It holds a pistol.* TRENCH *shoots. The chauffeur is killed.* TRENCH *stares at him from the hole in the canvas. The pistol smokes.*
>
> *Off, sounds of helicopters, cars, police dogs.*

HELICOPTER (*off*). Remove your clothes. Throw items well clear. Girl first.

SIX

Park.
TERRY, JOHN *and* BERYL *on a bench. A pram.*

BERYL. All this for a few measly quid. No wonder it take so long to change anythin.

JOHN. It'll pay for a proper holiday. If I don't get one I'm knackered for the rest of the year.

BERYL. There'll be a whip round for his wife.

JOHN. Who reckons the lads'll jack it in?

BERYL. The papers'll have a go. Not nice when you're called an animal. The kids read it.

JOHN. Bet Ray's havin a go.

BERYL. Non-stop. What'll we tell the papers?

TERRY. When?

BERYL. When they ask what we think now he's dead. They're bound to ask.

JOHN. We didn't know they'd kill him.

BERYL. We said take the risk.

JOHN. Anyway it was only the dead girl. The other two were in custody.

BERYL. What'll we say?

Press Release

TERRY. 'Militants condemn terror.' So everyone's still got their right label. We can go home happy. What good's that? If you're ignorant that's your excuse. But if you know what sort of world you're in you have to change it.

Well what world is it? The poor are starvin. The rich are
gettin ready to blow it up. Terrorists threaten with guns?
We do it with bombs. One well-heeled American with his
finger on the button. That's sick. And there's worse than
that. The ignorance we live in. We don't understand what
we are or what we do. That's more dangerous than bombs.
We're all terrorists. Everyone of us. We live by terror. Not
even to make a new world: just to keep one that's already
dead. In the end we'll pay for that as much as the lot who're
starvin now.

How long can we go on like this? Yet we sit here as if we
had all the time in the world. All of us: we sit.

When they ask me to condemn terror I shall say: no. *You*
have no right to ask. You are a terrorist.

*

The Activists Papers

The Activists Papers

The Activists Youth Theatre Club is part of the Royal Court Theatre's Young People's Theatre Scheme. Most of The Activists Papers were written when I rehearsed *The Worlds* with them.

A Fallacy, *Learning* and *The Theft of a Bun* were written while I rehearsed the play with students at Newcastle University. Earlier versions of *A Note to Young Writers* and *The Art of the Audience* were written for the Warehouse company of the Royal Shakespeare Company.

The papers are an introduction to the play. Extracts from them may be printed in theatre programmes. They need not be read in the order in which they are printed here.

MEMORANDUM

The word reason alienates many people. Especially in universities. They think of it as being inhuman and cold. They think of theatre and the other arts as being human and warm.

We live and relate to ourselves, others, technology and our environment by organizing our behaviour and consciousness, with its attitudes and concepts, into a society. These things interconnect and mutually form one another. By 'rational' I mean the condition that exists when this is done in such a way that we're as sane and behave as morally and humanely as historically possible at that time. All societies should desire this state of affairs. Few do. In most societies it's assumed that when technological change (from the stone axe-head to the electronic computer) creates new wealth and new ways of using resources and abilities, these things should be fitted into the existing social order. The consciousness and beliefs of the members of society are arranged so as to make this possible. I say arranged and not manipulated because it's not likely to be done by conspiracy. It's not even likely to be done consciously. This makes it harder to detect and describe. The ruling class doesn't know what it's doing. That's why it's always losing its temper.

There are two grounds on which the ruling class justifies its obstruction of rational change. First it maintains law and order. It sees this as synonymous with maintaining decent social relations. But social relations are based on a particular social order. In time if this order doesn't change it becomes unjust. The ruling class denies this. Its second ground is that it's better washed, better mannered, better dressed and is interested in cultural affairs that are far superior to mere labour and survival. In a word, it protects the best. It sees people in the working class as being almost animals.

It sees itself as being synonymous with civilization and its cultivation as coming from its natural abilities and not from its wealth and privileged opportunities. It doesn't see that the way in which it monopolizes these things distorts the culture it derives from them and that this makes its culture irrational and an enemy of civilization.

To keep society as it is the ruling class uses education, media, jobs, bribes, punishments and other means of informing, commenting and persuading to make people think and behave in ways that will justify its rule. It doesn't fight the bad with the good, it uses both in an infernal alliance. This means that when it acts moral distinctions break down. Clearly almost any good action can be used to corrupt and damage. Charity may support a system that impoverishes. Teaching may strengthen ignorance. What has to be understood is that the ruling class uses every means it can to create social conditions and attitudes that will justify its claim to maintain law and order. Guilt, greed, envy, sexual repression, public disorder, self-denigration ('we're all animals'), everything that turns men back to their past – these are its cultural foundations. Its claim to represent justice depends on its ability to create injustice.

Here is an example to do with education. People are educated according to their class and money. Rich parents can buy their stupid children the best education. The stupid children of the poor get the worst. But society must at least appear just so the bright children of the poor may be sent to the schools of the rich. Earlier this century a man who ran an almost feudal estate sent two such bright boys to university every year. This disguised his despotism as enlightenment. An apparently good action was used to strengthen a bad system. This is the point: the bright boys had to behave themselves – and so did their parents. It also took possible malcontents away from their natural allies. The working class is often clannish. Even now getting above your station may be risky if it exposes you and your friends. Employers (as once the gentry) can pick you out more easily. In this way intelligence is a danger to the community. This attitude can only change when the working class can properly educate and support all its members.

Our relationships are based not only on beliefs and ideas but also on emotions. That is very useful to a ruling class. Emotions are effected by both the mind and the body. The first is easier to understand and so I'll say something about the second. A drowning man is afraid and may panic. A man resting in the sun is likely to be at peace. All the while we react to our environment in this way. Housing, factories, streets, the organization of work, the amount and security of wages, all these things, the physical, institutional, legal, domestic environment – in a word the social environment – effect our emotions. If the social environment isn't one that helps us to live humanely (socialism) but helps in our exploitation (capitalism) or makes us beasts or machines (fascism) then our emotions tend to deteriorate into fear, tension and racial and religious paranoia which lead to aggression, vandalism, child battering and other forms of violence. By education and information in newspapers, films, entertainment and so on the ruling class stresses this condition and reinforces it with pseudo-science and folky mythology. Mind and emotions prey on themselves and on each other. Ideas become infested with illusions and myths. Men behave in ways which aren't based on the world they're in but on the one they believe they're in. This is irrational and when we're irrational our condition deteriorates. Fear and tension aren't static conditions. Irrationalism leads to increasing hysteria, paranoia, apathy and violence and so society declines. In this way capitalism uses law and order to capitalize on the damage it does to men. It claims that a destructive emotional state is part of 'human nature' – as is its final consequence, war. This is what passes for its culture. It's the commentary we live by. Surely to those who come after us it will seem madness?

As technology changes so the society and behaviour based on the earlier technology becomes unable to use the new technology properly. Industrial and social relations break down. Technology makes the old society unworkable and the old society can't change itself so as to make the new technology work. Nevertheless it must try to make it work: so Hitler buys a plane and goes electioneering. If you don't make society and consciousness more rational then they must become more irrational. As technology changes *they* can't remain the same. The aggressive emotional condition and the behaviour it provokes must become more irrational and violent. To combat this the ruling class becomes even more coercive, its culture more decadent and its view of human nature more pessimistic. This aggravates the condition it's supposed to prevent. After all, it's only a more extreme form of the reaction that created the condition in the first place. But the ruling class can't understand what's happening or what it's doing. That's why comparative affluence failed to make the West more civilized.

The decline has no set pattern. Variation is almost infinite. Lies and excuses give way to new lies and new excuses. Perhaps the ruling class claims that it's civilized and the working class is brutal. Or it may argue racially. The working class is brutal but less brutal than even the elite of another race. Or it may say this of a social group. Often it's created the group itself: vandals for example. Or it claims that it has all the managerial skills and so we must all support it for the common good. And so on.

Our ability to be irrational is the necessary condition but not the cause of fascism. Hitler came to power because the German economy broke down. Money was devalued and there was poverty and unemployment. But affluence doesn't prevent fascism. In itself affluence doesn't make society rational, it merely gives fascism a new form. An irrational society projects its irrationality into individuals in many ways. I've described only some of them. Unless technological, industrial, economic and political relationships – unless all relationships involving human beings – are rational or developing rationally, then they produce fascism. I say 'rational or developing rationally' because we should use 'reason' to describe either a rational state or its creation. The word culture should be used in the same way: to mean a state of culture or – the only possibility open to us – the struggle for it.

The struggle for rationalism is of course against irrationalism. That's why it may have to be violent. If it is violent then superficially it seems itself to be irrational. Nevertheless the growth of rationalism can be seen in history. There are two reasons why its growth may be unclear. Partly, as I've said, it's because of the nature of the struggle: rationalism may have to use irrational means. And partly it's because as the irrationalism of the old order dwindles advances in technology give greater power to what's left of it. If you wish to see the growth of reason in history consider this. What would a medieval pope armed with H-bombs have done to infidels if he believed (as he did) that if he spared them suffering in this world they'd suffer for eternity in the next – and so would he?

Irrational society can't reform itself or stay as it is. Neither force nor fear can save it. Nor can its attempts at tolerance, kindness or charity. As we've seen, it corrupts moral action and whatever force it uses must hasten its end. The social order is itself irrational and would collapse into barbarism if there were not rational forces at work in it. These forces are the forces of socialism. They change the relationships between the classes and therefore the society and culture based on them. Socialism is caused by the collapse of the old society and is a cause of its collapse. The collapse of the old society and the creation of the new are aspects of the same

historical event. The old society wouldn't collapse if socialism wasn't necessary. Socialism is the working of reason and
the foundation of human culture. What is at stake is the
human mind.

A FALLACY

Whether the stomach is full or empty
Whether the house is large or small
All men are equal in joy or pain
There's only one sound of laughter
One sound of tears
And all who go in darkness stumble
In the calamity small differences are swept away
Men are united in common suffering
Master and servants weep at the grave

And it's true that all hungry men
Reach for the plate with one appetite
But not that all men have enough to eat
Or that the old man wrapped in linen
And the thin youth shot on the square
Should be mourned with the same cry
Humanity isn't shared when the rest is shared unjustly
Yet the hypocrites go on braying
All men are brothers!
As if that were the password of thieves

LEARNING

In the House of Preliminary Detention
By copying letters from cigarette packets
The worker and socialist revolutionary
Nikolay Vasilyev taught himself to read

He then got books and using his new knowledge
Wrote in capital letters
'MR PROSECUTOR DEAR SIR I AM THROWN IN THIS
   HOLE
FOR NO REASON
WITHOUT LIGHT OR AIR OR SPACE OR THE COMPANY
   OF PEOPLE
HAVE YOU NO GOD?'

There was no answer
One night he heaped the books over himself
Set them on fire and burned to death

From this there's much to learn
When knowledge is taught by the ignorant
We should fear not only the burners of books
We should fear the builders of libraries

THE THEFT OF A BUN

When the boy runs from the shop
Into the arms of a priest who says
'It's wrong to steal'
He turns white and drops the bun in the street

He doesn't ask the priest why it's wrong to steal
So the priest needn't answer
'Christ shed his blood on the cross
For the three-in-one-and-one-in-three
To redeem sinners except those elected by god
To be damned...'

The priest would be speaking long after the bun was stale
Even when it had turned to stone

But the boy doesn't ask because
The priest has one word that stands for many
This is the way lies may pass unquestioned

If we'd answered we'd have said
'It's wrong to steal
But if you're starving it may not be wrong
Ask why you steal
Ask is the owner a thief?'

And then we'd need to use so many words
The spectators would have gone home to dinner
Long before we'd finished
That's why truth often disperses a crowd
And is met walking alone and is jeered at
She doesn't have one word for many

SONG OF THE TOP POLICEMAN
(To sad music)

In the old days when I was young I slogged the beat
I passed the time by picking pockets
Nothing like it in the gentle summer sun
Lifting wallets in broad daylight on the street
Some days I made a ton
Now I sit behind a desk
You can't hear a truncheon drop the carpet is so deep
And it's all taking bribes from villains on the make or toffs
    who made it
They pass it over with a handshake and I go back to sleep
Of course I'm grateful for the dough
But the fun's gone out of life as I knew it long ago

In the old days the good old days when I was young I slogged
   the beat
When I was bored with clear blue skies and sun
I'd run a blackie up a sidestreet and drop him in the doorway
   of a shop
Then put the boot in and make the bastard hop – well you
   need a bit of fun
When the rent's behind and you're quarrelling with the wife
My panting mingling with the laddie's screams
Brought back fond memories of my brief boyhood
When we played pirates by laughing sunlit streams
Now the fun has really gone out of my life

I sit alone in my big office thumbing catalogues of guns
Sometimes there's an exhibition of riot gear and tear gas
(One lad went on crying even after I'd hammered in his skull
   – it's top-notch stuff)
But I haven't seen a decent bit of action not since years
Never hear a bone crack or a yell as the lads wade in with riot
   sticks
In worldly terms I'm doing very well out of the reach of flying
   bricks
But all the same my life is very dull

THE TEAM

The dogs dragged the sledge over the ice. It was hard work.
Perhaps it was even harder for the explorer. He wasn't used
to the cold. Fortunately he didn't have to waste strength
whipping the dogs. They obeyed his voice. In camp at night
they were let out of harness and fed. After feeding they didn't
run away. They were tired. They slept. And there was
nothing to eat out in the snow. In the morning they were
strapped into the harness. The order was given. 'Mush!'

Young dogs don't run away from their mother. And when the trainer takes them they're kept in a pen. If a dog is lured away by the dark green forest he's caught and beaten. The trainer has a secret – or rather a knack, because he doesn't understand it himself. He teaches the dog to train itself. Even when the trainer's dead the dog carries him in his head. This isn't to say that dogs become men but that sometimes a man becomes a dog.

Dogs know that meat doesn't spring from the ground. Still, the explorer had meat in tins. Surely this was manna from heaven? His dogs believed he was god. That's why they worked for him.

God was overdue. He was lost. So he used the whip. He made the working day longer. There weren't many tins left. Even now the dogs stayed with him. They trusted him. He wasn't wantonly cruel. In the good times he hadn't used the whip. Besides, what else could they do? They were famished and tired. They worked as best they could and did what they were told.

One night a dog tried to slink away. God tied him to the sledge and whipped him. Afterwards he left him tied there. He lay in the snow beside the sledge and slept. In the night he whimpered in his sleep. In the morning he was dead. God stripped the carcass. He cooked and ate some of the good meat. He packed the rest in snow in a sack. He tied the sack onto the sledge. He threw the offal, hide and bones to the dogs.

Two nights later the dogs were still hungry after their meal. They quarrelled. God cowed them with his whip. Then he put them in the harness. They spent the night in it.

God went on with his journey. He travelled under the bright stars. Slowly the weather turned. The strong wind came. Steadily the temperature fell. God ran out of tins. Now the dogs lived in the harness. From time to time one was taken out and killed. That's how god fed himself and his dogs. Each time he killed a dog the dogs that were left pulled the sledge more slowly. God's face darkened. A dull light shone in his eyes. He cracked the whip as if he were dancing. He believed they were moving fast. If you'd watched from a hill you'd have seen the team crawl over the ice as slowly as a worm. Now the dogs were imprisoned in the harness. Otherwise they would have run away. The cold killed the last two dogs and the explorer. His body lay on the lee side of the sledge. The dogs lay in the harness.

We should be sorry for these poor creatures. The circumstances of their deaths were as absurd as their lives. But don't be greatly worried. Men are neither gods nor dogs.

SPEAKING WITH ACTORS

He writes a cheque
That only proves he's in cash
Does the mother hold the child because she's kind?
Wait!
The mother can't waste kindness on that
She holds it because it will fall
Kindness is a special thing
Only those who run in the street are kind
They drag their fallen friend to the doorway

Was this soldier merciful?
How can I know? His uniform won't tell me
All I know is he's dead
To learn how to kill he shot at targets
They told him 'be proud of your uniform'
No one told him it was only a target
Why do they wear targets?
It would be a kindness to tell them
You'd be arrested

Don't let's sit and talk of the good
Not even the air's good here
You actors! don't crawl on the stage and question your soul
If it hasn't already answered you're wasting our time
And don't tell us you have problems
We know the problems
But you act opening the door and forget to look in the room
Open your eyes as you go through the doorway
Then we see that you understand problems

You act what's happening
Only the dead do that and nothing much happens to them
Something's going to happen
Now that's interesting!
Where will we be in an hour?
What will we do next year?
As you sit at rest in the chair
Show us that next year you'll run for your life in the street
As you do one thing let us see in it what you'll do next
As we see what you are let's see in it what you'll become
Act what's going to happen and what you will be
How else can you act what you are?

It's not that you don't interest us
But when we know what interests you you're more
    interesting
Unless all that interests you is yourself

All our characters must be Lear Hamlet Cordelia and Helen
But that's only a start
Much more is happening
Lear sits in a corner and you're the storm
Is there peace when the storm dies?
No
Lear cried for justice and you have to give it
So act what's going to happen

ADVICE TO ACTORS

Actors
Don't try to make your character possible
Men do things that ought not to be possible
Don't say 'he'd never do this'
Men don't behave in expected ways
Don't make the character one man
Unfortunately a man is many men
Don't worry when an action isn't consistent
Men aren't consistent
Ask why they're not consistent
Find out the uncharacteristic in a character
Find out why the character stops being himself
In this world we're still not human
Some try to be human
Others are butchers or worse
Start work again when you say 'he'd never do this'
You may be close to understanding
Why this man seeks freedom and that man's a butcher

Don't search for a soul
A soul won't help you to understand what's done
It's a white rabbit pulled from a hat when the truth's hard to
    follow
It's not a motive for acting truth
Don't try to become the character
That's impossible and if you try you give up responsibility for
    what you do
You give up judgement and without it you can't create
Possess the character don't let it possess you
Take your life to what the writer offers as useful
Acting changes the written word and the described gesture
As much as wind changes the shapes of clouds and clothes

Words change as you speak them and again as they're heard
Without these changes the play is a paper ghost

The character is by nature angry or happy?
How little this tells us!
There's not one anger or one happiness or one courage
But there is only one justice
The SS guard is happy
Emotions don't make us human
It's not even true to say that virtuous acts make us good
Judge by the situation not by the character or his actions
A starving prisoner gives a child bread
The guard gives it bread
He knows tomorrow the child will be gassed
Is the guard kind? He's mad
But it's still an act of kindness?
No it's an act of madness
The same act has many meanings
There's no soul common to all men
All that we have in common is reason and some men use
    reason to defend madness
So show us the situation
Then we can see how vices and virtues
May pass through our minds under false names
As a man smiles when a pistol is in his back
Or a man disguises himself at the frontier post
You ask is he a bandit or friend of the people?
Don't expect his disguise to tell you!

A miner finds gold in the hills
He changes his clothes and eats well
You act this but what have you taught us?
Go to the hills!
The poor are still poor

The past still hides the past and the future is still uncertain
For shame! Why waste our time?
Don't show us a man who comes to terms with this world
His life isn't changed – only his way of life
There's nothing for you to act in that
The miner's nails are clean – that's all you act!

The fishwife is clever or stupid
You show which but you still haven't shown us the fishwife
The cleverness of the fishwife and her customer aren't the
    same
There's not one cleverness
The cleverness that makes the fishwife cunning
May make her customer a good mother
The fishwife can't be shown by her character
Her life's shaped by the stall
By the storm that blows on the quay
Till the canvas over her head flaps like a vulture's wings
By the sun that makes the fish stink when the passersby are
    too poor to buy
By hauling baskets and haggling with skippers
By speaking at the stall holders' meeting
By bribing the licensing officer
By all the business of selling and buying fish

Two lovers alone in a room
One leaves the bed and puts on his brown tunic
Two more lovers in some other room
One weeps
We don't share one love
You can't show a girl in a kitchen till you show us the landlord
And who runs the city
The clock stands at three
You can't tell the time till you know the century

A man tends the rosetrees in his garden
The city is run by gangsters
He builds a high wall round his garden to shut out the urchins
Who sees the beautiful roses?
The gangsters kill him behind his wall
Who sees the killers?

What does the character bring to his situation?
Characteristics? Temperament? Useless!
Is he proud? Of what? Angry? When? Kind? To whom?
Unless we know a man's situation we can't say if he's good or
    evil
How can the fishwife fix the price of fish till she knows the
    state of the market?
How can she know what she does till she knows what world
    she's in?
The pessimism of one man and the optimism of his neighbour
May change the world in the same way
What should a man understand? His life
That is his situation and what he does in it
His life isn't made by what he does to himself
It's made by what he does to his situation
The SS guard doesn't understand his life
You will act many men who don't understand their life
Not all wear uniforms to warn us
So how important that *you* understand!

It's clear a character can't be acted
You must act a life
I repeat a character can't be acted
This is a paradox but true
The parable of the leaf and sail will help you to understand
A leaf driven before a storm sought its tree
It called to the wind for help

But the strongest storm can't blow one leaf back onto its tree
On the lake a boat raises its sail
It takes the wind and crosses the sea
It can even make port in the teeth of the storm
The character can be compared to the leaf
What you should act can be compared to the sail
What you call character is only self
The self does nothing but call to the storm
The life of one man is explained by the lives of all men
You don't need to understand his character
You need to understand his life
You need a way to show this understanding
A man is either himself or all men
You must act all men
That is the theatre of reason
Act this understanding
Act learning
Don't reproduce – don't call the wind
Judge!
Let your playing show that you understand history
The changes that men make and that make men

The acting of knowledge is like a window
Of good proportion and clear glass
To show us the world
We bring the audience to the window
They see how they live
And how others have lived before them and made this world
And how they can remake it
This is of great use but it's not drama
This is drama:
'Man the seeker and finder of knowledge'
That men seek and when they find what is true they know it
That's why they're called men
That is the ancient lure that brings them to the stage

Cattle go to the pool to quench thirst
They drink and their thirst is quenched
Men go to the pool and drink with their parched throat
But they're not quenched till they see their face in the water
That's why they're called men
They see they are men who seek understanding
Oedipus is both foolish and wise
Knowledge is truth but not art
In art there's always justice
In drama the meaning of justice is clear
In drama man learns who he is

We also show that men question truth
We know things that to our forefathers were secret
But they sought!
Their plays bear the scars of reason and are among the classics
We have new weapons and tools of understanding
Justice is no longer the cry of the falsely accused
Justice is passed on the false accusers
In your acting guide us in our changing times
Show justice
And we shall know her when she comes to meet us on the
    street

ON WORKING WITH YOUNG ACTORS

The stage is the court of justice herself
Some players play in the masks they wear off-stage
They're like the curteous men in striped suits
Who step from the pavement to let evil pass
Don't learn their tricks!
When an actor goes onto the stage he shows what he lives for

How else could he act other men's lives?
And there's justice in this
The way you judge them is the way you judge yourself

Actors! understand that each word and gesture shows why
   you live
We don't hear the human voice but the human brain
When you speak you show us all that's in your mind
Remember the distance between the brain and the voice
Is the longest way in the world
Did you die on the way?
What is this stranger saying? In what tongue?
How can we understand – he can't even tell us where he came
   from?
Well who has something to say?
Those who watch and listen
And speak when silence would make them
Accomplices to the crime

Lies too need time to grow
But perhaps you've already run on ahead
To lay traps and snares on your way
In time you'll meet yourself
Waiting on corners and sitting in strange rooms
Offering yourself coins or a knife
Or in too much despair to look up as you enter
Already some of these meetings have been arranged

Then how will you live? What can you do?
Work for evil or good
Nothing else can be done with your life
No other choice
The stage shows how you choose
Help us to choose
Choose well

A REHEARSAL IN THE GARAGE

If you were learning to kill they'd give you weapons
Hot food a uniform and a dry hall

Their pals give you bright lights and music
That's why they give you money
So they can rob you
Sure! you need to dance
And who dances better?
But they grab everything
They'll leave you nothing

We work in the cold garage till eleven at night
When you came you were tired
From carrying bricks and studying primers
Rain weeps through the ceiling
But listen how joyfully it's hammering on the roof!
Wind comes through each hole in the wall
Is it that curious to see what we're doing?
It must be interesting!
When we work the world tries to burst in
Those others, they're trying to shut it out

A NOTE TO YOUNG WRITERS

Perhaps every twenty years there will be a new generation of
angry young writers. They'll have a right to be angry.
There'll still be many things to be angry about. But what use
is it that five times in a century young writers tell us they're
angry? Anger may be caused by impotence.

We haven't done much when we've abused the stupid and
presumptuous people in power. Abuse won't take away their

power. And it's not enough merely to point out where their misuse of it leads. We must say how they got it and how they keep it.

Capitalism needs to understand the nature of things. It uses science to do this. It doesn't want to understand people. Such an understanding would destroy the deception on which it bases its confidence. It would also make it easier for the people it controls to understand themselves. This would make them harder to control. Capitalism doesn't want to know what we are but merely how we can be manipulated. To this end it creates a mythology about men and society. This passes for its culture – and it's almost feudal.

When capitalist culture controls science and technology we're in danger. Dramatists are right to warn of an apocalypse. But that's only part of the truth. Capitalism doesn't have to lead either to a stable fascist state or to the end of the world. That sort of pessimism is irrational.

Capitalism sees men as bestial. They must be restrained by law and order and manipulated by incentive and coercion. This is its image of man. It's mythological. But it can't free itself from this mythology. To do that it would have to stop being capitalism. That's why capitalism can never again be fit to control science and technology. It uses them irrationally. It's rational only about things and the way they work. It's not rational about men or their relation to things or to each other. In other words capitalism no longer expresses reality in an accurate or even adequate way. It no longer has a culture.

Capitalism uses education and morality to teach men lies about themselves and society. It starts doing this when they're children and that's one reason why the teaching has an effect. But people have no lasting need to believe lies. Indeed, the lies they are taught go against their daily experience. For many reasons all people try, sometimes more and sometimes less, to express their experience in an adequate and accurate way – that is, rationally. In a time of capitalist irrationalism a rational culture can be created only by the expression of working class experience, and the working class must obviously take the major part in creating it. This rational culture will need new political and social forms. It will also need a new image of men and women – and new artistic forms to create it. Writers can create art only by working to create this culture. It's the only way they can record the truth. Writers who don't help to do this peter out in silence or hide their increasing superficiality under deeper obscurantism or run for the bolt-hole of reaction. Contemporary theatre has examples of all three.

The form of the new drama will be epic. This name is often misunderstood, partly because the form isn't yet fully developed. An epic play tells a story and says why it happened. This gives it a beginning, a middle and an end joined together in a truthful way. This isn't true of the theatre of the absurd. It sees life as meaningless: it has a beginning and an end but no middle. The bourgeois theatre is concerned only with anecdotes: they have a middle but no beginning and end.

Epic plays don't need to cover centuries or have a cast of armies. The essence of epic theatre is in the way it selects, connects and judges. Even when it deals with two people quarrelling in a kitchen it draws its method and values from the understanding of the history of all people. How else should you judge between right and wrong? Bourgeois writers believe that only they write with subtlety and sensitivity. They see epic theatre as abstract, inhuman and cold. But what they call subtle and sensitive is only arbitrary and incomplete. They try to derive meaning from the incidental. No, the broad structure of history must be understood before the incidents in it can be given meaning. That's why the epic is the only form of theatre that can be subtle and sensitive – and have good taste, wit, nuance and human intimacy.

Bourgeois theatre lacks this sense of purpose and this makes it inhuman. It would be unfair to judge its subtlety and sensitivity on the fodder it gives to tired businessmen and their bored clients. That would let it off very lightly. It ought to be judged on the crudity, shallowness and vulgarity of the plays admired by its intellectuals.

Anger and apocalypse aren't enough. Theatre must talk of the causes of human misery and the sources of human strength. It must make clear how and why we live in a culture of nihilism. And because the understanding of history has been contaminated with mythology it must rewrite it to make sense of the future. To do these things we need a rational theatre.

ANTIGONE

In the old plays kings fought kings
Quarrelled with princes and queens
And told the people when to take the leather tool-bag
From the worn skin of their shoulder
And strap on the knapsack
Because in those days power went to the kings
And as art deals with justice
It told how the kings used power

The king took the people's power
His small hand was a giant's
It sent ministers from the room
And drove armies into mud on the broken banks of the river
If his mood was bad he sat down with sycophants in a corner
    to corrupt justice
His family quarrel was the state quarrel
His fate was the people's fate
Because power went to the kings

And whether Antigone or Creon is right
Is a question that has no answer
How can a man of power be human?
How can he use his power for good?
Antigone and Creon are vultures who fight for a corpse after
    battle
Antigone's screams can't tell us
The meaning of justice

Men with great power don't govern a human state
They take the people's power but can't take their wisdom
When the people have lost their power
Their wisdom is lost to the state
And the people who say it's right that the king should take
    our power
Will be wrong in all matters of law and justice that follow
As much as a man who can't tell you the day he was born
Can't tell you his age

All giants are tyrants
No tyrant is human
If Creon has power he can't be just
And Antigone's weakness can't make her wise
Or her pain teach her the law
But the people who know their right to power
Are wise in all that follows
Then power itself is wise
And the wound that divided power from justice is healed
So that the human smile is stronger than the armies
That once roamed the face of the earth
    Then we'll know how to bury our dead
    And how to live

THE SIMPLE IMAGE

In the time of the hand-held plough
Of kings in purple and gold
And inquisition into the mind
When the poor woman served her children
Bread at the scrubbed wooden table
The bread was pure and her smile without guilt
And her hands were clean
Because she worked in a field that wasn't stolen
And though her husband rused like a raddled fox
He was honest and stole only what had been stolen from him
And at play his children sang in joy of the world

And now in the time of bombs
And troops in the drab overalls of mass executioners
And inquisition into the mind
When bad bread is served from a plastic bag
On the formica top of a plastic table
To a man who works in armaments
And to children who sing commercial jingles
Where shall we find the simple image of truth?

The family is still exploited
Still suffer all that follows
When the mind's coerced for profit
And is not free to create a decent life among neighbours
There's still unemployment and debt
The crime of all preying on all fills prisons
Hospitals are full of sick in body and mind
Education is superstition
And morals are fraud and violence
That's still how we live

Don't be misled
The exploiter tells cynical tales
In schools he teaches despair
His theatre shows the slave's mind as enslaved
He fears the truth because the exploited speak it
In his language only lies can be spoken

In the simple house in the east quarter
Mind isn't formed by money
Or character by hiring and selling
Instead hand and brain work together
And the brain sees what the hand does
So that the value of all things can be seen
There you'll find the simple image of truth

The woman who watches at night by the sickbed
Not reading the open book on her lap
The care of the father who serves at the table
The children's mouths as they hold out their plate
The frown of the anxious mother as she enters the shop
In all these things there is beauty
And beauty always gives warning of storm
Of change
There is the simple image of truth

ON WEAPONS

It's in the nature of things that we have buses before we know
how to ride in them, cars before we know how to drive them
and spades before we know how to dig with them. We have
machines before we know how to use them because at first we
don't know all that they do. A machine doesn't merely make a
glass or a shoe. Those who make and use the machine are

changed by it. It doesn't give them a new purpose but it makes it necessary for them to live in a new way. Machines demythologize the earth, men and their societies. They make the old expression of humanity, and the old society connected with it, inhuman. All technology changes us and our society. It changes the way we live and so our beliefs, attitudes, customs, behaviour, consciousness itself – all change. And as consciousness is both mental and emotional the change in us is great enough to make us different people. We become either more rational or more irrational.

Our species innovates. When we change the mechanical means by which we live we have to change our social relationships. We develop new attitudes to the rest of society and what's in our heads changes. In the business of maintaining ourselves we change ourselves. How else could we co-operate in new ways? And how can society work without co-operation – either forced, as in the past, or freely as is made possible and necessary by modern technology? There's a constant mutual influence between technology, the human mind and social order. Society changes so that it can use its new machines and the users of new machines change so that they can use them and live in the new society. If we're to remain human these changes must be rational. In fact it's by making these changes rationally that we create our humanity. Each generation inherits its humanity from its society but it retains it only by recreating it in solving its new problems. That's what humanity is: each generation is faced with new problems and in solving them it creates its new humanity. Obviously feudal society couldn't run modern technology. But more important, if we try to run modern technology on the consciousness and social relations of feudalism we don't get feudalism. Instead what are now irrational social relations distort consciousness in order to bridge the gap between the old social order and the consciousness made necessary by the working of new technology. That distortion is fascism.

A weapon is a machine for causing respect, fear, pain or death. It has a good and a bad use. What good use? When technology changes human consciousness, social change is also necessary. Society resists change. It's based on laws and property relations that benefit the rulers of the old social order. They run it on the old form of consciousness calcified in universities, churches, theatres, customs, opinions and so on. We live in societies that are both new and old and which are therefore unsuited to many of our needs. If a society isn't changed rationally then the consciousness of many people in it is distorted so that they become, in effect, less human. Many resist this distortion but even so rational change is often late. It can't always be brought about by peaceful persuasion. Every day men learn the ways in which society doesn't meet human needs but they may not understand how much must change before it can meet them. Perhaps it seems a few small changes will do. But often small needs amount to vast social desires. For all to eat well there must be liberty and governments have had to fall before children could wear shoes. Society can't be just and rational in part. What we do and are depend on the relationships between everyone in society. The force and mythology needed to hold together an unjust society damage everything in it.

From time to time the conflict between society and the new needs and new consciousness of the people in it falls into crisis. Then the old society is destroyed by force. This is revolution. That is the good use of weapons. They're used to create a society in which consciousness doesn't have to be distorted and our needs can be met in a human way. It's not merely a struggle to take power and wealth from some and give it to others, it's a struggle (as we see) for the freedom of the human mind to express its humanity. Power and wealth in the hands of the old rulers dehumanizes society. It must be put into new hands before we can recreate humanity. So it's easy to see why change comes late. Revolutions aren't caused by those who desire them but by those who don't, by those who lose not those who gain by them. Many who read this will be against revolution and many of them will be the cause of revolution. This paradox shows the irrational way we still run our affairs. It's why reason still has to use irrational means.

Not all revolutions serve reason. Often the old society uses revolution to attack the new consciousness. It captures the new technology and tries to use it to drive men back to their past. Think of Hitler's electioneering planes and the death factories that came later. Fortunately totalitarianism must perish in a machine age. Superficially it seems that machines might help it (1984) but they only help it to get power not to keep it. Totalitarianism conflicts with the needs of the new consciousness created by technology. A modern totalitarian society becomes increasingly irrational and as a result unworkable. It can only tolerate the violence and hysteria needed to keep it going by apathy – and this makes it even more unworkable. In a modern totalitarianism the trains wouldn't run on time. It would bleed to death internally or if like Hitler's Germany it tried to save itself by going to war it would die of external wounds. It can't fight efficiently. A totalitarian soldier in a tank is as useless as a bushman handling a rifle for the first time. It's not that the soldier can't handle the tank efficiently but that his society can't. The only war a modern totalitarianism could wage efficiently would be total nuclear war – and it couldn't win that because it has no winner.

It's confusing to use the word revolution to describe the reactionary use of violence to save an old society. We should use it to describe only rational change. The confusion arises because in the past social change was studied in the universities, military academies and theological seminaries of the old societies. There all violent social change (even their own when they had to use it) was seen as bad because it disturbed the status quo. They classified by method not cause and this was misleading.

Affluence isn't an alternative to rational change. It makes that change more likely. It can't preserve an unjust society. Even a just society that was starving would have more chance of preserving itself. In an unjust society (and therefore in one which teaches, encourages and forces people to behave irrationally) the bribed can't trust the briber to go on paying. And anyway if the society is unjust the bribed will always want more. Really the briber is hostage to the bribed. Could there be a more absurd way of running our affairs? Affluence with socialism could bring peace, affluence without it must bring fascism. Affluence meets the needs only of an unjust society, or rather the needs it knows it has. Just societies need not only affluence but reason. Since western society doesn't understand this it can't do anything to get it. So it falls apart.

History needs weapons and revolutions. In time it won't. One day the old society will learn how to change peacefully into the new. But now it still clutches at power and tries to force its primitive forms onto our new, restless, changing world. It can neither work nor peacefully make way for the new. It produces discord, then reaction, then fascism. This delays rational change but it can't stop it.

THE NEW FASCISM

Technological and economic change make greater freedom possible and necessary. As human consciousness develops men demand more freedom. When they use more complicated machines, so that economic and social organization is made more elaborate, then as a rule they demand more autonomy. This is true even if their own job is simplified. It's enough for the machinery to be more complicated and the organization of the economy more complex. Men who accept more responsibility as workers or consumers demand more responsibility in the rest of their lives. Technological change destroys the old social structure, and the changing people construct a new one. They demand not just a society in which technology can work properly but one in which they can live together in decency. Unfortunately the demand can be corrupted. The old society tries to use technology and comparative affluence to cling onto power. This accelerates irrationalism, as we see, and leads to fascism. The fascism of affluence isn't the same as the fascism of poverty. The new fascism is the H-bomb, the mechanical Hitler. It's the product of irrationalism in affluent societies. Progress from scarcity to affluence doesn't make fascism impossible. It merely changes its form. Both forms may exist together.

Not only capitalist societies have H-bombs. Socialist societies have them. That's the ancient dilemma of good and evil. If reason could always choose its own weapons the history of man would have been different. Both capitalist and socialist societies have H-bombs but they're not both morally guilty for having them. Wherever technology is owned irrationally the production of H-bombs is likely and this makes their production necessary in societies which are becoming increasingly irrational. If technology is owned irrationally anywhere in the world then H-bombs will be made there and in many other societies.

Irrational societies create H-bombs. Irrational societies deteriorate through internal stress. It seems to follow that irrational societies must use their H-bombs. Affluence is as vulnerable before the new fascism as poverty is before the old. Socialism is the only alternative to fascism. On the road to hell there is no half-way house run by a liberal landlord. Socialism is the political definition of reason and without reason fascism grows.

THE STRUGGLE FOR REASON

The relationship between technology, consciousness and social order must be continually adjusted. This is in the nature of the relationship. History makes it increasingly possible for the relationship to be rational. As technology makes it possible for more and more people to become autonomous so the possibility of reason is made greater.

As the relationship between technology, consciousness and social order changes, so the relationships between workers, men and women, parents and children – all human relationships – change. If we make these changes rationally it doesn't mean that we lose our humanity, warmth, spontaneity, enjoyment and creativity – all those things which are the concern of art. Rationality isn't their enemy or even an alternative to them. They can't exist or be protected without it. Our wide use of technology to change our environment and our way of living has created problems in all human relationships. We've not yet solved these problems – and this is one reason why we misuse technology.

We use technology before we fully know what it does. When we use it we begin to live in new ways, create new experiences and gain new knowledge. We use all this to understand our new life and this understanding changes us again. All the time we behave differently and become different people. Each generation lives in a new world. Each generation must create its own humanity. If it's to be human it must develop new social relationships in which reason can flourish. Our minds can't be modern when we work and consume and feudal when we think and relate socially. Yet that's what capitalism demands. It brings chaos – the inarticulate cry for reason that can for a time be used to support the enemies of reason. Men long to be free of these ancient problems. With such burdens how can they live and work together in human decency? It's as if to free itself from the past our species always had to struggle for reason and cry for justice. That's what human societies do, that's what men are. Reason struggles in the whole world. Our lives invite us to reason and make it necessary. The cry for reason could only be stopped if we destroyed ourselves with nuclear weapons.

But before we can live in reason and justice – in accord – we must end the class order. Socialism makes the old idea of the classless brotherhood of man possible. It's the political work-ing of reason. With it men can recreate their humanity in the time of advanced technology, even in the time of the H-bomb.

A STORY

The man-beast pulls the plough. If it pulls the plough in an orderly way the owner feeds it. The man-beast eats its fodder as all beasts might. If it's unruly the owner beats it. If it's dangerous he kills it.

A horse pulls the plough. The man-beast drives the horse. The man-beast learns he's not a beast. He's like the owner. The old rewards don't work. But the owner doesn't want to kill him. If he did who'd drive the horse? The man must be rewarded or punished in new ways. The owner tells him of heaven. He turns him into a religious-beast.

Next a tractor pulls the plough. The religious-beast drives the tractor. He also makes it. The owner owns the factory where the tractor's made. The religious-beast buys corn so that the owner makes a profit to invest in the factory to make the tractor. 'Wait a moment! I work for the boss so that he can make a profit to afford to hire me?' The man talks this over with the men who help him to make tractors. They ask the owner for more of the profit they make for him. The owner says no. The men stop work. They are many, the owner is one. It may be said that the men are masters but not owners.

Why isn't the factory working this morning? We could say that when the factory works the man pulls the plough and is driven by the horse. That's the easiest way to describe what happens when the master works for whoever he's master of.

Is this the modern world? Clearly it can't go on like this. What happens next? That depends. The master must become the owner. Then he'll be master of himself. Till then the horse goes on cracking the whip and calling him animal and nothing works.

THOSE WHO GO BEFORE

Machines changed our world and our minds
But we served the old ways
Things broke
Old customs and old beliefs – the old world itself
Didn't work
But we kept to the old ways

In change we saw only decay
The thin line of dawn was a blade at our throat
Roof tiles were blown through our windows
We spoke only of young vandals
We didn't inspect the roof or name the wind
We talked of peace and reason
Longed for lost courtesies
Sighed at the ugliness of the old world we wanted to save
Shuddered when it was said revolution controls change
And despaired when the mob that had always begged bread
Now wanted money

Only we could pay the artists and buy books
Only we had a use for quietness
See how we wrung our hands with gestures from attic friezes!
We cried with great beauty
We clung to the rags
We didn't see they made our hands dirty

And so we dug the deep dark pit
And over it spread the few yellow straws
Our slogans were tolerant! Our creed human!
We never spoke of our new masters
Or the empty streets of curfewed cities
Or neat rows of bodies outside the new annex
Each labelled at the wrist
Or the unlabelled dead who came later

THE THINKERS

In the concrete factory yard it drizzles
The stewards' mike catches the wind
Strikers with faces still oily frown as they
Strain to hear and stamp to keep warm
They ask will my opinion be heard or my question taken?
And start to bellow and wave their arms
These are signs of clear thought and judgement
To the TV screen a rabble of louts

The director doesn't open the door
It's held for him by the chauffeur
Paper and pen before each chair
Glasses and a decanter of water
Whispering in carpet-dust parches the throat
Here the workers were once sifted for profit in a giant sieve
Now the hands holding the sieve shake in fear

Hurling the workers from side to side in chaos
Things can't go on as they are
No control!
Calm voices can't hide the panic
The porter opens the door as the director leaves
On the TV screen a courteous smile on top of a white shirt
'Let's hope the men see reason'

When the men have the table and pen and ink
The view from your window will change
At one stroke you'll see many things differently
Paper and pens are the tools of reason
Who knows how to use them?
The lathe operator works to the thousandth of an inch
He's schooled in the art of discrimination
His owner demolishes houses and builds empty towers
Who knows the craft of choosing?
The lathe operator counts shillings
His owner moves millions over the board
Who knows the value of money?

The clouds didn't soak your black coat
So that it shines like the river as you run for shelter
It's the drops of rain that did it!
The icy wind didn't make the girl shake with fever
It's the little crack in the window that killed her
But round here you know nothing!
You dress the criminal in red robes instead of pulling him
    from the chair
You put his victims in thin prison overalls!
You people would let the killer come up to you with the knife
    in his hand
If he disguised himself as a surgeon!

How confused you are
It will be hard for you to think till reason wears its own
   clothes
And speaks in its own voice

ON VIOLENCE

It's said violence creates violence
Violent man is chained to a wheel
His struggles to free himself turn the wheel
Day after day he's knocked off his feet and stood on his head
There are three sounds in the world
The grinding of stone
The racing of chains over the stone
And the man's groans

If this is true the state must create revolution or war
The state is the greatest user of force
If the wheel turns the state must cause violence
It may be said the state doesn't use force in violent ways
Instead it has preachers teachers and judges
So there is no nightmare
No war dance of the devil mask with the red mouth waved on
   a stick to frighten children
No puppet of stuffed denim with helmet and gun
To kill as if it were a child playing with clay
And so the wheel stops

Consider
The scrupulous judge weighs the law in his white hand
Politely he sends a man to prison for ten years
Or he says 'Go
Take this chance to be a good worker and live by the law
I wish you well'

The last sentence is more violent than the first
It condemns the man to give his life to the judge
Teach his child the judge has a right to send its father to
    prison
Respect the school that made the judge
Build a wall round the judge's house to protect his loot
Hurry to work each morning to make guns for the judge to
    fire in the square
And be told to die in his own house or kill in his neighbour's
Or worse worse day after day to live quietly
So that the judge may give mercy that's harsher than prison

All this might be justified if in the place of violence it put
    order
So that the wheel stopped
It doesn't
Whatever stops man knowing himself is violent and the
    cause of violence
How shall a man know himself?
Let him know where he is and what he does

Consider
The man who stands in freedom on the street corner
Holds by the hand an unseen man
For twenty years this man has been mad
He is old and lies at the foot of a damp wall with his dead child
    in his pocket
His heart beats only to pump out his life through his wounds
He's too weak to staunch it or call for help
Who is this unseen man he holds by the hand?
Himself
If the mind had a human shape it would be this
These things were done to it by the judge who said mercy
These are the wounds of peace
The violence of freedom

More bitter than famine
Crueller than war
Deadlier than plague
It's not seen
It's hidden under the head as if that were a stone to hide truth
In such a world there is no peace
The man walks from court in freedom
The university market library broadcasting station are
   prisons
The street is the gallery of a prison
The houses on either side are cells in a prison

We're told violence is caused by violence
The argument proves the state must create revolution or war
You priests why do you pray to the god of war for peace?
You comedians why do you dance in the temple of reason?
Violence will cause violence till men know themselves
Know where they are and what they do
Know the working of judgement and mercy
Till then the strongest prison is freedom
Few try to escape from its walls
But in it we're knocked off our feet and stood on our head
As we walk in the street

TYPES OF DRAMA

The remnant theatre of the old society uses a particular sort of
dénouement. There's a problem in social life. It may be lack
of money or an unhappy marriage or something else. The
dénouement solves the problem without changing society. A
will is found or a poor man turns out to be a rich orphan.
Unhappy marriages are more difficult to deal with. Though
wills are rarely found the idea of finding one is easily understood. But what is 'happy ever after'? So the theme of

unhappy marriage is usually avoided. Instead there's frustrated romance. If only the people could live happily together they'd live happily ever after. If they can't live together they may have to die together. The thing is to fit everyone back into a changeless society (the 'found will' and all bourgeois comedy other than some satire) or to give the social conscience a bit of a dusting (the tragedy of dying lovers).

In these plays the people on stage are themselves. In many ways they're like the audience but they're still private individuals. This doesn't seem to be true of bourgeois epic characters. King Lear and Hamlet aren't presented as themselves but in a sense as all who live.

Problems that concern everyone (not individual problems common to everyone) aren't private problems so they have no individual solutions. Lear's experience and thoughts are his own but they're also everyone else's. The resolution of his play is that although evil is virulent and the good must suffer yet they may endure. Because it's corrupted by human nature society is irredemiably evil but we're formally assured it will be better governed. This assurance isn't derived from Lear's experience and his thoughts aren't an adequate philosophy for it. Shakespeare says that Lear's suffering and partial, ineffective illumination represent the fallible condition of all human goodness. The problem is seen to be political but the solution given isn't – it recommends calmness and acceptance. Shakespeare tries to give the public problem a private solution. Lear finds his own peace and dies. This means that he finally relates to the audience in the way all other characters in bourgeois theatre relate to it. He's an individual with buttons on his jacket who resolves an epic problem – in a private way. This sort of drama was still possible when Shakespeare wrote.

Lear is a feudal king with great political power. That he gives it away doesn't affect this point – it's merely Shakespeare's device to allow him to examine the problems of goodness. Characters such as Lear contain the personal and political in one image. To him the loss of an army is personal in the way the loss of a child is to one of his soldiers. His psychology effects his political acts. If he's rash he loses battles. This means that Shakespeare can use personal imagery and the personal expression of emotion to describe political causes and events, that he can transcribe historical cause into the emotional expression of personal motives. Lear represents society in his person and mind. All members of society are members of his body and their ideas and feelings are in his head. Political determinants seem to filter through him so that he can express them as direct, subjective, human experience. That's a very powerful dramatic tool. But we have to deal with new political relationships that can't be dealt with in the same way. We can't use strikers in the way Shakespeare used kings. The defeat of a strike isn't the same sort of thing as the abdication of a king. An individual biography can't show historical movement or be a pattern for the historical understanding of society. Nor (and perhaps this has the greatest significance for drama) can individual emotions still be used to transcribe historical causes. Hamlet's poetry is put forward as the voice of history itself. But emotions only tell us how it feels to be in history not how history feels. The swimmer's feelings don't describe swimming. His feelings of determination don't tell us why he won the race. Bourgeois theatre assumes the swimmer's determination is so great that he rises out of the water and runs across it. We have to show the real mechanisms of history – the dreamtime is over. We can't use a general to encapsulate an army. A private soldier can't represent a historical pattern, as interpreted by socialism, in the way a general can represent it as it's interpreted by capitalism.

A play can show characters resolving a problem by using socialist consciousness. They may win a strike or decide to build a factory or hospital. Marriage could be looked at in the same way. These would be socialist plays to be understood and enjoyed most by socialist audiences. They're incident not propaganda plays. A propaganda play must be able to tell its message to an uninformed or resisting audience. It must stress its characters' class functions. If it's to work it may be necessary to show them as types. If the propaganda is a straightforward piece of information, such as what medicine to use, types may have a direct effect. If the information is more complex – perhaps about picketing or landlords – the audience will have to translate the types back into their own experience. Obviously general statements aren't always true about individuals. Types may draw out truths from collective experience and make them easier to see. But the audience must still compare these truths with their own experience. One woman's landlord may be better than the others. She has to understand that his 'goodness' won't provide good houses and in fact that he stops her son being educated and her daughter-in-law cured. A propaganda play may make these points too. But what it does is limited by the proper need to simplify. The audience has to develop a socialist consciousness able to reflect and judge from its own free will. By themselves propaganda plays can't create this consciousness. Theatre workers who don't understand this ignore some of the needs of their audience.

Both incident and propaganda plays are important parts of socialist theatre. They don't try to fit people into an unchanging society but to help them to change society – the only unsentimental sort of modern drama. Both may be written with wit and grave feeling. Is there another sort of socialist play, another sort of epic, in which the characters aren't only in history but are its representatives? Aren't only class types but types of history or spokespeople of its forces, so that the play embodies history itself? Such an epic wouldn't only be an account or story, it would be a poem. It would put history on stage as a dramatic reality. In it subjective qualities could again be used to transcribe history. It might help us to see and understand people in a new way.

In this form, characters, events and incidents wouldn't only be aspects of historical movement. They'd show the pattern and nature of that movement. Instead of history being filtered through an individual, reduced to him (as in King Lear), the play's figures and incidents would embody and demonstrate the total historical movement. History wouldn't be shown as immanent in an individual, individuality would be transcended by the historical pattern which it represented. Incidents would be chosen to show how historical problems arise and how they lead to resolutions. Movements spread over long periods and involving masses of people might be reflected in stories, often in simple stories. The characters wouldn't be moved by personal motives but by the forces of history. They'd be epic in analysis but not necessarily in size – after all a mouse can be the hero of an epic. The forces wouldn't be shown as abstractions. We need to show the historical abstraction but at the same time we need to show the individual characteristics – they're the means through which history works. That's really the reason why we have art – we need to show the general in the particular in order to understand ourselves. So we'd show individual quirkiness. Indeed we'd show the power of historical forces by showing the individuality, ordinariness and human vulnerability and strength of the characters who live it.

In epic theatre the individual's involvement in society is seen to be a full involvement in himself. This is possible because every life is part of history. In epic theatre dramatic development doesn't come from the individual coming to terms with himself but from his changing society so that everyone in it may be more human. This broad category includes incident and propaganda plays. And it may be that socialism needs and makes possible this other, poetic drama which impersonates history.

Perhaps the epic that was possible in the classical world will again be possible. The classical world believed (and as it was then a reasonable belief it could produce art by it) that it either understood the world or that when it didn't it understood why it didn't. In this way all was understood and accepted. Homer wrote on this assumption. All events were contained in the relationship between gods and men. The gods were knowable. Of course, to men the gods' behaviour didn't always make sense as behaviour of gods. But it made sense as behaviour of men – and gods were seen as men, different only in having superhuman powers. They didn't live in the sky but in another part of Greece. Their footprints were in the dust. Street, field, plain, quay, market, house, landscape – the home of men was the home of gods. The utensils and clothes of men were also those of gods. So accounts of daily life could describe the individual and the historical pattern at one and the same time. Christianity did away with all this. To the Greeks a god might appear anywhere. The christians didn't expect to see him. He sent a sign. Often it was the virgin – a woman who conceived without intercourse, a denial of earth, a miraculous sign-in-itself. Epic doesn't deal with signs, it is itself a sign. Christian epic wasn't possible after the Bible, and even that's said to have been written not by men but by god. In the Old Testament god makes man in his image and behaves like a man himself. But by the end of the New Testament god doesn't behave like a man anymore. He's truly mysterious. His last human act is to murder his son. After that he can't be understood. He certainly can't be understood by epic. At most he can be understood in mysticism. His power isn't superhuman but supernatural. His ways can't be explained to man. He can be known only by faith. Epic has nothing to do with faith. It's created when reason and poetry are one. That's why it should be appropriate to our age.

Socialism is a philosophy of the relationship between

people and their world. People are the measure of all things. They may speak all things that are true. How people, society, technology and their environment relate isn't fully understood. Cause and effect aren't completely observed and explained. And some things aren't illuminated by explanation but by experience – love for example. But it's again clear what sort of explanations have meaning for us and what experiences don't need explaining. God doesn't play dice with history and men can understand how reason works in it. That's why epic is possible again.

All art aspires to the lyrical, just as truth tends to the simple. And in epic the lyric becomes objective. The artist tries to show reason in experience and appearance – and lyric is the daily appearance, the commonplace dress, of reason. It shows us the rational. It makes the epic pattern human. It's the footprint on the pathway. In the epic-lyric the individual and particular are no longer isolated but are placed in a historical, social, human pattern. That's why there's a political way of cutting bread or wearing shoes. That way is described in the epic-lyric. In it there's no conceptual division between descriptions of a battle or a meal, between a battlefield or a dinner plate – no bewilderment, no creative no-man's land. Battle, meal, field and plate are all contained in one epic-lyric form of expression. They occur in one pattern of knowable causes and recognizable appearances. Each guarantees the existence of the other, each makes the other real. The family at table, the soldiers in the field, the refugees, the children playing, all human actions, human objects and the human mind may be completely shown in the arc of one story.

ON TEXTURE

We should let the audience follow the story but we shouldn't let the story run away with the play. We should let the audience enjoy the texture.

Texture concerns what someone does, why they do it at a particular moment and how they do it. It's very like the thing we often call character. But the notion of character buries something important. It makes the source of action secret, spiritual, mysterious and in the end unknowable. It's the conjuror's white rabbit, hidden away so that at any moment it can be pulled out of the hat. But when the character is treated as part of the play's texture it's placed in its social context. Instead of being abstract and spiritual it becomes political and is seen to be a matter of class. It's no longer judged as abstract kindness, anger, pride and so on but put in a context where such abstractions can be morally judged. The ability to interpret such texture is a basic human skill although the use of the skill has to be learned. When it's learned it helps to make social living pleasant.

A young office worker takes the day off. The other office workers know he went with his girl to the country. Next day he tells them his mother was ill. He explains that she wanted him to go to work but like a good son he stayed with her. On his face: the candid expression of a good son. Perhaps it will remind his audience of their feelings for their own parents? They observe how he sits down at his desk and eagerly pulls up his chair. He works a little harder than usual. How hard is finely judged. Hard enough to show he'll make up for lost time so that extra work won't fall on others but not so hard that it shows guilt. His audience are skilled observers and they take delight in using their skill.

They even enjoy the way the boss tells them he can't increase their pay. He talks and unconsciously opens the palms of his hands to show how bare they are: nicotine stains. He is eloquent. He gestures and accidentally knocks the cigar from his desk. Stooping to get it he sympathizes with them and likens his problems to their's. The cigar rolls under the desk. He has to burrow for it. He straightens and eases the pressure of the tie on his neck. There is a slight whiff of burned carpet. After enjoying all this the office workers go on strike.

You enjoy a meal. The next day you eat the same sort of food. Between the two meals you've learned how many people suffer from malnutrition. This time you don't enjoy the food. It doesn't chew in your mouth. It chokes you. Knowledge has changed the taste. Cruelty tastes like this.

A table at the end of the room. It's beautiful, its proportions are harmonious. We can also admire the beauty and grain of wood. We know how grain is revealed by polish or wear. So we go to the table to admire the grain. It's chipped and scoured. The table was made for a ballroom or a minister's office but now it's a carpenter's workbench. We're not deceived by the elegant proportions or antique design. We look and see a workbench. We learn to know what things are by their texture. Texture is evidence of truth. Because of texture we're less easily deceived. We don't judge the office holder by his desk or uniform. We look closer to see if he has a right to office.

By understanding texture the audience admire what's good, forgive what's untrue but innocent and see through hypocrisy. It gives them insight. So don't let the story completely take over. Give the audience opportunities to use and strengthen this social skill. Think of certain moments of texture as set-pieces. Don't always astonish and surprise the audience but give them time to observe and consider. Reveal truth patiently, if necessary step by step. Enjoy the flow of the dialectic and the turns it makes.

We have to think rationally. Texture can't do the work of concepts. But in texture we can see and enjoy the physical appearance and working of reason.

IF WE WERE HERE

The consciousness of feudal men was limited by their primitive social world. The serf wasn't much different from the cattle he tended. He was fixed rigidly in his place by the feudal god. The renaissance made society more complex. This meant that human consciousness had to become more complex. Everyone had to take more responsibility for their social role. They either had to accept it or change it. In either case they had to reconcile their behaviour with their subjective sense of autonomy, to explain their life to themselves in the light of their sense of free will. This new subjectivity wasn't just the way a man related to himself. It was also the way he related to society and judged it and his place in it. So it had a moral aspect. It wasn't only consciousness, it was also conscience.

Shakespeare helped to create this new subjectivity. One way he did this was by using the soliloquy. In a soliloquy a character talks directly from his subjective self. He comments on the play and tells us his subjective relation to it. Imagine Hamlet without the soliloquies. The play's politics would have to be made far more feudal. Hamlet wouldn't solve his dilemma by searching his conscience. The drama would be theocratic and the solution would be what god or the Bible said it was. As it is, when Hamlet is confused and perplexed he searches for moral meaning in himself. He finds it and acts. Iago also soliloquizes. He tells us he's evil but he can't tell us why he's evil. God made him evil. Shakespeare is better on goodness than he is on evil but he's usually wrong on both. There is no evil will. The evil are banal and empty, mere functionaries of each other. Modern drama must show that the origins of good and evil are political.

Hamlet is son and heir. When he talks subjectively he talks as both. His soliloquies are both political and personal. His actions as son have subjective motives which are at the same time his objective causes as heir, politician and agent of justice. By a literary device history seems to speak its purpose directly in flesh, blood, mind and passion. Hamlet's consciousness speaks as if it were the conscience of history itself. Shakespeare doesn't have to make a distinction between subjective and objective, between motive and cause. Yet this is confusing because a motive may be mistaken but a cause cannot. When Shakespeare wrote the court had political power and the rulers were a private family as well as a state institution. This meant that Shakespeare didn't need to distinguish clearly between public and private, political and personal. He could handle the two things together so that it seemed as if political problems could have personal solutions. The state was still small, uncomplicated and mysterious enough to be described by the imagery of the human body. I Hamlet the Dane! It could even seem as if in Hamlet we felt the will and emotion of history, as if the movement of history was conveyed directly in transcriptions of human emotions, so that when Hamlet is angry history is angry and Hamlet's emotion of anger triggers a historical movement.

This made it easier for Hamlet to express a wide view, to unite individual and political morality. But now political power (or at least political weight) has passed to the mass of people. A soliloquy at court isn't the same as a soliloquy in the kitchen. The connection between personal and political can no longer be shown so simply or if it comes to that so mistakenly – because the mistake couldn't be made to seem so plausible. Hamlet is the king's son. The factory worker isn't the boss's son. His actions are collective, he isn't their sole agent. In talking from his private, subjective self the worker wouldn't describe his political world in the way Hamlet did. It's not that in Shakespeare's time anymore than in our own history moved through purely psychological drives but that people could more easily act as if it did. It seemed to

Hamlet that when he talked of himself and his family he talked of his objective political relations: the rottenness in Denmark. But when he acts he doesn't see himself, his consciousness and conscience, as a product of politics. He thinks that he dips into the great bowl of truth in his mind and takes out clean water to wash the state. When Hamlet was most private he was really most public. The Hamlet soliloquy was spoken by society and this made it politically and morally urgent. Now society can no longer be expressed politically and morally in terms of the individual and so soliloquies don't work in the same way. The individual is no longer a metaphor for the state and his private feelings can no longer be used to express cause in history or will in politics. Changes in social and political relations make a new drama urgently necessary. Poetry must also change. Until it does we can't talk rationally about ourselves. The bourgeois theatre clings to psychological drama and so it can't deal with the major dramatic themes. Hamlet's soliloquy has withered into the senile monologue of Krapp's last tape. In bourgeois drama subjectivity has replaced politics and so broken Shakespeare's joining of the two. Hamlet has nothing more to say.

Hamlet's play was called 'The Mousetrap' and ironically the detective play is the atrophied remnant of the bourgeois political play. With this in mind we can see that *Waiting for Godot* is a degenerate thriller which morally says rather less than Agatha Christie's thriller. When my play *Stone* was rehearsed I was asked who'd killed the Irishman. I said I didn't know. The answer wouldn't have helped the actors to play the play or me to write it or the audience to understand it. It would have misled all of us. The play wasn't about a murder but about its cause and all those on the unjust side of the social confrontation were guilty of it. Calling one character guilty would have been as arbitrary (as to guilt) as the conviction of a murderer is by a bourgeois court. The court isn't concerned with justice, with creating just social relations. On the contrary it wishes to maintain law and order, to strengthen the unjust social relations which are the real cause of most violence. Obviously a new drama couldn't depend on the cliff-hanging trial verdict which openly or in disguise is the essence of all remnant bourgeois drama. There the dénouement depends on individual guilt and motive is substituted for cause. Such plays can't describe our times or solve our problems. They're as irrelevant as asking why Lear gave away his power. We still have to take it from him.

The Worlds is an experimental play. It tries out various dramatic devices. It tries to find new ways to tell and prove the truth. It's not the sort of experimental play that tries to reveal the truth 'from itself', from its purely aesthetic content. There are no aesthetic answers to political problems and so none to the problems of drama. There are only political answers to aesthetics problems – which is harder to prove. It implies there's a political way to cut bread, wear shoes and see sunsets. Or rather it implies that all the ways of doing these things are political and that there's a politically right way of doing them. I've always written on the assumption that this is so and in 'Types of Drama' I have tried to show why it's so. Aesthetics are often misused. This doesn't mean that we should try to write plays without aesthetics but that we should use them properly. Human beings relate through the sensory aspect of things, through appearance, sound and so on. All communities translate knowledge and social practice into aesthetic terms. Aesthetics should be thought of as ideas translated into sensory terms and art as aesthetics with true ideas.

In *The Worlds* I tried to find contemporary equivalents for Shakespeare's soliloquy. I wanted to give the characters a means of informed, personal comment in the play. At the same time I wanted to show the force of history, the causes of historical change. This is the dilemma. If the working class character isn't politically conscious his subjectivity is false. It's false because his owners – his employers – and their representatives manipulate it by education, news services, welfare, law, entertainment and so on. The brain in his head isn't his but theirs and so he can't talk from his subjective self objectively. His introspection wouldn't tell the truth as Hamlet's did, or at least the truth as it appeared to be to Shakespeare and his audience. The worker in this condition is riddled with false subjectivity and mythology precisely because he has no objective self, no valid interpretation of objective experience. But even when the worker is objective, when he's political and understands society and his role in it, he still can't talk directly from his subjective self. He knows too much. Now what he has to say is so urgent he becomes a messenger. The Greeks – who were wise – didn't make messengers their main characters. It's clear that in time a whole new world of subjective truth will be available to socialist art. But we have to solve this problem first. You could put it in this way. Hamlet can be two-dimensional in a three-dimensional way. Of course I don't use two-dimensional pejoratively. On the contrary I use it to refer to the knowledge gained from experience and in more abstract ways, which we must have and use before we can know our real political situation, make our society more rational and develop our humanity. Often what passes in drama as profound and three-dimensional is really superficial and cheap: the individual relating only to himself. Strictly this relationship isn't possible. We still think of consciousness as reflecting itself but really self-consciousness is consciousness of the world. An individual can't be true to himself but only true to the world and whether his understanding of the world is true or false is an objective matter. Strange that 'being true to yourself' isn't usually seen as the pettiness it is when compared to being 'true to the world'. Originally it was said that the 'self' to which we were to be true was given to us by god. This vouched for its value. Now god is removed but his commandment remains: so we're left to be true to the nakedest egotism. The confusion arises in the modern mind because we still think we make our own consciousness and not that it's made by our society and what politically we do in it. Our consciousness can be compared to a machine that takes in finished products (social teachings) and either reproduces the same products or creates a new understanding of the world. What goes on in the machine – what grinds out truth and sifts knowledge – is practical experience.

If we want to show a worker as two-dimensional (or objective) then unlike Hamlet he doesn't share his subjective self with us (which Hamlet does because he's three-dimensional) but becomes a teller of slogans and theory, a bringer of the message. That's the dilemma. Without political analysis there's no socialist theatre but how can we show socialism, above all things, without showing full human beings?

The dilemma is full of opportunities. First there's a mistake to avoid. We mustn't treat personal dramas which are only a consequence of political dramas as if they were themselves full political dramas. A shop steward or lecturer sacked for being a socialist isn't dramatically interesting – politically – because he personally suffers. This would let bourgeois theatre in by the side door. We need to make objective political analysis fully dramatic in its own right. This seems harsh but if we do the last properly it will include the first.

In the speech beginning 'If we were here' I've tried to push the character, for that speech, not into his Hamlet-self but say forty years ahead in time. He then talks not as he is but as he would be after we have been there. His age stays the same but he speaks with historical hindsight, with greater political consciousness and stronger political presence than he yet has. Because of this his language changes. But this is essential: the audience mustn't feel that the character has suddenly stopped being himself (he hasn't, anymore than the actor playing Hamlet stops acting when he talks directly to us) and become the spokesman of the author. What the character says must still be right for his character. His subjective individuality then helps to explain the truth of his objective, generalized statements: in the future these things will be because there are *now* people like him. So it would be nearer the truth to say that the author becomes the spokesman of his character. The actor doesn't step out of character but the audience sees the character's potential self, sees him as he could be. I call this device a public soliloquy. Perhaps Chekhov meant Vershinin to do something like this when he 'philosophizes'. But Vershinin hides in visions and expects to be laughed at. He isn't a cause of change, he stays the same and we're to accept change because of his personal faith in it. This limits his dramatic use. He doesn't speak for the author. Really he speaks against him.

Shifting time in this way isn't doing anything more awkward than Shakespeare did when he let a character 'talk-to-us-in-himself'. If it seems awkward that's because writers and audiences haven't learned to live in our time as fully and perceptively as Shakespeare and his audience knew how to live in their's. We haven't learned what's possible and necessary for us as well as they knew what was possible and necessary for them. Their drama exploited subjectivity more subtly and efficiently than ours. We should develop public soliloquy and other devices till we can use them without confusing the audience. If we understood ourselves and others more we would see people differently. Showing people in this way on stage would help our audience to create this understanding. They could delight in these new devices and see their own strength in them.

The quality of public soliloquy, of a commentary which the character has the right to speak (and which the actor and the writer have won for him) needn't be confined to moments in a play. A large part, perhaps all, of Scene Four (Part One) of *The Worlds* could be acted as a group public soliloquy. Whole characters or groups could be permeated with public soliloquy so that we feel they're both in and outside their time and aren't eternal prisoners of the present appearance of things. Such a play wouldn't just record events but would be a sustained public soliloquy, a politically informed commentary on what the play records. Otherwise how can socialist writers put three-dimensional characters on stage? We risk showing characters merely as schematized class functions or as still being essentially bourgeois. That's no better than showing them as bluff jokers who try to slip in a message when no one's looking. Unfortunately that's also when no one's thinking.

Actors must act lives not abstractions. Otherwise one of the main strengths of drama is wasted. Class functions must be shown or the drama is meaningless but we need to extend our ways of showing them. We must show that politically conscious figures are full human beings, that their class function is a complete self function and that in consciously being members of their class they're also fully themselves. Socialist art has nothing to do with the arbitrary, fanciful rigmarole of bourgeois art but neither is it a restriction. It is the way the truth is told, and that makes it synonymous with freedom. Our audience is new, it is not the audience of the earlier socialist theatre. The continuing industrial revolution and comparative affluence have satisfied some of their needs, hidden others and given new ones. They behave and see the world differently. We have to deal not merely with the crimes of capitalism but with its excuses, evasions and superficial successes. As capitalism becomes cruder it becomes more sophisticated – and the working class more subtle and clear-sighted. Drama must deal with the world as it is. It must find its use. When society changes it mustn't repeat itself. Capitalism has a need for nostalgia because the quality of its culture and intellectual life deteriorates no matter what goods it provides. But we have no need to look to the past in this way. We should create a new culture.

Tackling the dilemma in this and other ways would let us create real sensitivity and subjective discrimination. These qualities are necessary to human society. Sensitivity is still associated with Bloomsbury but that sort of sensitivity is false, cut off from knowledge of the real world by an escape into a dark, fragile, ghostly world of eccentrics. It sees political relations and the use of power as always barbarous. Well, since it discards social and political obligations in this way it has no moral aspect. It merely feeds on aesthetics, which by itself is a poison. The subjective self becomes sensitive and discriminating only when it's shaped by objective knowledge, when knowledge and experience of the real world illuminate and reform subjective individuality. It's a form taken by reason and morals, the individual's way of possessing the truth. In the past sensitivity was often pale and fanciful because it belonged to a culture which instead of revealing the world concealed it. But we cannot be human without moral, discriminating sensitivity. It expresses understanding of history, society and the world in subjective terms. How can we be rational and human without that?

The renaissance developed subjectivity but at the same time prostituted it to the objectivity of the business ethic. This was reflected in subjectivity in the haunted puritan conscience and the witch-hunt. Its modern counterpart is fascist racism. Socialism could resolve most of the antagonisms between objectivity and subjectivity. It would let us live in the world as it is and so be our true selves, instead of living in the world as it is run for the benefit of a few – with all the mythology, injustice and distortions in consciousness and conscience that follow. All this was historically necessary and it had the justification that for a time it created order. Now it creates disorder. Feudalism saw workers as purely objective: as little more than beasts, and the church said beasts had no souls. And even what little subjectivity workers did have wasn't owned by them, it was owned by god. Capitalism sees workers as machines and all that goes into them as raw materials. It sees a holiday on the Costa Brava or a colour TV set as raw materials for making cars or cans. No doubt many who tell us socialism and technology will turn us into robots would like us to be beasts or machines. But socialism could create an objective sensitivity and so make us fully human.

A character strengthened with two-dimensional political analysis has three-dimensional wholeness. He has a rational, moral psychology with which he understands the world as well as himself and is able to develop humanely in step with changing technology. His humanity and sensitivity are strengths. He is whole, not the rump Hamlet of late bourgeois theatre, the Krapp with nothing to say. His public soliloquy is spoken for himself and for others too. In this paragraph I've dropped the distinction between characters in the play and in the audience. Culture is our means of understanding and saying what we are and ought to be. This image, with the appropriate mind and conduct, changes historically. Theatre workers are part of the audience, at most no more than its spokesmen. We can say that the audience is ready to create a new image and a new culture.

THE ART OF THE AUDIENCE

Eagerly the dumb hear the singer
And the crippled still run the race
So strong do men struggle
But actors are only shadows
The stage is an image of the world where the audience act
We move with their gestures
We speak language they have refined.
We mourn because they mourn and we study their mourning
We have wit because they laugh

We wear their clothes
The fire doesn't set light to itself.
There's no foreign land called art
Art doesn't create its own truth
Our blood is paste
We die and return with the living

Scrupulously we enter their struggle
To show the clash of classes
To speak precisely the concepts to be drawn
From their experience
To sharpen the sharp mind
To show iron freedom
To show that at the horizon where light enters the world
A world is still hidden

What is art?
It puts the incident into the concept
The stone into the mosaic
It fits each word to the epic
We march over continents in a small room
In two hours we pass through centuries
And show how every hour leads to the next
And the years that wait in a day
We show how a soldier stands in a corner of every kitchen
Like a sentry over a pass
We study the waves
They remind us of the worker's creased brow

Our form: clarity order precision
Our tools: colour action sound
Our weapons: anger laughter judgement
Our face is a mirror that shows the spectator his face
In us he studies himself and his friends
He learns to know himself and to fight the exploiter

We wish to show how the crisis leads to the solution
How shall the audience judge what we show?
Art is more than the intellectual knowledge of truth
It's social
The audience ask will this solve the crisis played on our
    streets?
If our solution is wrong we've pretended their houses are
    painted flats
But they built the houses
Carrying bricks and pouring concrete
And the knowledge of how the world works
Gained by carrying and pouring
Is the knowledge by which truth is judged
In art and everything else

Who are our audience?
We write for those who carry bricks
Not those who hire builders
The hirer's world is a dream that floats on painted clouds
We speak to him if he sits in our audience
But he's an onlooker
Only the others can judge
Only they have the knowledge to judge
The hirer reverses all human values
We write for those he exploits
If we give them a key they know if it will open the door
They made the door
It's as simple as that
If our theatre shows beauty wisdom and skill
It's because our audience knows how these things should be
    used

So we show the audience its great talents
We study the art of the audience

A POEM

In things there is order
Stone is hard
Water is liquid
We drink water
When we don't drink we die
When we drink poison we die
Little grows in sand

There's order too in human affairs
Not so simple as the order of stone and water
Harder to see but with laws as strong
They're part of the order of all things
Part of the iron law
Stones water men and all things are in iron law

The tree has roots
Through them it takes water
We don't take what we need in so simple a way
We take what we need through society
It's as if the tree fetched water to its roots

The tree doesn't think how to take water
Or imagine it's stone
The tree doesn't move
Roots are the way it's in the world
Men move and make new ways to be in the world
Plough
        Sledge
                Tractor
                    Plane
                        are ways to be in the world
They are ways as roots are a way

Stones trees and dogs evolve through eons
Such creatures and things change as their place changes
Evolution makes mountains trees and dogs
It's slow
Trees rarely change their way
The way of the dog rarely changes till we change it
In the way of man there is great change
When our way changes we change
We change our way
We change the place where we are
We change it quickly
We must change as quickly as we change the place where we
     are
We don't change in eons we change in history
What wonder the change we bring to the world!
We make history and so make ourselves
We change quickly but still in the iron law
The means by which a thing is in the world is its way
Trees may not move from their place
Fish may not fly
And men must follow the way of men

If trees lost their roots they wouldn't be trees
When the ground's parched the roots are dry and the tree
     withers
We change the place where we are
We change the means by which we live
We change what we are
We change our place quickly
It's not enough if our feet change as feet change in eons
Feet can't change quickly enough
We change our mind
The mind changes quickly
We must change quickly
History is fast

We imagine
We couldn't think unless we imagined
We couldn't work unless we imagined
We couldn't make a machine unless we imagined
We couldn't make a poem unless we imagined
We can't know everything
There's no time to see round corners
We need imagination to understand what's real
We need imagination to live in history
If we didn't imagine we'd be as slow and cumbersome as
    wooden puppets
We'd be in eons
We may imagine the real to be false
With a new strength a new weakness

Imagination helps us to learn
It makes thinking more skilful
Imagination is iron law yet free to be false
We imagine we're wise
We imagine blackmen or whitemen are devils
Trees and stones can't imagine
They're in the world of iron law
It's also in iron law that to live in history we must imagine
In imagination there's freedom and slavery
Imagination to men is as the pole star to the sailor or the axe to
    the tree
On us lie the burdens of morals and choice
These like roots are a way to be in the world
Without them we'd be in eons

Roots and leaves are the tree's way to be in the world
By these means it makes part of the world into itself
All our abilities are means in this way
They're iron law

We're free yet in iron law
We imagine and think
These are means by which we're part of the world and make
    part of the world us
They're the way we're in the world

History is the way we're in the world
Society is the way we're in history
Society organizes us into a way to be in the world
So we eat drink and build
This is a means as roots are means
Society organizes us to live together and make tools
We prosper and win great power and learning
Those who can be taught can be told
We're told what we are
But we are what we do because that's the means by which we
    are
We're told but we also learn by ourself
Society tells us what we are in society
The branch doesn't tell the leaf to be part of the tree
We're not as safe as the tree from the axe

We're born in ignorance
We're born to question
That's why we're men
When the tree first grows it's already a tree
We're not men when we start to live
We don't know what we are till we learn
We learn to be men
To be human or inhuman
The tree can't learn to be stone
We must be born in ignorance or our minds would be as rigid
    as stone
We change the world
As the world changes our mind changes

We are free to change
We must be free to learn

What a thing is depends on what it gets and how it gets it
The tree takes water through roots
We take our share of the world through work
We're masters servants workers and children
All men breathe and sleep in one way
They're not all in the world in one way
They're master or servant
They're in the world in two ways

We're in society
Society tells us our place in society
Society tells us what we are
Society calls us master or servant
Society tells us that's also our name in the world
We are the way we're in the world
The world can't lie
Trees are trees
Men are in the world only as the men they are
Society can lie
Men are in society and society is in the world
Men are not in society in the same way they're in the world
We change the world and this changes what we are
What we are in society changes
Society may not accept this change
But if society lies it's still in the world
All things in the world are in iron law
Iron law is the way all things are in the world
Men are society's way of being in the world
As men change their world they change themselves
Society doesn't change as quickly as men change
Men must change society because that's the way they're in
    the world

Wind and fire make things in eons
Society teaches us and makes us
We have two conducts and two minds
What we are in the world and what we are in society
Men must be in society in the way they're in the world or
    there's chaos
We must change society to complete the change in ourself
As we change society we must change ourself but society tells
    us who we are
It's as if the roots could tell the tree to fly
We may not be what society tells us we are
How shall we judge?

Society is the way the world's farmed and mined
It's the way we share what we take and make
It places us in its organisation
Earth doesn't own the tree or the tree the earth
The means by which it takes water isn't owned
No owner tells the tree what it is
What a tree is isn't owned
Society owns the earth
Society owns the means by which we live
Society owns the way we're in the world
Society owns men
Society owns the image of man
Society tells each man what he is and what all other men are
Society owns
Society is owned

To farm mine and fish there must be order
Society is order
Without order we can't farm mine and fish
There's chaos
As much as if the water turned to stone and the tree withered

Men live together
Men must work together

Some men know they lie
Others lie but don't know it
Men who imagine are free to imagine the false
Here are two lies

   1.
   This world isn't real
   The real world is in eons
   Our conduct in the unreal world decides what we do in
     eons
   2.

   The tree is still
   Men move and cast stones at each other
   We're animals
   Society is the way we stop tearing out our neighbour's
     throat
   Those who own society stop us tearing out our neighbour's
     throat
   The owners are strong with the wisdom of sages

If goodness is weak and must be protected by society then
   society is more evil than those who're in it
If goodness is weak it can't get power and so society is ruled
   by the evil and strong
If men are animals society must be more corrupt than the
   animals in it
If we're good and wise enough to create societies we're good
   and wise enough to live without them
If goodness and wisdom weren't stronger than ignorance and
   evil we wouldn't have created societies
Instead of society there could be friendship

All that's in history changes
The society slow to change when men change is soon corrupt
Reason works quickly or slowly
Gradually or in crisis

The tree isn't taught to be a tree
Society teaches us the conduct of men
We farm and mine and make and conduct ourselves in the
　　ways to do this
Otherwise we couldn't do what we do
We're free to imagine but we're not free to imagine we don't
　　do what we do
We have the mind of the people who do it
Society can't give us the mind of those who don't do it
Anymore than roots can tell trees to fly
Our way to be in the world is to have the mind to do what we
　　do
We make our mind by what we do
Our mind makes us what we are
We learn what we are from what we do
We're what we do and this is our way to be in the
　　world
But society teaches us what we are in society
It teaches us that what we are in society is also what we are in
　　the world
It tells us our social position is given to us by nature
That would be reasonable if we were in society what we are in
　　the world
Then reason and nature would be one
But society stands between us and the world
It may teach us falsely
It may deny what we learn by what we do in the world
Teaching may conflict with experience
Teaching may conflict with the conduct we need in order to
　　live in society as we are in the world

If trees were in society society would often tell them to fly and
   punish them for not flying
When we change we must change society
The mind enshrined or encrusted in social institutions may
   be the mind of men who lived long ago

Trees and stones are hard
We struggle to change them
Hardness resists change
Society is hard
Society is owned by the past
By the dead bones who own flesh
Society tells men how to live
But they also learn how to live from what they do
They learn from experience
From working together
Men change when they learn new ways of working
Society has schools churches and courts to tell us what we are
Social institutions are the means by which we're in the world
They're also the means by which society is owned
Owners of society own its institutions
They own the image of man – of what man ought to be
Owners of society don't own men's experience

Society must be in the world in the way men are in the world
   or men have two minds and two conducts
Then it seems to them they're in two worlds
But the world is real and we're what we do in the real world
Society has pilots and tractor drivers
Society has the minds and conduct of pilots and tractor
   drivers
That's the way society is in the world
Pilots and tractor drivers are made by what they do
Society is owned by the past but needs pilots and tractor
   drivers

Society owned by the past teaches tractor drivers they're
  ploughmen and pilots they're waggoners
Society owned by the past puts men into society in a false
  way
When men are in society in the way they're in the world
  society is rational
Their minds and conduct are rational
And they live in reason
When men are not in society in the way they're in the world
  society is irrational
And their minds and conduct are either irrational – dictated
  to them by society
Or rational – formed by what they do in the world and their
  struggle to change society

Irrational men can't co-operate
Their society is organised by force and myth
Force and myth can't make irrational society stable
Irrational society deteriorates
A pilot with a waggoner's mind can fly – even a charioteer
  could drive a tank
But a pilot can't be human in a waggoner's society
In a waggoner's society a pilot understands planes but
  nothing of men
His society isn't human and he isn't human
Men with two minds and two conducts aren't human
They can't treat themselves or other men as human
They become human only when they struggle to make society
  rational
Men with two minds and two conducts can't know them-
  selves or other men
They're irrational
Irrational men fear and panic
Men who fear and panic believe what they imagine
Men act on what they believe

The society of pilot-waggoners and ploughmen-tractor
    drivers falls
It says men behave badly because they're animals
It's easier to justify force when it's used against animals than
    when it's used against men
Irrational society uses fear fraud and force against men
    because it thinks they're animals
There is chaos!

Courts universities and other social institutions often repress
    the needs of those who work in factories power stations and
    other modern institutions
All irrational social institutions conflict with human practice
This is the dilemma
Society must control men so that they can live and work in the
    world together
Men must control society so that they can live in society in a
    human way
Otherwise society is inhuman and men are inhuman
Social institutions don't change as men change
Men change as they change the world
Men can't resist this change – they change because of what
    they do
Society resists change
Society is owned
All changes in society change the ownership of society
Societies that can't change in peace change by force
Iron law

The tree bends in storm
We make the storm that bends us
So strange are we!
As if we created the elements in ourselves
Jove-like we hurl the thunder bolt
Scamander flooded the plains of Troy

We flood history
Men become their own chaos because they're their own creators
There's danger in freedom
But freedom is iron law

Iron law
When men are in two minds and with two conducts society is torn apart
We who live in history are free to fall into chaos
We're not free to fall out of history
We fall into chaos when we're false to what we are
We are what we do in the world
When we don't follow the iron law it judges us harshly
But men will have reason – what they do in the world demands it
If history is about to turn back men take to the streets and bring her home
Once men are in history they can't be animals
Those who own society seek unreason
Their hirelings teach it and their soldiers kill in its name
But reason comes to the world because men work
We work and change the world and change ourselves
That's the way we're in the world
Let us talk of these men of change
Men who change the world and themselves so that they're also the men who change their society
Men who change society so that it's in the world in the way they're in the world are the seekers of reason
They seek reason in society because of the way they're in the world
They can't be in the world without seeking reason
Men can't pull back from being men
The horses of history can't shy in the shafts or men jump from her cart

Men must know who they are
That's the way they're in the world

Society organizes us to farm mine and fish
Men change when the way they work changes
Then the dealings between men change
Society doesn't change as we change
Society does nothing to the world
Society does things to the minds of men
Yet it's as if it were a tree that grew from men's brains
Of trees we say this: when the soil changes the tree changes
Society teaches and organizes men to do things in the world
Society has no way of changing
Society can only make men in its image of men
Men must make society in their image
When men change as what they do in the world changes they
    change society so that they can have one mind and one
    conduct
Men change their society or the farming fishing and mining
    go badly
The tools are misused
And men can't live in co-operation with one another
They are inhuman
They will not take responsibility for their society
Society is full of panic and fear and violence

Men change but the world doesn't tell them they're changed
The world tells nothing
Men are the way the world says what it is
The world is the place of trees and stones
Men know they change but not what they've become
They see and think in new ways
Society doesn't teach them how they've changed
It gives the child's book to the man
There is chaos

Men must speak the truth to one another
Talk together so that they understand one another
When they know what they are they're human
When they don't know what they are they're inhuman
If they're taught myths there's chaos
If they believe myths the axe is brought to the tree
If they're taught truth then experience and teaching are one
The machines and tools are well used
All men are human
The image of man is human
And men treat each other as friend

Grain isn't taken straight from the field to the table
Coal isn't taken straight from the mine to the furnace
Cotton is woven before it's worn
All that a man uses passes through the hands of all other men
Bread passes through courts universities and prisons before
   it's eaten
Yes it passes through the empty mouths of the starving before
   you eat it
That jacket's handled by kings beggars teachers children and
   madmen
It's covered bodies and mothers have wept beside it before
   you wore it
What's in a room is also in a city
The way it's owned depends on who owns the city
We own wear eat and learn prisons courts hospitals schools
Do I take food from a beggar?
Do I take my coat from the poor?
Do I learn wisdom from a madman?
Is my house a resting place for the dead?
I have two conducts: I steal the coat and wear it as if it were
   not stolen
Yes I wear his coat when I send him to prison!
When I strip am I covered in stolen flesh?

Write down on this all that I say said the doctor of law as he
    tore a strip from his dunce's cap and handed it to his
    student

Iron law
We eat lies or truths
We wear lies or truths
We teach lies or truths
We walk in lies or truths
One or the other
If we're in society in a false way we're the tree growing on
    rock
Owls fly from her branches they do not trust her
The fox will not house her cubs under her roots
The mole will not dig in her shadow
What's irrational offends the elements in man
There's chaos

History is the struggle for reason
Without reason we fall into chaos and suffer in chaos
So we seek reason
It's the way we're in the world
There's no other way men can be in the world
Men who don't seek reason seek the irrational
Such men destroy themselves
The owners of men don't seek reason
That have weapons to destroy us
The greater the weapon the faster history runs

Iron law
We can't be destroyed because the animal in us overtakes us
History outran the beasts long ago
We can't be destroyed by what comes from the past
We make the future
Make it irrationally and it will destroy you

History can't forget

Destroy the tractors and planes – you're still the men who
   made them!

They made you

Understand what you are

Men who don't seek understanding destroy society

Unless we seek understanding society is barbarous

Men revolt against barbarity

Men struggle to be what they do

Men struggle to be what they are

Men struggle to learn what they are

Men struggle to be human

We long to live in a society which tells us what we are

Our struggles to change society are our struggles to be
   ourself

The old society stops us being human

Men are what they do but they must learn what they are

The mind needs schooling in concepts

We need reason in social institutions so that society may live
   in accord

We need society in which human gestures have meaning

An action must mean the same in society as it means in the
   world

Yet it's still not so!

They throw bones to the beggars

Men's bones? Who can tell in this place?

If I'm kind will those who torment the poor sleep sounder at
   night?

What men do has two aspects

An action is done in society and in the world

Men can't be human in an irrational society

They revolt against unreason

The seeking of reason is the seeking of justice

Wherever men are there is the shout for justice

The call for reason

Men can't stop their struggle for reason till they have it or are
   wiped from the face of the earth
Men don't seek justice because some of them are born just or
   with this strange desire
Men don't seek justice because their souls seek it
Men seek justice because that's the way they're in the world
Justice is making the two worlds one
We can't be in the world in another way
We can't be water or stone
We're in the world in the order of the world
In iron law
The iron law is that men seek justice and reason
We seek it because we change the place where we are and so
   change ourselves so that we must change our society
We seek it because the stone is hard and the tree's branches
   shake in wind
We seek it because of what we do
We seek it because we eat sleep dress build love and
   work
Our hands as they till the earth and tend machines gesture for
   justice
When the two minds and two conducts are one there'll be
   reason and justice
A good act will be good in both worlds
Not good in one and evil in another
If I feed the beggar at the wayside the prince will not sleep
   sounder in his tower
It is down
Evil will be the same in both worlds
And men won't be torn apart
The judge will be just

Iron law
There must be this order because of the way we're in the
   world

The tool which makes change –
The tool-user's mind and conduct –
The society which teaches him to use tools and live together
    with other men –
All must relate together in reason
Then society will be the home and guardian of friends
The elements in man be at peace
And the image of man be human

The search for reason shapes history
The sleeper struggles to find comfort
He calls in his sleep
History is the human day and already the sleeper wakes
He will not struggle in dreams but walk the earth
He will talk reason to friends
Two minds and two conducts will be one
We will know the world we're in
And what we are

Tools change the world and the tool-user
Only the tool-user knows how to use tools
Only he knows the tool-user
Only he knows what men are
Only he knows what society ought to be
The tapping of tools are the seconds of history
We struggle to make society a tool to make men who live and
    change in peace
So that man is the image of man

Then the ploughman won't be flogged to the tractor
The tractor driver will sit in the tractor and plough over
    common fields
Not rake the rubble of Lidice
Schools will teach truth written before men could read and
    truth men have written

Reason will not go in prison uniform or the scientist in fool's
    motley
The boats will put out to sea and cast nets for fish
And the world will be run by the fishers of fish
Not by those who cast nets to fish in the sea for statues of
    stone

ON AESTHETICS

The trees at Auschwitz were beautiful but did the guards and
prisoners see the same beauty?

Prisoners painted pictures of camp life. Their pictures
showed what that life was like. They're images of the truth.
They're beautiful. Could an overseer have painted the same
pictures? No, we paint what we see. The overseer couldn't
have seen what life was like in the camp. He'd paint an image
of a lie. It would be irrational. I don't know of such a painting
but imagine how it would show a guard.

Some prisoners were killed for painting pictures. Were
they killed because of what they painted or how they painted
it? The paintings were beautiful because the painters wanted
to record the truth and had the skill to do so. The overseer
wasn't interested in truth and so couldn't see its beauty. It
would be impossible for him to say 'This hanging shouldn't
have been painted. All the same the painting has great beauty
and must be shown to all who love beauty.'

Aesthetic judgements aren't based on the abstract appearance of things but on what we know or think we know about
them. Aesthetic appearance changes as knowledge changes.
If our understanding of the world is rational we can discrimi-
nate between beauty and ugliness. If it's irrational we can't
make this discrimination clearly.

The tree is beautiful. It grew at Auschwitz and this makes
it more beautiful to those who see the world rationally. To

them a tree is more beautiful because it grows anywhere in the world in which there is Auschwitz. It's more beautiful because they understand why Auschwitz was built and can use their understanding to defeat its builders.

If men and all other creatures were immortal and all things immutable then men wouldn't find anything beautiful. We have a sense of beauty because we're mortal. The sense comes from knowledge of change. All beauty reminds us that we're human. But the sense of beauty is political and not metaphysical. It doesn't come from the banal confrontation of life and death. If it did beauty would always be sad. As it is, it's always joyful. This is because the confrontation is between cruelty, stupidity and waste and reason, love and humanity. Between death and life that's decent, moral, human and sane. This sort of life is created by reason working in history. It means that beauty is politically determined. Some things are more beautiful than others. But to the rational all things in nature are beautiful and most other things are beautiful as well.

Beauty isn't what we see or sense in another way but depends on our relation to what we see or sense in another way, on what we know or think we know about it. Aesthetics isn't about abstract seeing but our human relation to things. We can't be taught to see abstract beauty. We can be taught what stops us seeing beauty or makes us see it as ugliness. How clearly we see depends on how well we understand.

All ugliness is made by men. Only they are able to see ugliness, desire it and bring it into the world. They often call it beauty. When men assemble or disassemble things they may make them less beautiful. Ugliness is the image of the irrational. The irrational see beauty as ugliness and ugliness as beauty. But the ugliness which they see as beauty doesn't appear as real beauty even to them: it's clouded, phantom-like, a dream. The irrational can't see real beauty. All that the irrational see as real is ugliness. That's why destruction attracts them. The rational see that all things not made ugly by men are beautiful. Men may themselves be ugly. The face of the SS overseer is ugly. He and others have made it ugly.

Men may make things more beautiful. Rembrandt makes a painting by arranging natural aesthetic elements (such as colours and shapes, the abstracts used in representation) and images or parts of images of things that are partly natural and partly made by men and their society (such as clothes or the human face with its images of nature, biography and history). Artists arrange images and natural qualities into new forms. When they create art they don't use aesthetic qualities in an arbitrary way. Riding a bicycle over a wet canvas creates beauty when it's confronted (in the mind) with the decadent arbitrariness of the disciplined, dead photographic realism of the academic portrait.

A work of art is seen politically. Aesthetic elements, considered apart from images, are also seen politically. Art adds comment to aesthetic elements. This increases our enjoyment of them. Good form is produced by the working of reason in history and by the understanding of this working. We see things historically. This is true of whatever we reproduce in art: scenes, still lives, portraits, abstracts and so on. The way men recreate natural qualities and images into works of art (or see works of art) is the same as the way they see the real world. What creates excellence in art? Seeing rationally. That is, to see the world as it is, or rather as real as it can rationally be understood and therefore seen at the time. As men increase their understanding of their relationship to the world so the appearance of the world changes. As time passes it's possible for more people to understand the art of the past because in some ways it becomes easier to understand. Often understanding is first achieved through struggle and effort. To portray the world more rationally the artist must also struggle. Human knowledge and experience, and the creative work of the artist, elucidate and strengthen each other. An artist shows the rational appearance of things at a particular time. He records historically. If rational art shows the reality of the appearance of things it follows that it can also show the reality in and by which they change – that is, it can show the force of history itself revealed in the present. When he does this the artist shows the lasting strength of human reason. He also shows our reason for living, since we're the expressors of the force of history. This is the most creative form of art. The pot doesn't show the marks of the potter's hands or his wheel. The form is created by the two forces working on the clay. From the pot we read the strength of the elemental forces that make it. The image of the force of history should be thought of as appearing in works of art in the same way.

The world is a place of natural aesthetic qualities. Socialism is produced by being in the world in a creative way. Socialist consciousness sees the world differently from other forms of consciousness. It sees it to be more beautiful than it is as seen by earlier forms of consciousness that survive but have out-lived their creative period. When these earlier forms were created they would (provided they were the rational forms of their time) have seen the world to be more beautiful than it was as seen by still earlier forms. In our time the confrontation in our species between reason and irrationalism – a confrontation made necessary by the biological and physical nature of things – is between socialism and fascism. Of course not all prisoners in fascist concentration camps are socialists. But all enemies of fascism see more rationally (and so distinguish more accurately between beauty and ugliness) than its supporters. However not all who fight fascism are its rational enemies. Some, such as English tories, are merely its political opponents. They can't create rational art and indeed most of them insist on the practical irrelevance or even the nihilism of art. A humane artist who isn't a socialist may make images that contain the ideal in an abstract way. They are dream images, phantasmagoria. But rational art is practical. The final, ideal appearance of reason will be created by the struggle for reason. Only artists involved in this struggle can see and paint (according to their skill) the reality of its image in the present. They see the ideal as practical and man-made, not as a visionary dream. Abstract idealized images lack the moral authority of rational art. They're not proved to be art by the practicality of reason in them. In them the ideal is static.

We see objective things subjectively. Different men see the same painting differently. Not all men see the same Giotto scene. The artist sees a chair in one way. X may see the chair differently. The artist and X may see the artist's painting of the chair differently. Those with a rational consciousness see things as they really are, or rather as they really are for their time. They will really be different for later times. Beauty has a historical form. Shakespeare didn't have to wonder if an aeroplane is beautiful. He saw *his* world in a rational way and recorded what was seen by the rational mind of his time. Because he did this with skill he created beauty. Rational men can see the historical appearance of reason in earlier art but irrational men can't. That's why the academic understanding of Shakespeare usually trivializes him. Seeing things as they really are is like seeing them in a practical way. Beauty and ugliness are real when they're seen rationally. When it's seen irrationally beauty is dream-like and phantasmagoric. When the irrational see ugliness it has the quality of nightmare of which the dreamer is in charge. All societies and all people live in one calendar time but many live in many cultural times. Hitler is a medieval man seeing an aeroplane. He sees a vision, it might be a god. It doesn't have the reality which belongs to beauty. This means that Hitler can't understand the world in which the aeroplane flies. He sees the world irrationally, that is destructively. Reactionary artists create reactionary images, dream-images that obscure the truth. They are like a screen of dreams wrapped round a reactionary's head.

An artist can help us to see more clearly. He's in a special rational, moral relation to what he records. But a work of art doesn't reveal truth to everyone who looks at it. The SS man sees what the artist records and may even recognize some of its truth. The enemy in the dock may be beautiful just as the innocent may be sinister. But the SS man sees the picture as tainted, as beautiful *and* ugly. It repels or fascinates him. He wants to destroy it or is obsessed by it in another way. These aren't his subjective reactions to a common appearance shared by him and the artist. His mind distorts what it sees. He doesn't see the objective beauty created by the artist because he can't judge it rationally and morally. The beauty the artist creates is an image of the rational understanding appropriate to the time it's created. It combines moral imperatives with political imperatives rationally appropriate to that particular stage in human development. The consciousness of the SS man doesn't belong to the present. His head is here but what's in it is in the past. His cultural time isn't his calendar time. When he paints the picture is being painted hundreds of years ago.

Intellectual discourse is rarely poetry. But conversation on factory floors and in bread shops is a form of poetry. In these places people relate ideas to words and their voice to each other's in a poetical way. If people didn't normally speak poetry they'd sound odd. One aim of culture is to change the concepts in colloquial speech so that people aren't mystified and made to despair by the irrational appearance of the world. But even in a mystified world ordinary people must usually speak poetry in order to survive, to be accepted in ordinary social relations. This is because ordinary people are ordinarily practical and this places them close to one element in reason. It's only in a wholly irrational world (SS soldiers in their barracks for example) that they stop speaking poetry and speak melodramatically instead. Formal poetry is only more beautiful than bread-shop conversation when its concepts are more rational. Often out of sheer practical necessity the concepts used on the shop-floor are more practical than those used in a university. A machine either does what it's made to do or it doesn't. This produces a practicality in its makers and users (not necessarily in its sellers, of course) that can extend to the rest of their consciousness. A university doesn't produce a machine, it produces a mind. A mind that doesn't know reality can invent a false one. Probably most literature teachers find more poetry in their mortgage than in Shakespeare. They understand their mortgage better and it means more to them and so they can interpret it practically. If this wasn't so universities would be very different.

An SS man and a socialist see the same sunset differently. Seeing depends on the seers objectivity: how objective is his subjectivity? This depends on his culture and this depends on his class and political position. We see what we know or think we know. We don't see a Rembrandt portrait of a jew as Hitler saw it. We don't see the tree at Auschwitz as Himmler saw it. If the biological act of seeing had a built in moral discrimination then the SS and the socialist would see the same aesthetic qualities, the same beauty, in the same things. Things would appear the same to them. If they did seeing would be a very privileged activity – all other forms of moral judgement may be mistaken. It can hardly be denied that our moral apprehension of something changes the way it appears to us. I think our moral state (which depends on our rational state) changes the appearance of all things to us. We think that the way we see is analogous to the way we feel. Usually if we put our hands into a bowl of hot water all of us who do so feel the heat. But not if some of us have first put our hands in ice. Cultures can act like the ice. We see through our culture and so we see through extremes. Men see sunsets differently

just as they see prisoners in the dock differently. If Hitler saw
the Rembrandt portrait of a jew as we see it he wouldn't have
been a racist who gassed jews. If Hitler saw the Rembrandt
portrait of a white arian gentile as we see it he wouldn't have
been a racist who gassed jews. If Hitler saw the sunset as we
see it he wouldn't have been a racist who gassed jews. We
can't put ourself into a state of moral and political neutrality
when we look at the world or a painting of it. All seeing is like
an identity parade. We look for the truth. Only those who
help to make the truth can know it and recognize it. Truth,
morality and the appearance of things are politically determined.

The tree is there for everyone to see but we create what we
see. We see subjectively. Usually we broadly agree about
what we see. The SS man and the socialist see a teacup. The
different ways of seeing the teacup aren't a problem because
they usually have little practical consequence. Differences
are usually noticed only when they have a marked practical
consequence. Most of us see the red traffic light in the same
way. Or at least we see it as a traffic light in the same way – not
for example as part of our reflections while we wait at the
crossing. We see the red traffic light and stop. We don't all
see the red flag in the same way. The response to this isn't as
simple and uniform as stopping at the red traffic light. The
question is, do we see the sunset in the way we see the red flag
or the way we see the red traffic light? When we see the red
traffic light we're in a car. When we see the sunset we're in
our life, we're aware of the world and the men in it. Clearly
this is also the way in which we see the red flag. Finally of
course that's also the way we're aware in the car, because the
car's in the world. So there's a political way of seeing and
doing everything. But aesthetic appearances don't call out in
us a conventional and conditioned response in the way the red
traffic light largely does. They call out our whole life. The SS
man can't see the tree as beautiful because he sees it in the

way the motorist sees the traffic light. But a man may see the tree to which he's taken to be hanged as beautiful.

People might disagree if you told them their neighbour sees the sunset differently from the way they see it, that in effect he sees a different sunset. They're less likely to disagree if you said that Rembrandt saw a different sunset. This is because Rembrandt is thought to have been more creative than ordinary people. In fact he wasn't. Creativity is seeing the world rationally, that's all. Rembrandt saw more rationally than some but not all people in his time. He was exceptional not in creativity but in skill. His skill allowed him to record what he saw. Seeing a picture involves as much creativity as painting it. Fortunately creativity is very common. It would be even more common if society didn't so often try to repress it. Most people can be as creative as Rembrandt. If they weren't we couldn't live in human societies. The same creativity can be used (depending on the skill) to paint, compose music, run a home, teach, change society, care for others, live a decent life and so on. All these activities may call out the whole of our life.

ON PROBLEMS

The creator needs problems
The problem is an unlearned skill
In solving problems the creator learns skills
He uses skills to make new skills
Out of problems

The worker has only problems and skills
Respect the problem!
Don't turn back or aside when you see it
Go to it
It holds the secret of change

Look at the problem closely
Understand it has many sides
But few solutions
Before the solutions are known
You must know the sides

This is the law of nature
The chain snaps at the weakest point
Follow the same law
To release the prisoner
Search the chain for the weakest point
Then aim the axe

At each new step in the race
The runner places his foot
On the edge of his reach
Each step touches this boundary
How else can he win the race?

Sun ripens or scorches
Frost may kill the young shoots
Wind scatter the sheaves
Drought turn fertile earth to dust
Or rain mire it
These are the farmer's problems
When he knows his problems the harvest is safer
He studies the earth and the sky
Or plants in the wrong season

A storm may sink the ship
Or a hurricane sweep the sailor into the sea
And the black waves devour him
As if the whole sea were leviathan
But whoever takes to the sea must go with the wind
Seas and shores are the homes of wind

The sea and its wind are the sailor's problems
He weighs anchor and leaves port
He knows the wind and the currents
Or he will not reach home

With the sea there is wind
With men there is struggle
The struggles of men are the artist's problems
He must know men and their history
They are his means of creation
Show the audience the solution
But show them the problem
Make the problem fruitful!

Restoration
A Pastoral

Restoration was first presented at the Royal Court Theatre, London on 21 July 1981, with the following cast:

BOB	Philip Davis
LORD ARE	Simon Callow
FRANK	Nicholas Ball
MR HARDACHE	Wolfe Morris
PARSON	Norman Tyrrell
GABRIEL	John Barrett
MESSENGER	Kit Jackson
GAOLER	Patrick Murray
ROSE	Debbie Bishop
MOTHER, *Mrs Hedges*	Elizabeth Bradley
ANN	Eva Griffith
MRS WILSON	Darlene Johnson
OLD LADY ARE	Irene Handl

Directed by Edward Bond
Music by Nick Bicât
Designed by Hayden Griffin and Gemma Jackson
Lighting by Rory Dempster

England, eighteenth century – or another place at another time

Part One

Part Two

Note on the songs

In the first production of *Restoration* 'Hurrah' was cut from Scene Eight. It would be possible to cut 'Dream Song' from Scene Eleven and sing it between Scenes Ten and Eleven. 'Suddenly' would then have to be cut.

It's a Big Broad Fine Sunny Day

It's a big broad fine sunny day
The black clouds are gonna blow away
It's true that the rockets are aimed in their pits
But they wont be fired, not this time
This time there ain't gonna be any crime
This time we're gonna say no
This time we're gonna be wise guys
And tell the bastards where to go

It's a big broad fine sunny day
It's getting more sunny all the time
It's true that the bombs are stacked in their racks
But we won't load them up, not this time
This time there ain't gonna be no more war
This time we're gonna say no
This time we're gonna be wise guys
And tell the bastards where to go

It's a big broad fine sunny day
It's getting better all the time
And this time the soldiers will not march away
So they won't be shot at, not this time
This time they ain't gonna die for the sods
This time they're gonna say no
This time they're staying here to play
And tell the bastards where to go

It's a big broad fine sunny day
And the sky gets bluer all the time
From now on we'll live in the way that we say
And we won't be told, not this time
This is our world and it's staying that way
This time we're gonna say no
Today we'll live till tomorrow
And tell the bastards where to go

Part One

Scene One

London.
The Park of LORD ARE's *house.*
ARE *and* FRANK. FRANK *is in livery.*

ARE. Lean me against that great thing.

FRANK. The oak sir?

ARE. Hold your tongue. No no! D'ye want me to appear drunk? Nonchalant. As if I often spent the day leaning against an oak or supine in the grass.

FRANK. Your lordship comfortable?

ARE. No scab I am not, if that gives ye joy. Hang my scarf over the twig. Delicately! – as if some discriminating wind had cast it there. Stand off. How do I look?

FRANK. Well sir . . . how would yer like to look?

ARE. I wore my russet and green of a purpose. Must I sprout berries before I am at home in the landscape?

FRANK. Not seen your lordship –

ARE. Pox! ye city vermin can't tell the difference between a haystack and a chimney stack. Wha-ha! I must not laugh, it'll spoil my pose. Damn! the sketch shows a flower. 'Tis too late for the shops, I must have one from the ground.

FRANK. What kind sir?

ARE. Rip up that pesky little thing on the path. That'll teach it to grow where gentlemen walk. (FRANK *offers the flower.*) Smell it! If it smells too reprehensible cast it aside. I hate the gross odours the country gives off. 'Tis always in a sweat! Compare me to the sketch.

FRANK (*checks sketch*). Leg a bit more out.

ARE. Lawd I shall be crippled. *Do* they stand about the
country so? When I pass the boundaries of the town I lower
the blinds in mourning and never go out on my estate for
fear of the beasts.

FRANK. Cows aren't beasts sir.

ARE. The peasants sirrah. Don't mar the sketch with your
great thumbs. I had it drew up by a man renowned for his
landscapes to show me how a gentleman drapes himself
across his fields. That I call a proper use for art. The book
oaf! Well sirrah open it! Must I gaze on the cover as if I
wondered what manner of thing I held in my hand?

FRANK. Any page sir?

ARE. The blanker the better. (*Looks at the page.*) Turn sir.
The poet spilt his ink and scribbled to use it up before it
dried. A poem should be well cut and fit the page neatly as
if it were written by your tailor. The secret of literary style
lies in the margins. Now *that* sir could only have been
written by Lord Lester's tailor, whose favourite colour is
woad. Turn me to something short. Your master is a man
of epigrammatic wit. About your business. I must pine.

FRANK *goes.*

What a poor gentleman I am! Town house and park,
country house and land as far as the eye can see, they tell
me – for I never look out, 'twould remind me how far off
was the town – debts to honour a duke, and broke. So: a
rich bride. Yonder, about to rise over the horizon like a
pillar of smoke, is Mr Hardache, iron founder, ship builder, mine owner and meddler and merchant in men and
much else that hath money in it. With his daughter, who
must have a title and country estate to go with her fortune.
Well marriages have been built on weaker foundations.
The heart changes but pride does not. So here I am set,
imitating the wild man of the woods. An extravagant ges-

ture but I would have the gal love me at sight and be spared the tedium of courting an iron master's daughter. Faith boys what would one do: rattle a spoon in a tin mug and call it a serenade? Peace good soul! You have but to glance up from this bundle of tasteless moralising – the relief itself will bring rapture to thy face – and the slut's fate is sealed. I hope I am not to wait for a change in the season? I shall put out branches or turn white in a hoar frost.

BOB *enters*.

A swain wanders o'er the landscape.

BOB. Well London here I am! What strange sights I hev seen!

ARE. Why does the fool gawp so impertinently? Lawd it grins!

BOB. Mornin' my lord.

ARE. Gad it addresseth me! Oaf be off!

BOB. Ay sir, where to?

ARE. Where to? What care I where to? To hell! Wha-ha! (*Aside*.) Dear heart do not discommode thy complexion. A raw face is a countrified look but I would not have one even to gaze on the blazing of the bankruptcy court! Dear gad my foot is misplaced!

BOB (*aside*). Doo a London gentleman complain when his foot move? However do they git into bed – or out of it? – Shall us carry yoo sir?

ARE (*aside*). I am dealing with a harmless lunatic. The iron people have turned into the avenue. Soon we shall hear them clank. – Good fellow, take the run of my grounds. Go and play.

BOB (*aside*). This is a test Bob. Don't git caught out. (*Idea*.) Drat what a fool I am! That owd rag round your neck hev hitched yoo up in the bramble! Tell by the look on yoor face! I'll soon haul yoo out sir!

ARE (*pushing* BOB *away*). Off sir! Back to your bedlam!

BOB. Why sir 'tis Bob – come of age and sent up to serve as yoor man, as laid down in the history of our estate: eldest Hedges boy hev the right to serve his lord. Steward writ an' say he were sendin' me up.

ARE (*aside*). This comes from opening a poetry book. – Sirrah . . . ?

BOB. Bob sir. Or Robert Hedges.

ARE. Bob, yonder is a paddock. Go and graze.

BOB. Graze sir?

ARE. A country lad must know how to graze!

BOB (*aside*). I must learn their ways if I'm to survive. – Ay sir.

ARE. Then graze.

BOB (*shrugs. Aside*). I'll chew three stalks t' show willin'. That'll hev to doo.

BOB *goes.*

ARE. Yonder comes my money. (*Reads.*)

HARDACHE *enters.*

HARDACHE. Lord Are.

ARE. La sir ye surprised me!

HARDACHE. My girl's back of the hedge, studyin' the shop window. (*Calls.*) Come daughter, or his lordship'll think you don't know your manners. A retiring lass.

ARE (*aside*). Good. Let her retire to the country and leave London to me.

HARDACHE. You'll soon know her ways. Mind, she has a temper – like her mother. That blessed woman ran my shops like an empire. (*Calls.*) Pst! Come daughter. – She has all the airs of a lady. Learned it from the customers. Not that she works in the shop now, O no! Last week the soup was cold. She hauls the cook in and rows her out in front of the guests till she shakes like a dog being shown the well. Anything she likes, she must have. Saw a carriage with a new fancy way of panels – must have. A duchess with diamonds in her hat – must have. Skrawky pet dog – must have. Little black maid – one of them too. I don't begrudge. She's all that's left of her mother to me, barrin' a few shawls. That good woman worked all her life – till we had a penny to spend on ourselves and tuppence to mend the damage – and died at the counter with a slice of dinner in her hand. We're a family sort of family –

ARE (*aside*). Lawd he'll quote me the jingles on his family tomb-stones.

HARDACHE. – and I intend to make you part of us!

ARE (*aside*). Pox if I call him father!

ANN (*off*). Pst!

HARDACHE. You call my sweet?

ARE. Fetch her sir – (*Aside*.) ere the ivy grow o'er me.

HARDACHE (*calls*). I'll meet you halfway.

> ANN *comes on downstage and*
> HARDACHE *goes down to her.*

ARE. Not uncomely, but the neglect is beyond redemption! Style cannot strike at any age like a conversion. Its rudiments are learned in the nursery or never. That redness of cheek might be had off a coster's barrow for ha'pence. But I'll take her, as she comes with money.

HARDACHE. Well sweetheart? (*By her.*) Hussy you're fit for nowt but an errand boy but you're my daughter and you'll marry an earl.

ANN. But father! He's got four limbs and his wind. He could last for years.

HARDACHE. Shan't I buy good stock?

ANN. O you are a fool father! Lucy married a count with gout who lasted no more than three months. And Audrey's old baron died of overeating in a year – and he was no trouble

while he were alive. He chased her round the bed but were
too fat to catch her. She lost pounds and looked better after
her marriage than she did before – and few girls can say as
much!

HARDACHE. Come miss.

ANN. Even that ugly Mary Flint. Her father got her an earl of
nowt but twenty-five. But he was so eaten up with the
diseases he was born with and those he'd acquired – and
mad, she had three doctors testify to him before she signed
the settlement – that when they came into church the poor
parson didn't know whether to turn to the marriage ceremony or the burial of the dead. He were right too: they'd no
sooner left the church than they had to go back in for the
internment. She went with the peeling and came back with
the tolling. But what have you ever done for me father?

HARDACHE. Presently my lord!

ANN. Can't you find one in a wheel-chair or at least on a
crutch, so a body might hope? Did you enquire if the
family die young? No – you are a thoughtless man father.
And what does it matter that he has land in the country?
You know I abominate the place.

ARE. Pray unhitch me.

ANN. Can't we leave him to see if he hang?

HARDACHE (to ARE). My daughter's too well brought up to
touch a gentleman's linen in public. (Releases ARE.) Now
sir.

ARE. Servant ma'am.

ANN. Good day sir.

ARE. Let me show you the grounds. A few roses, a planta-
tion, a pretty forest, the best kept wilderness, and a jungle
in the hothouse. We will not bother with the water gardens
– a puddle compared to the lakes of Hilgay!

ANN (aside). Perhaps he's prone to accidents. – Did the scarf
wound you sir?

ARE. Wound! Fwa! when I take a toss out hunting the ground cracks.

ANN (*aside*). Well, best know the worst. He's still the first box at the play, eating out in great houses, orchestral balls. I'll be presented at court and dance with the prince the second time he asks – the first time I'll be in one of my pets and give him a great yawn.

ARE (*aside*). Cupid has lodged his shaft. I'll beat up my price and set her onto that old maker of cinders. That light in the eye of a slut or a countess is the true lust for money.

> ARE *and* ANN *go.*

HARDACHE (*calls*). Rose! – You youngsters go and look at the flowers. I'll wait up at the house.

> ROSE *comes in.*

Call me if the hussy runs off. He can fondle her hand and rub up against her – but nowt else.

ROSE. Yes sir.

> HARDACHE *goes.* BOB *comes on. He has already met* ROSE.

BOB. Shall us follow?

ROSE. No.

BOB. Hev you notice the sky is gold? Knew the streets ont paved with it. If I was towd the sky was I ont believe that neither.

ROSE. The sun shines on the smoke.

BOB. Lawd. I'm Bob. What yoo called gal?

ROSE. Rose.

BOB. Will yoo show us London Rose?

ROSE. Won't get time for sightseein'.

BOB. Ont mind that, rather kip busy. But I intend to see the churches an' palaces an' docks an' markets. Whey-hay!

Rose if yoor lady an' my lord git wed, as yoo say, us'll see a lot of each other, which us'll like. Make a bargain: yoo say everytime I goo wrong.

ROSE. That'll keep me busy. You run up here to get away from some poor cow carryin' your bastard.

BOB. Thass a lie! Ont ought a charge a chap with that!

ROSE. Keep yer shirt on.

BOB. Thass all right then, s'long as we know. – Look at the way *they* go on! Could drive a cart between 'em. Treat a Hilgay gal like that she'd reckon there was summat wrong with her. I'll show yoo how that ought to be done. First yoo take the gal's hand an' walk her up an' down. Bin a hard week so she soon git tired an' goo a bit slow.

ROSE. She's not goin' too far. She might have to come back on 'er own.

BOB. He's a thoughtful chap so he steer her to a bank an' pat the grass. 'Take the weight off yoor feet gal'.

ROSE. No, I'm wearing my best dress.

BOB. Yoo hev t'say yes or I can't show yoo how to doo it. 'Look' he say 'yoo're a pretty gal an' he give her a (*Picks up* ARE's *flower.*) Lady's Smock. Then yoo give him a kiss.

ROSE. Why?

BOB. You hev to!

ROSE. Why?

BOB. God yoo're a disconcertin' woman gal! Thass considered very rude in Hilgay. Yoo hev the flower, yoo hev t'kiss – or thass bad luck for both parties for a whole year. Ought to give us some luck Rose – (*Kisses her.*) on my first day in London.

Roses (BOB)

I lay a red rose on your breast
A red rose on a dusky flower

It rises and falls in the scent of your mouth
Your breath is a breeze that blows
In the silent world where the ice walls tower
And melts the snows to sparkling streams
And brings the swallows home from the south . . .
In the scent of your breath and from the rose
The petals open and fall apart
Scatter and lie upon your heart
And there I lay my head in repose
I kiss the petals
They stir and close
Close to the secret bud again
The bud in which are hidden away
The breezes of spring
The gentle rain
And the warmth of a summer's day

Scene Two

Hilgay.
The Hall.
Porch.
MOTHER *and* PARSON.

MOTHER. Upset yoo ont let 'em parade in a line. Ont often
   git a bit of fun.

PARSON. Let them work – that's what his lordship would
   wish to see.

   ARE *and* ANN *enter.*
   FRANK *goes in and out with boxes.*

ARE. Faw! The dust! Parson ye have emptied your graveyard
   on my doorstep!

PARSON. My lord I shall pray for rain.

ARE *enters the house.*

ANN. Every bone in my body's broken. My stomach's changed places with my liver. (*To* FRANK.) Mind that box man!

PARSON. My lady welcome to Hilgay. We asked a blessing on the wedding –

ANN (*to* FRANK). Get them away from his feet!

PARSON. – and would gladly have held the service at St John's. His lordship's father was christened, married and buried there, as were –

ANN (*to* FRANK). Don't slam it man!

FRANK. 'S heavy.

ANN. So will my fist be round your chops!

MOTHER. M'lady, Mrs Hedges yoor housekeeper.

ANN. Make someone keep an eye on the carriage! Who are those ruffians loitering round the back?! Be off! They'll steal my new things!

BOB *comes on. His livery is the same as* FRANK'S.

PARSON. My lady the parish has had an outbreak of methodists! On Sunday I took the horses from their stalls and drove the fanatics through the lanes. 'Tis no boast to say that on Monday the beasts were so weary 'twas painful to lead them to the shafts.

ANN *goes in. The* PARSON *follows*

BOB. Ma.

MOTHER. Boy yoo look smart.

They can't embrace because BOB *is putting down a parcel.*

BOB. Keepin' well?

MOTHER. Gittin' by. Dad's out the back, brought him up to the house. She the sort a creature she looks like?

BOB. Yes if thass cow.

MOTHER. I can handle cows.

BOB. Tell dad I'll be out soon's I git his lordship straight.

BOB *goes in*. MOTHER *examines the luggage*.

MOTHER. Huh load of old stuff. Ont need that here.

ROSE *comes in*. MOTHER *straightens up and sees her*.

MOTHER. Eek!

ROSE. Mrs Hedges.

MOTHER. Thought the devil catch me pryin'. Give me a turn gal.

ROSE. I'm the lady's maid.

MOTHER. Ay. Heard the London servants was getting black. Sorry I shouted my dear. The house is my territory by right and conquest. What goo on outside come under the steward or head gardener – I ont responsible for their lawlessness. Mr Phelps is the parson when yoo goo to church – which yoo better had, doo they complain – an' the magistrate when yoo goo to court – which you better hadn't. Yoor regular duties come under her ladyship but anything relatin' to the runnin' of the house come under me: where yoo sit at table, upkeep of yoor room an' any set-to yoo hev with the servants – I'm the law, an' the mercy if yoo're lucky. That clear my pet? Disorder's unprofitable all round.

ROSE. Ta I like to know where I am.

MOTHER. Git her ladyship settled like a good gal and come down to my kitchen. Must be famished. (*Idea.*) Yoo ont eat special?

ROSE. No.

MOTHER. Jist as well cause we ont hev it. I'll find yoo summat tasty.

BOB *comes in and embraces* ROSE.

MOTHER. You two know each other.

ROSE. We're married Mrs Hedges.

MOTHER. Married? Well. (*Pause for thought.*) Black cow give milk same as white cow. They say black the grate an' the fire burn better. Still, god doo goo in for surprises. Hev a daughter-in-law! Well send a lad to London he's bound to come back different. Could hev got someone to write a letter. I'd hev got it read.

ROSE. Their weddin' kept us busy.

BOB. We're very happy ma.

MOTHER. They all are t' start with, otherwise they ont git married. Well. Us'll hev to –. Fancy hevin' a daughter! Take a minute to git use to! Need a double bed. I'll invite both on yoo to a glass of wine in my pantry. Settle her ladyship first. Don't want a paddy on her first day in the house.

ROSE. Let the cow wait. I haven't had five minutes with Bob all day.

> FRANK *comes in.*

FRANK. Nobs gone up?

ROSE. Yeh.

FRANK. Dump ennit? Cruel to animals keepin' 'em here. All the trees look alike. Don't yer get lost? 'Fraid to stick me head out the winder 'case I can't find me way back. Do all right though! What's the talent like? Smart lad down from London, good looker, spin a yarn, knocked about a bit – what? Answer to a maiden's prayer. Yoo bin prayin' ma? 'Ere, yoo speak English or do animal imitations like Bob?

MOTHER. Mrs Hedges the housekeeper. Pleased to make yoor acquaintance Mr . . . ?

FRANK. Frank love, I dispense with the title: don't pull rank. All them bulls an' cows runnin' abaht in the altogether – gals must go round ready for it all the time. But I don't

fancy them fields. Now a back alley's been the scene of
many of my –
BOB. Pay no notice.
FRANK. Speaks English though don't she Bobby. Well sort
of. She yer ma? Pleased to meet yer Mrs Hedges.
MOTHER. If they bought a donkey for its bray I could sell yoo
to the lord mayor. Git all that stuff out my porch –
FRANK. Your ma gettin' at me Bobby?
MOTHER. – before we break our necks.
FRANK. Ask me, put it back on the coach. Don't see madam
stickin' this caper.
MOTHER. Yoo jist git them cases –
FRANK. Not me Mrs Hedges. I'm the outdoor servant. Bob's
indoors. I fetch an' carry outside – *an'* not all this junk. In
London it's letters, presents done up in little boxes, pick
up from the florists, or follow yer lady when she's shop-
pin'. If this was London an' his lordship stood on that line
I'd have to clean the front of his boots an' Bobby'd have to
clean the back.

Song of Learning (FRANK)

For fifty thousand years I lived in a shack
I learned that a shack is not a place to live in
For fifty thousand years I built mansions for men of wealth
That's how I learned to build a mansion for myself

For fifty thousand years I hammered and toiled
All that I made was taken away from my hands
For fifty thousand years I ran factories for men of wealth
That's how I learned to run a factory for myself

For fifty thousand years I waited at table
I learned to cook and how to unbottle the wine
For fifty thousand years I watched rich men tuck in like
    swine
From now on the food is gonna be mine

For fifty thousand years I printed their books
I learned how to read by looking over their shoulder
For fifty thousand years I built libraries for men of wealth
That's how I learned to write the books I need for myself

For fifty thousand years I fought in their wars
I died so often I learned how to survive
For fifty thousand years I fought battles to save their wealth
That's how I learned to know the enemy myself

For fifty thousand years I gave them my life
But in all that time they never learned how to live
For fifty thousand years I was governed by men of wealth
Now I have learned to make the laws I need for myself

I have known pain and bowed before beauty
Shared in joy and died in duty
Fifty thousand years I lived well
I learned how to blow up your hell

Scene Three

Hilgay.
The Hall.
LADY ARE's *Drawing Room.*
ANN *with a book.*

ANN. Last night I had a wonderful dream. We were walking
    arm in arm. A perfect day. Suddenly rain bucketed down.
    We sheltered under a tree. Wind howled in the branches –
    and a bolt of lightning hit it. It crashed down, struck my
    husband on the head and drove him straight into the
    ground like a hammer striking a nail. He weren't there!
    Vanished! Killed and buried at one blow! I wasn't even

brushed. Then the sun came out. Well it would, wouldn't it? And Lucy and Peg – my best school chums – rode up in a carriage sat on top of a great mountain of my luggage. And I'm whisked off to a gala given by royalty at Covent Garden for all the people to celebrate my release. Ee I was that happy!

ARE *comes in. He carries bills.* ANN *curtsies.*

ARE. If ye've crooked your ankle try cow liniment ma'am.

ANN (*aside*). I shan't be provoked.– O what a lovely thing!

ARE. What ma'am?

ANN. That jacket.

ARE. D'ye like it? My plum red. Ye begin to have taste.

ANN. And that other thing round your neck!

ARE. The cravat? Pox ma'am 'tis a disaster! Odious! My oaf of a man left it out and hid the rest. Had I been visiting anyone but your ladyship I'd have stayed in my room.

ANN. O no it's a picture!

ARE. Well insult me to my face. It but confirms that your tailor's bills are wasted on you. Pox ma'am, one of us must give up this damned foolish habit of followin' the fashion – and I'm damned sure it ain't me. I'll get something from the marriage! Ye have the title and may be thankful that unlike the fashion that has not changed in the last six hundred years and will not in the next. When my mother departed this house in haste she abandoned her wardrobe. Hitherto it was a supply for dusters but ye may sort out something to wrap in. Her taste was execrable but it will do for the servants.

ANN. Your lordship will tease.

ARE. Tease ma'am? I never tease about fashion. On that subject I am always serious – and correct. Well today ye're pleased to ogle me like an ape, but ye commonly find my society tedious –

ANN (*aside*). At last he's said something I agree with and I can't tell him.

ARE. – and as I never willingly discomfit a lady I'll relieve ye of it. I depart for London within the week to see to the refurbishments ordered to my house to console me at the time of my wedding. I told the designer the dining room should be apple green. He hath sent me a sample. If any apple were ever that colour Adam would not have been tempted and mankind would not have fallen. Next I asked for a crimson drawing room. 'Tis a modest wish. The rogue hath sent me a specimen of wincing pink – the colour of his cheeks when I kick him from the house.

ANN. O lawd sir why wait a week? I'll pack my things and we may be off –

ARE. 'Twas agreed ye spent six months in the country learning manners. A wholely optimistic time but a newly married man is fond and believes in miracles – as well he may. Six months. 'Tis not my fault the designer hath gone colour-blind in one. Ye stay.

ANN. But sir how can I learn manners here? What refinement can I get from a duck pond?

ARE. Try the parson's sister. But keep her off Deuteronomy. She once went to Bath. The visit was brief but she heard a concerto. She will hum ye the tune if ye ask her – and indeed, I believe, if ye do not. I assure ye that if in six months ye are totally transformed none will be more thankful than I.

ANN. Oh you pig! Pig!

ANN *throws a book at him. He picks it up.*

ARE (*reads*). 'The Duchess of Winchelsea's Guide to Conduct with Notes on Presentation at Court and Selected Subjects for Polite Conversation with Examples of Repartee, Condolence and so forth.' I see ye have read it. Winchelsea is an illiterate hag whose conduct would have her expelled from a madhouse. Repartee? – no one talks to her but Lord Lester and his repartee is as sparkling as a judge passing sentence of death. Ho! ye have much to learn.

ANN. I'll learn you this my lad! Your title lasted six hundred years but it'll likely die with you! I shan't enter your bedroom till you can hear the singing at Covent Garden when the window's shut!

ARE. Fie ma'am! I intend to bequeath posterity the memorial of my life not some snot-nosed brat! If I have a boot or cape named after me – as I hope to have a hat – I shall be content. I tell ye ma'am, your father palmed me dud coin. I've had ladies swell for far less labour and far more pleasure.

ANN. You monster! You promised me –

ARE. Ma'am a gentleman will promise anything to avoid quarrelling in church with a parson.

ANN. Not his vows you ape! My vows! You promised me theatres, parties, dining in palaces, footmen, clothes. I was to meet the prince. I didn't expect you to keep all your promises. But you haven't kept one!

ARE. Why ma'am if a gentleman kept his promises society would fall apart. I promised? Forsooth and is that not enough? Have ye not had the pleasure of the promise? Your feet tapped when I promised you the opera! Your mouth watered when I promised you diamonds! Your knees shivered when I promised you the prince! What happiness I gave you! I denied you nothing. I was a prodigal of promise. Why ma'am have ye not noticed I promise all the time? I am a christian. I go about the world scattering promises on the suffering and destitute. Would ye have me hard-hearted and not promise my fellow man in his misery? Fwaw! Be silent ma'am! Ye asked to learn and ye shall. I promised! Ungrateful gal was that not enough but that now you must have the promises kept? What fool doesn't know that promises are better not kept? 'Tis plain folly in a gentleman to keep his word. I verily believe that is the cause of half the world's miseries. What surer way have we to drive our friends to despair? I shall not be so cruel to any man that it can ever be said I kept one promise I made him. Why I promise ye the stars! The Atlantic ocean! There is no limit to my generosity! I promise ye the moon! Now ma'am must I keep my promise? Do ye not know that every man who ever sighed has promised the moon to someone? Will ye all go a-squabbling for it? Ma'am I wonder that ye can live in this world at all with a mind so unschooled in polite society. The sundial is promised the sun – yet is content to read the shadows! And hath it not snowed in June? I shall now promise to pay your tailor and if he hath wit enough to thread a needle he'll know what that promise is worth.

ARE *goes*.

ANN (*calls*). Rose! O I have a new purpose to go to London. *Revenge*. I'll shame him at the greatest soirée of the season. I'll wait till the prince, to further his cause with me, is about to offer him some high office and then say in a whisper loud enough to wake the postilions in the street 'Nay, sire, make him an admiral and your chance of a liaison is gone' then sit back and watch him cry in some magnificent palace.

ROSE *comes in*.

ANN. Can you do voodoo?
ROSE. Voodoo?
ANN (*indicating a jewel*). I'll give you my pin.
ROSE. No ma'am.
ANN. O you heartless brazen liar! I'm sure your mother

taught you. It comes naturally to you people. You cut a chicken's neck and say spells.

ROSE. I don't believe in all that.

ANN. If only someone would help me! I tried sticking pins in a doll when we were married. This house is haunted. A girl was bricked up for carrying on out of wedlock. She comes out of the wall of a morning and wails. I don't have to keep you on when I get to London. Black girls aren't the novelty they were Miss Will-when-she-wants-to. You're two a penny. Rose you could dress up as the ghost and threaten him.

ROSE. My husband wouldn't let me.

ANN. We shan't tell him.

ROSE. If his lordship found out he'd sack me and my husband.

ANN. Very well. You had your warning. I'll do it myself.

Dream (ROSE)

I sit in a boat and float down a river of fire
The boat is cool – it doesn't burn in the heat
The flames hide us from the banks
Where the whiteman aims his gun
The boat sails safely on
The whitemen rage and stamp their feet
Then the fire flows up the banks and into the trees
The whitemen run and the fire comes on
The river of fire chases them till they fall
To their knees and crawl about in the flames
The river burns everything that stands in its path
Forests and men all are consumed in its wrath
    I am black
    At night I pass through the land unseen
    Though you lie awake
    My smile is as sharp as the blade in my hand

But when the fire is spent
The ground is not scorched
The trees are not charred
The land is green in the morning dew
The cattle passed through the flames yet are not dead
Only the whiteman's bones are black
Lying by his burned out tanks
Now cattle graze the river banks
Men and women work in the fields
All that they grow they own
To be shared by old and young
In the evening they rest
And the song of freedom is sung
   I am black
   At night I pass through the land unseen
   Though you lie awake
   My smile is as sharp as the blade in my hand
   The venom does not kill the snake

Scene Four

Hilgay.
The Hall.
'The Thieving Scene'.
Workroom.
Chest and chairs.
MOTHER *and* ROSE.

MOTHER *cleans silver and* ROSE *sews.*

MOTHER. Ont lose things. Thass took. Knife an' fork. Be the
    devil to pay. Yoo can write it in my Loss Book so I ont hev
    to bother parson. Yoor mother alive gal?
ROSE. Yes. She was a slave. Her boss got rich and came to

England an their kids cried so they brought her with them.

    FRANK *comes in dazed, exhausted and filthy. He drifts like a ghost and talks like a somnambulating child.*

MOTHER. Mornin' 'outside'. Don't mess in here, nough t' clean up.

FRANK. Bloody hole! In London yer work all hours but yer not an animal. More'n two parcels an' yer call a porter! But what am I here? Muck out the yard. Heave pig shit. Ashamed t' smell meself. If I got back to London I wouldn't get a job in this state. Never wash the muck off me hands. Like bein' branded! Night time I'm wore out. Creep into bed. If I had a bird I'd fall asleep on her. Fat chance of that! (*Without humour:*) Their fellas guard 'em with pitchforks. O Rosie I'm so tired I could cry. Why did we ever leave London?

MOTHER. Jist upset his-self.

ROSE (*cradles* FRANK'*s head*). Hush.

    He instantly falls asleep.

MOTHER. Yoo London folks are a proper laugh. Bit a hard work hev him cryin' like a babby.

ROSE. He's not used to workin' in the yard.

MOTHER. Git used, same's everyone else.

ROSE. He don't mind working with his hands but that's *all* he does now. Likes to use his brains. He's smart – aren't you Frank? (*Shakes him awake.*)

FRANK (*as if waking from a dream*). Hens cacklin'. Cows roarin'. Horses kickin'. Dogs snarlin'. Bloody great curs! Dogs in London sit on cushions an' say thanks when yer feed 'em. These bloody mastiffs 'd rip yer hand off. Me nerves are in shreds.

ROSE. Sit down.

FRANK (*sits in* ROSE'*s chair*). Ta Rose. Yer a saint.

Wood Song (MOTHER)

The wooden cradle the wooden spoon
The wooden table the wooden bed
The wooden house the wooden beam
The wooden pulpit the wooden bench
The wooden hammer the wooden stair
The wooden gallows the wooden box
The iron chain the brass locks
The human toil the earthly span
These are the lot of everyman
The winds that drive the storms that blast
For everyman the die is cast
    All you who would resist your fate
    Strike now it is already late

MOTHER. My family polished this silver so long the pattern's
   rub off. Mother say 'Fruits pluck and birds flown'. Her
   mother an' her mother polished 'em in the winder to git the
   best light. Howd 'em up an' see the colour of your eyes in
   'em – then they're clean. Show the babbys their face upside
   down in the spoon, turn it round an' they're the right way
   up: one of the wonders of the world. Kip 'em quiet for
   hours. Saw my face in that when I were a kid. Mother
   say 'When yoor turn come, yoo clean 'em as good as
   that gal'. She's bin in the churchyard twenty years. Wash
   'em an' set 'em an' clean 'em after but ont eat off 'em
   once.
ROSE. Use 'em tonight. Have a feast. I'll lay the table an' the
   parson won't have to pray for yer.
MOTHER. Don't be cheeky. Bad 'nough clean 'em t' let
   others make 'em dirty. What I want goo dirtyin' 'em meself
   for? Food taste jist as good off mine.

   BOB *comes in.*

BOB. Parson's called.

MOTHER. Goo upstairs?

BOB. Yip. Says a prayer – an' then off up to see her ladyship.

MOTHER. Git his glass of wine out on the hall table. Allus set it ready. Old man his age need summat t' set him up.

MOTHER goes out.

BOB. Look at that lazy sod.

Takes some tape from the work-basket and begins to tie FRANK *to the chair at the ankles, knees and elbows.*

ROSE. What's that for?

BOB. Teach the lazy pig to sit.

ROSE. He's wore out. (*Helps* BOB *with the tying.*) Go easy. I have to account for every inch of that.

BOB. 'He's wore out'. So 'm I dooin' his work. Truss up lovely me old darlin'. There! Bet he's hevin' all sorts of dreams. Ont know whass in store.

FRANK opens both eyes.

FRANK. Bob. Undo me.

BOB. Ont fill the horse trough.

FRANK. Did. Buggers drunk it to cause a ruck. I'll fill it up again. Come on, don't get us into trouble.

BOB. Whass a matter boy? That old chair so fond of yoo it ont let yoo goo.

FRANK. Rose.

ROSE. He'll pay later.

BOB. Ho-ho a bit of hankypanky?

MOTHER comes in.

MOTHER. There. Thass set on the table with the saucer on top. Keep the flies out.

FRANK (*trying to stand*). Come on Bob. It's no joke.

BOB (*tickling*). Ickle-wickle piggy goo to market. Ickle-wickle piggy stay at home. This ickle piggy goo wee-wee-wee!

FRANK. Git off! Bloody lunatic! Don't muck abaht. Me foot hurts, the blood's cut off.

BOB. Whass the difference, yoo ont use it?

MOTHER. Spoon gone.

ROSE. Can't have. Count 'em.

MOTHER. Can't count. Tell it's gone by the pattern. Knife, fork – where's the spoon? Who's bin in?

FRANK. Well I'm clear. I was tied up and fast asleep.

MOTHER. Bob yoo ont got it?

BOB. No.

MOTHER. Rose? Hev to ask. It's my job. Easy git swep off by yoor skirt. Look in the pocket.

ROSE. Don't be daft.

MOTHER. Look.

ROSE (*looks*). No.

FRANK (*wriggles*). This is bloody stupid. Parson nipped in on his way up. Yer left it in the cupboard. (*Stands.*) Rose get this off.

MOTHER. Turn his pockets out.

FRANK. Now wait a minute! How could I do it? Trussed up like a chicken.

MOTHER. Could hev took it afore.

FRANK. Well I ain't.

MOTHER. Bob.

FRANK (*jerks*). Now look here. I'm not havin' this.

MOTHER. I'll hev to look.

FRANK. Don't accuse me Mrs Hedges. Yer didn't use that tone to them.

MOTHER. I know they ont took it –

FRANK. O do yer!

MOTHER. – and I'm me own judge a character. Ask to see in yoor pockets, yoo ont hide nothin' yoo ont make a fuss.

FRANK. You'd make a fuss if yer was bloody tied up. What yer do round here to prove yer innocent? Float in the pond?

MOTHER. I lose my silver I lose my job. Out that yard 'fore I turn round. Ont git another job with a bad name.

BOB. Hand it over.

FRANK. Look son – get this bloody chair off or I'll break every bone in yer –

BOB. All right I believe yoo: yoo ont took it.

FRANK. Ta. Now undo these bloody –

BOB. So we'll jist look in yoor pockets to satisfy ma.

FRANK (*tries hitting the chair on the floor*). This has bloody well gone –

ROSE. Let him go!

ROSE *tries to untie* FRANK. BOB *moves her aside.*

BOB. I'll settle this Rose.

FRANK. Keep off son! I warn yer! I'll bloody cripple yer! Treat me like an animal, I'll be one!

MOTHER. Grab him Bob! He ont got the strength to hurt a fly!

BOB. Us'll hev to see Frank.

FRANK. Look I didn't take it – an' what if I had? Thass my wages – by agreement. I get paid bugger all. Why? 'Cause in London I get tips. Take a letter get a tip. Keep yer wits open an' there's plenty of ways to pick up a bit on the side. All yer pick up here's the shit on yer boots!

BOB *tries to search* FRANK. FRANK *spins and tries to defend himself with the chair legs.* BOB *and* FRANK *fight.*

BOB. Quick mum.

BOB *grabs the chair and forces* FRANK *to sit.* FRANK *struggles and jerks.*

BOB. Ont help boy: truss up like a rabbit.

MOTHER tries to search FRANK.

MOTHER. Howd him steady! He's gooin' like –
FRANK. Bitch! I'll kick yer bloody – smash yer bloody –
MOTHER. Beast! Beast! Beast!
ROSE. Stop it! All of yer! Yer like kids.

ROSE starts to untie FRANK. She releases his arm. He takes the spoon from his pocket and holds it out.

FRANK. There's yer spoon. I hope it chokes yer.
MOTHER (*takes the spoon*). Any damage t' that chair make it worse.

FRANK begins to untie himself. ROSE helps him. Suddenly BOB turns the chair upside down. FRANK's feet are in the air and his head is on the ground. BOB jerks the chair.

BOB. Where yoo hid the rest?
FRANK. That's the lot. Crowd round here it's a wonder there's anythin' left to nick.

BOB lets the chair fall flat on its back on the floor. FRANK again begins to untie himself.

BOB. I'll search his loft.
MOTHER. Git Ronnie off the field an' tie him up proper. I'll tell his lordship we've bin thief-catchin'. Parson's happen lucky, so I ont hev to send out for a magistrate.
FRANK. Hold on. Yer got the spoon. That's the end of it.
MOTHER. Us'll tell boy.
ROSE. Don't be daft, mother. There's no harm done. Frank'll go and get the knife an' fork – (*To FRANK.*) an' everythin' else yer took – (*To MOTHER.*) an' yer can put it back. (*To BOB.*) Yer ruined my tape. Who's paying for that?

FRANK. It's just the knife an' fork – god's honest.

BOB. Us'll hev to tell.

ROSE. What's the good of that?

BOB. Ten't a question of good. Question of law. Ont break it us-self, an' if someone else do: we stay on the right side an' tell. 'S only way. He's been stealin' for years. Steal himself if it had any value.

MOTHER. Fine Christian I'd be turning him loose on my neighbours. He'd hev t'steal to live on the road.

FRANK. Yer have to steal in my job if yer wanna live. Yer fetch an' carry for 'em, pick 'em up, get 'em upstairs, put 'em to bed, clean up the spew. Stands to reason they drop anythin' – it's yourn. That's only right. Chriss! yer go through their pockets out of self-respect! Give it back, they'd drop it again or lose it gamblin'.

ROSE. For chrissake Bob. They hang yer for stealin'.

FRANK. Gawd.

MOTHER. Could of thought of that. If he was hungry I'd hev understood.

FRANK. Look forget it an' I'll scarper. Down the road an' yer'll never see me ugly mug again. Vanish. Now that's somethin' to look forward to eh? No hard feelings. (*Finishes untying himself, stands and offers his hand.*) Say cheerio ma? (*No response. Offers his hand to* BOB.) Come on old son. Don't upset Rose. She didn't know yer could be like this.

BOB. Ont trust yoo to goo through the gate: yoo'd nick it.

FRANK. Gawd you peasants drive a hard bargain. Stickin' pigs, twistin' necks, carvin' balls off calves – no wonder they treat people like animals. (*To* ROSE.) They after a cut? How much?

ROSE (*to* BOB). That lot can afford a bit of silver. Chriss the work they've got out of him, he deserves it.

MOTHER. Can't Rose, only do us a disservice.

ROSE. Please.

BOB. Yoo ont understand. I hev to take care of yoo now as well as ma.

FRANK. Gawd gal yer married a right little hypocrite there. Nasty little punk. Rotten little git. Arse-crawlin' little shit –

BOB. Thass enough of that before my mother.

> BOB *struggles with* FRANK. MOTHER *opens the lid of the chest and* FRANK *is bundled in.* BOB *closes and bolts the lid.*

Soon settled his hash.

FRANK (*inside*). It's a madhouse!

BOB. Yoo stay quiet an' think up a good excuse.

MOTHER. Phew he git me hot!

> FRANK *starts to kick and punch inside the chest.*

MOTHER. Ont yoo harm that chest boy! He's a proper vandal!

BOB (*aims a kick at the chest*). That ont help. Doo yoorself a mischief!

FRANK (*inside*). Rotten bastards!

BOB (*to* MOTHER). Git parson an I'll git the rope. Rose yoo wait outside, ont stay an' be contaminated by his filth.

FRANK (*inside*). Filthy rotten swine! Shit. Rotten sod. God rot yer yer bastard!

> BOB, MOTHER *and* ROSE *go.* FRANK *rattles the lid, trying to shake it open. Then he tries to knock off the end of the chest by kicking at it violently with both feet together.*

FRANK (*inside*): O gawd they'll hang me. (*Thump.*) Please. Why did I come to this madhouse? (*Thump.*) Please Bob. Bastard. (*Thump.*) Can't stand bein' shut up! Go off me head! (*Violent shower of footfalls on the end of the chest.*)

ROSE *has come in slowly. She stands and watches the chest.*

FRANK (*inside*). Can't breathe! Help! I'll die! (*Shakes the lid with his hands, then tramples his feet on the end of the chest.*) Never do it again pal. Promise. I learned my lesson. O please Bob.

Kicking and struggling, changing to regular thumping, and all the while he groans. ROSE *goes to the chest and gently sits on it. Immediately* FRANK *is still.*

FRANK (*inside*). Bob? The spoon fell on the floor an' I was tempted. Honest. I know it's wrong but I –. No no, it's dark Bob, I'm confused. Listen. I'll tell the truth. I took it to get me own back see? You had yer head down tyin' me feet. I winked at Rose. She'll tell yer. O dear Bob yer fell for a trick there. We're gonna laugh. Come on old sport.

ROSE. Frank.

FRANK (*inside*). Rose.

ROSE. Listen carefully. Yer life depends on it. I'll let yer out –

FRANK (*inside*). O bless yer –

ROSE. – if yer do what I say. Hide in the yard in the little barn till it's dark. Then go. Stay off the road an' keep to the hedges. Yer –

FRANK (*inside*). No, I'll scarper as fast as I –

ROSE. Listen. If yer go on the road now yer'll git caught. Where's the knife an' fork?

FRANK (*inside*). Rose what if they search the –

ROSE. Promise or I won't let yer out.

FRANK (*inside*). Promise.

ROSE *stands and unbolts the chest.* FRANK *opens the lid and steps out.*

FRANK. Yer darlin'!

ROSE. I'll get the stuff from yer loft.

FRANK. Keep it angel! I'll help meself!

> FRANK *grabs the rest of the silver, drops some, grabs it again but still leaves a few pieces.* ROSE *watches him.*

ROSE. O Frank.

> FRANK *runs out.* ROSE *shuts the chest, bolts it and sits on it.* BOB *comes in with a heavy rope. He goes to the chest and* ROSE *stands.*

BOB (*bangs the lid with the flat of his hand*). Gooin' to open yoor lid Frank. Yoo let me tie you up. No language – parson'll think thass Hebrew an' hev to look it up. Now then, git ready. (*Opens the lid.*) Ont git far.

ROSE. Yer like a stranger. I don't know yer.

BOB. Seem hard but it's for the best. Meddle in somethin' like this ruin yoor whole life. We think of us, can't afford to think of no one else. Hard times but we got jobs, we could be happy – but we ont if we meddle. He took the risk, now he hev to pay. Ont no way out of that.

Song of the Calf (BOB)

You take the calf to the slaughtering shed
It smells the sweat and blood and shit
It breaks its halter and runs through the lanes
The hollering men run after it

It snorts in the fresh clean morning air
It bellows and lows and tosses its head
And after it with sticks and ropes
Come the hollering men from the slaughtering shed

It reaches the town and runs through the streets
It tries to hide but the children shout
It turns at bay and trembles and groans
The hollering children have found it out

It scatters the mob and flees the town
It stops to rest in a quiet lane
Then peacefully strolls back home to its field
And enters the wooden gate again

And there stand the men from the slaughtering shed
In a circle with sticks and a halter and chain
They seize the calf and fetter it fast
And lead it back to the butcher again

For though it run and bellow and roar
The calf will be tied to the slaughterhouse door
The butcher will cut its throat with his knife
It will sink to its knees and bleed out its life

The morning is over, the work is done
You eat and drink and have your fun
The butcher is sharpening his knife today
Do you know – do you care – who will get away?

BOB. Best git started.

ROSE (*points*). He helped himself again.

BOB (*stares*). Rose yoo git us into terrible trouble.

ROSE. If yer catch him he'll tell – anythin' to get back at you. Let's hope he gets away.

BOB. Well thass a rum un! I come to tie up a thief an I hev to help him git off! (*Tugs the rope between his hands in bewilderment and frustration.*)

ROSE. He's hiding in the yard in the little barn. I'll take him some grub later on. My mother told me what the slaves do. The owners never search the backyards, go tearin' down the road, even the dogs – glad to be off the chain. Some of the overseers go mad – off their head – bound to if yer go round with a whip all day – an' start killin' the blacks. One or two a year, then one a month. Use the whip so it's legal – well it may be against the law but the whites run that. So

the blacks scarper or wait till it's their turn. Yer didn't
know yer'd married all that. Me mother said stay quiet an'
wait for the chance: it'll come. Yer were all rushin' round
shoutin'. So I waited quietly – d'yer know, I felt happy? –
an' let him out.

BOB. Rose yoo scare me. Ont talk like that, ont even think it.
Yoo're one of us now, yoo hev to think like white folk. We
ont hev madmen with whips – 'less we step out a line an'
meddle: *then* they goo mad! From now on yoo be guided by
me.

ROSE. Take orders? No. I 'ave to take them from them, but
not from you.

BOB (*quietly*). Ont row. Yoo ont understand yoo'll hev to
accept an' thass that. Yoo're a soft gal Rose, too easy
touched: thass a canker.

ROSE. I can be as hard as you. But I won't do things I grew
up to hate.

BOB (*holds her*). Wish I ont married if thass only gooin' to
bring this sort of trouble. O Rose, Rose . . .

PARSON *comes in.*

BOB (*holding* ROSE). Beg pardon parson, wife's upset . . .
He's gone.

PARSON. Dear me.

BOB. Ont set the bolt proper. Shook loose. My fault. (*Steps
away from* ROSE.)

PARSON. Bob you cost your master dear. Get after him. Take
every horse and man from the fields. I accept responsibility. We have taken a viper to our bosom. A stranger who
does not love our ways. Pray he has led none of our flock
astray! Thank heavens there are hours of daylight before
us. Scour every road. (*To* MOTHER *as she comes in.*) Did I
spy my glass of madeira under its friendly blue saucer? If
you would be so kind. The excitement has parched my
throat. Bob take my horse too.

BOB. He took the rest of the silver.

MOTHER (*stares*). O the wicked man! (*Bursts into tears.*) My silver gone! I polished it for years! The wicked man! Wicked! (*She weeps and sobs the word 'wicked' as she crawls on the floor on her hands and knees, collecting the silver.*)

PARSON. There: see how the guilty afflict the innocent. This woman learns of a lifetime's wasted labour. The cherished things on which she lavished her affection are gone. How will she occupy the time she would have devoted to cleaning them? I cannot lend her a consoling book, she cannot read. And who is to say that in the hotness of pursuit fear has not triumphed over greed? Even now the loot may lie in the mud at the bottom of a ditch.

MOTHER (*weeping*). O parson don't say so!

PARSON. Or be hurled down a well, lost forever!

MOTHER. Whatever shall us do?

BOB. I'll take the men right out to Coppins Point. He'll hev made for the coach road.

PARSON. Ten commandments! That's all that are asked of us. One little law for each finger, to bring peace to the lord in his palace and the goodman in his cottage. Yet ten are too many. They live by one: self – and seek perdition. Are you confirmed my dear?

ROSE. Yes.

PARSON. A pity. O I rejoice in your salvation. But the darkness of this day would have been lightened by the conversion of a heathen in my own parish. O you mustn't think all Englishmen are rogues my dear. I assure you most are as upright and sensible as your dear husband. Well, I'll fetch the madeira. (*He goes.*)

Man Groans (ROSE *and* MOTHER)

The house is on fire

Dark figures wave from the roof!

Shall we fetch a ladder
Or light brands to burn down the rest of the street?

> You to whom the answer is easy
> Do not live in our time
> You have not visited our city
> You weep before you know who to pity
> Here a good deed may be a crime
> And a wrong be right
> To you who go in darkness we say
> It's not easy to know the light

A man sits hunched in a cell
People dance in the street
Shall we stretch our hands through the bars
Or run to the street and dance in triumph?

> You to whom etc.

A man groans in a ditch
We take off our coat
To cover the man in the ditch or give to the man who runs
away?

> You to whom etc.

Scene Five

Hilgay.
The Hall.
Breakfast Room.
Table set for breakfast. Two chairs.
ARE *reads a London newspaper.*

ARE. When I go to the city of light Hedges stays here in outer
darkness. Because my forebears had the lice combed from
their beards by yokels must I have my cravat ruined by

one? I shall – (*Stops short at what he reads in the paper.* ANN *comes in as a ghost.*) That damned little Lordling Lester! The ninth time he's squirted into print since my departure! Plague rot his little ermined soul! I'll rout that martinet at his capers and see –

He sees the ghost.

Why I'll put on last year's breeches! The family ghost! (*Puts down the paper.*) Mother I beg your pardon. I thought 'twas the gin when it grinned at ye through the windows.

ANN. Woe!

ARE. Be off with ye! Disturbin' a gentleman at his breakfast! (*Picks up his newspaper and shoos it.*) Shoo I say!

ANN. Hear me Lord Are!

ARE. Hear ye? What listen to an ague-ridden corpse! When I want news or advice I'll go to someone a damned sight livelier than thou art ma'am. When were you at court or the play? Ye gad! what d'ye know of fashion? I'll wear something a sight more sprightly to be buried in! It amazeth me ye are not ashamed to be seen so in modern times!

ANN. Thy poor wife!

ARE. My wife? What of my wife? (*Aside.*) Here's a to-do, discussin' me wife with a ghost – though the subject is fitting. Have ye come to tell me she's to join ye? I thank ye for the good news and bid ye be gone so I may celebrate in peace!

ANN (*aside*). The monster! – Thy wife must flee to London. Flee!

ARE. To London? Why?

ANN. She is with child. If 'tis born here 'tis forever cursed.

ARE. Forsooth? And who will bear the expense of a London lying in? Let the cow doctor child her, as he did all my family. A curse? Lawd 'twill curse me for cursing it with its mother! But 'tis to be hoped it's a sensible brat and will understand it was the she-cat or poverty – and his poor papa made the best of the bad bargain.

ANN (*aside*). O my London revenge! I'll smear the paint on his face in the royal presence! – Alas that noble woman!

ARE. If ye pity her go and keep her company. I am not so hard put that I must seek the society of a ghost. I tell ye this spirit: I had thought to have been too harsh with the slut, but if it's with brat I'm off tomorrow. Her morning sickness will be nauseous.

ANN (*aside*). I'll frighten the monster to death!

ANN *goes.*

ARE (*muttering to himself as he settles at the table and resumes his newspaper*). Damned impertinent she-spirit, to disturb a man outside calling hours. I see the editorial doth not advise us the ghosts are walking. 'Tis a good story – yet I cannot use it. I'd have the methodists roaring hymns at my door and asking to see my spirit. Still, the news gives a man relish to his breakfast. London! Blessed city! Our new Jerusalem! Soon my shadow shall fall on thy doorways, my sprightly foot ascend thy broad stairs, my melodious voice sound in thy tapestried halls. London London London thou art all! I thank thee spirit and shall drink thy health when I come to town.

ANN *comes in.*

ANN. Woe! Woe!

ARE. 'Tis intolerable! Have ye come to tell me the news was mistaken?

ANN. Thy poor wife. That dearest, loveliest creature, that paragon of –

ARE. Pox! If thy news is so great it brings thee from the grave twice then tell it!

ANN. If thy wife goes not to London thy wealth is lost!

ARE. This is arrant posturing! She hath raised thee to badger me. She stays. Go! I defy thee. (*Aside.*) 'Fore god I am taken with my style. Who'd have thought I'd unloose such a show of bravado?

ANN. Thy wife –

ARE. Stays.

ANN. Then curses on your ugly face! Your evil old –

ARE. I shall not have my face insulted at breakfast by a zombie!

ARE *goes.*

ANN. O the wretch! I'll poison him! No I'll poison myself and haunt him!

ARE *comes back with a drawn rapier.*

ARE. Out vapour! (*Whirls his rapier.*) I shall stir you up and blow you off in a mist!

ANN. O wretch!

ARE. It backs! What – ye remember cold steel? Have at ye! I would not be inhospitable to anyone but ye have a place: the wall – or anywhere at all of Lord Lester's. A man may breakfast at peace in his home before he's reminded there is religion – or it's not England!

ARE *runs* ANN *through.*

ANN. O. (*Falls.*)

ARE. Why 'tis a heavy ghost! I had thought to go whisk-whisk and – as I am a gentleman – opened the window for it and it had vanished in a puff of smoke. The ghost bleeds. (*Stoops, examines.*) 'Fore god 'tis flesh and blood. My wife. (*Steps back. His voice falls and he presses the index finger to the side of his mouth.*) Hsssssssssssssss ... here's a fine how-d'ye-do. My wife. Stretched out on the floor. With a hole in her breast. Before breakfast. How is a man to put a good face on that? An amendment is called for. It were a foolish figure I should cut. A buffoon. Murdered his wife. Got up as a ghost. Before breakfast. I break into cold sweat when I think of how I should use it had it befallen Lord Lester. I could not put my foot in a duke's door again. Never ascend the stairs to a hall blazing with chandeliers. Or ogle the ladies from the *balcon réservé* of a pump room. My life would be over. (*Nibbles toast.*) Cold. Faw! (*Puts toast down.*) A fine kettle of fish! (*Rings.*) Well you'd best sit at your husband's table. Hopefully 'twill look as if our quarrel had been less violent. Stretched out on the floor can only encourage the lowest surmises. (*Sets* ANN *in a chair.*) A man cannot think with his dead wife sprawled on the carpet. And I must think – after I've tired my brains with choosing a suit for the day.

BOB *comes in.*

ARE. Toast. This is as cold as a corpse – yea, and as hard as a tombstone.

BOB. That be all my lord?

ARE. For the moment.

BOB. Right my lord.

BOB *takes the toast rack from the table and goes.*

ARE. O thou Great Boob. Thou art my deliverer. Thou mayest be relied on. I do not see it yet, but thou art a loon and shall serve. (*Adjusts* ANN.) To arrange thee better. Faith thy silence is wonderful! Hadst thou behaved so when thou livst thou mightst have lived longer. Thy costume becomes thee. At last thy tailor hath done thee justice. Thy face had always a lowering look. You played death to the life. A performance to retire on.

> ARE *goes.* BOB *comes in with toast in a silver rack, goes to the table and steals a cup of coffee. He sees* ANN. *He drops the toast.*

BOB. Eek! Lawd defend us! The dead are risen!

> ARE *comes back.*

ARE. What man?

BOB (*points*). Th – th – th –

ARE. Ye have burned the toast? Twice in one morning!

BOB. No' – th' – no' – th' –

ARE. Is the child possessed?

BOB. Th' – *there*!

ARE (*goes to the chair and looks at* ANN). There is a ghost. O Robert thou art possessed! What have ye done?

BOB. Eek! A ghost!

ARE. How it spies at thee. It comes for thee Robert.

BOB (*sinks to his knees*). O no am I goin' to die? O lawd defend us!

ARE. What venom! Shut thine eyes Bob lest it ensnare thee.

BOB (*shuts his eyes*). Ah! Eek! Oo!

ARE. Take the rapier.

BOB. The –?

ARE. Beside thee. (ARE *kicks the rapier along the floor.*) Hold the handle as a cross.

BOB. Lawd! Lawd! (*One arm across his eyes, the rapier held out in the other hand.*) Mercy! Save us!

> ARE *lifts* ANN *from behind.*

ARE. Robert! Robert! Take care! It advanceth at thee!

BOB (*peeps from under his arm*). Ah! O!

> ARE *manipulates* ANN.

ARE. I struggle with it. It tears itself towards thee. God what strength! It will have ye!

BOB. No! No! No! No!

Terror! ARE *makes ghost sounds and lifts* ANN *towards* BOB. BOB *points the rapier.* ARE *leans* ANN *on the rapier's point.*

ARE. O Robert. Open your eyes.

BOB (*eyes covered*). Hev it gone? (*Uncovers eyes.*)

ARE. See! the ghost – the rapier – you: joined. Bob what have ye done? (*He pushes* ANN *with a finger: she topples.*) Murdered your mistress.

BOB. My mistress?

ARE. 'Tis – 'twas – she. I cannot say why she is so dressed. I do not recall she mentioned a fancy-dress breakfast. It seems unlikely. Who can fathom the mind of one suddenly raised to the peerage? Did she suppose society breakfasted in this extravagant fashion? We can never know. Impetuous Bob, how often have I warned ye?

BOB. Impetuous?

ARE. Certainly. Ye have murdered your mistress. Before breakfast. What greater proof of impetuosity?

BOB. But I – took it for a ghost!

ARE. As I say: impetuous Bob. I struggled with ye, but thou art a robust fellow and overcame me – and then, I had not breakfasted.

BOB. What have I done?

ARE. Murdered your mistress. Before breakfast. Pray do not stand there with your rapier dripping blood on my carpet. Hand it to me (*Takes the rapier.*) lest ye turn it against me –

BOB. Never my lord!

ARE. – in your present rashness. In one of your sudden fits. I see it now. A practical joke, a jape. Her ladyship ennuied by rural life – which must be said in her favour – tried thus to brighten our morning. But Bob you have no sense of humour.

BOB. No sir. I just do my job.

ARE. This morning you were overzealous. Well 'twas a paltry accident. Pick up the toast.

BOB (*picking up the toast*). What's to be done sir?

ARE. The future rests with the authorities – as it always does. (*Looks at a piece of toast.*) Blood. I shall not breakfast this morning. Forget the toast. One shudders at what you would do on your third attempt to bring it.

BOB. I begin to see what I hev done: I hev widowed my master.

ARE. Before breakfast. Few can say as much. I shall miss her pranks – this is presumably the last. Bob was I ever a bad master?

BOB. Thass what make it worse! Her poor ladyship.

ARE. Well she was not altogether without blame. Never play jokes on the servants. It agitates them into dropping the toast. That at least we have learned this morning. (*Rings.*)

BOB. What yoo dooin'?

ARE. We have a difficult road ahead. Turn to me at all times. I shall lead ye to the promised land. Hold no conference with others, who will mislead you.

BOB. Yes sir. I've made my mistake once. O thank yoo sir.

ARE. Do not fumble my hand Bob. Ye have slain my wife and I have completed my toilet.

MOTHER *comes to the door.*

ARE. Mrs Hedges her ladyship is dead.

MOTHER. Beg pardin' sir?

ARE. Her ladyship is dead.

MOTHER. Dead?

ARE (*aside*). O the tedium of a tragedy: everything is said twice and then thrice.

MOTHER (*flatly*): Dead?

ARE (*aside*). Twice.

MOTHER (*flatly*): Dead!

BOB. Dead!

ARE (*aside*). I have survived the morning tolerably well, now I shall spoil it with a headache.

MOTHER (*suddenly realising*). Her ladyship is dead!

ARE (*aside*). If she is not she is a consummate actress.

MOTHER. Is her ladyship dead?

ARE (*aside*). O god is it to be put to the question? We shall have pamphlets issued on it. There are really no grounds for this aspersion on my swordsmanship.

MOTHER. Ah! Er! O! (*Weeps.*)

ARE (*aside*). Now the wailing and hallooing. Lungs of leather from coursing their dogs, throats like organ pipes from roaring their hymns. Well I have an immaculate excuse for retiring to my room, and as it cannot return I shall use it. – Mrs Hedges if ye have no pan on the fire pray run to the magistrate and tell him Bob has murdered his mistress. Before breakfast.

MOTHER. Eek! Murdered? Bob?

BOB. Alas!

ARE. (*aside*). And now the convulsions they learn at country dancing. – Mind, not parson Mrs Hedges. Captain Sludge. I could not endure parson's consolations on an empty stomach. (Bob throw the toast to the hens on your way to prison.) (BOB, *weeping, picks up the toast rack and nods.*) I shall have to contend with parson at the graveside. Sludge is a plain bluff man who made many fields sanguinary with the blood of his sovereign's foes. He won't set the windows rattling at the sight of one dead woman. Mrs Hedges to Captain Sludge.

BOB. Ought to give her ladyship a sheet. Ont decent lyin' there.

> BOB *and* MOTHER *wail.*

Captain's is too far for mother in her state of aggravation.
I'll hand meself in.

ARE. 'Tis handsome Bob, but I cannot let a murderer wander
the fields. Superstition is rife: the hands would refuse to
harvest. – Mrs Hedges the chimney tops will rattle down
scattering fire and ash as if Hilgay were the sister city to
Gomorrah. Your wailing will start the dogs, the dogs will
start the cows, the cows will start the farm and so the next
farm and the news of my wife's death will reach London by
neighing and mooing. I would have it arrive by a more
conventional conveyance. Bob wait. I'll send a man from
the kennels. The dogs have been walked.

    ARE *goes.*

BOB. If it weren't for his lordship I'd kill meself.
MOTHER. Don't talk so daft. (*She hits him.*) Put a brave face
on it. Parson'll speak up for yoo if his lordship doo. Whole
a Hilgay'll rally round. Yoo ont step out a line before – not
till yoo married. An yoo married her in London (*She hits
him.*) so it ont count. Why! if they had to find an ordinary
chap they ont find one more ordinary than yoo boy.

Part Two

Scene Six

Peterborough.
Gaol.
Cell. Upstage door to another cell. ROSE *and* BOB. BOB *is shackled to the floor.*

ROSE. What happened?

BOB. O I on't know.

ROSE. Let me help you.

BOB. Can't help. It'll be all right. (*He tries to comfort her but she walks away.*)

ROSE. Show me what happened.

BOB (*half demonstrates*). I goo to the table. Toast. She's sat there. Hands like so. Blood. (*Puts finger on chest*). Yell. Lordship run in. Took howd of sword –

ROSE. Blood?

BOB. He tries to howd her. She howl. Stick sword out. Open me eyes. (*Uncovers his face.*) Sword in her. Topples down dead.

ROSE. Yer said there was blood on her before you stuck her.

BOB (*confused*). Ont know. (*Shakes his head.*) 'S'n accident.

ROSE. They have accidents, we make mistakes.

ARE, PARSON *and* GAOLER *come in.*

ARE. Robert you bear up bravely.

BOB. Sir. Parson.

PARSON. Bless you. (*To* ROSE.) Bless you child.

ARE (*aside* to PARSON). This is a sorry sight: my livery in a
cell. Cannot ye find him suitable clothes in the charity
bundle?

>   ARE *tips the* GAOLER. *He goes.*

PARSON. My lord. My sister shall attend to it.

BOB. We're jist tryin' to sort out what happened.

ARE. Bob Bob, why trouble your head with things that don't
concern it? If I can't manage the affair as I see fit I may have
to withdraw.

BOB. Ont do that sir.

ARE. I cannot be made a public lampoon. The good shepherd
who found his sheep and lost it on the way home.

ROSE. Her ladyship was bleedin before –

ARE. Like a loyal wife your head is in as great a whirl as your
husband's. (*Aside.*) The turnkey shall forbid her the cell.
'Tis seemly in a hanging.

ROSE (*to* PARSON). Her ladyship was sitting in the chair
bleeding.

ARE. Bleeding? (*Aside.*) I repeat words like the rest!

FRANK. (*off*). Pleasure brought me to my end! What brought
you, yer cantin' hypocrite?

ARE (*to* PARSON). My former footman. When we're finished
here I'll go and rattle my cane through his bars.

BOB (*calls*). Ont hang. His lordship stand by me.

FRANK (*off*). Trust that fox an' yer deserve t' hang! Bang the
door in his face! Yer no friend of mine Bob Hedges but I
don't wish him on yer!

ARE. Don't heed him Bob. His present position don't qualify
him to give advice.

ROSE. So she was bleedin' before Bob stabbed her.

PARSON (*shrugs*). Child the whole thing is beyond human –

ARE. Have ye never took a flower from a vase in the hall and stuck it in your coat as ye left the house? She sprinkled herself with paint on the way down as a final touch.

ROSE. We can see if there's paint on the sheet.

FRANK (*off*). Ask 'em to hang yer to music! Show the girl's yer fancy dancin' kicks!

ROSE. And the sword on the floor? How –

ARE. Mr Phelps next door.

PARSON. My lord?

ARE. We cannot let that fellow die with his soul in such neglect. For charity, go to him.

PARSON. Your lordship is a wonder! Even now I was silently praying I might be asked.

> PARSON *goes out to fetch the* GAOLER.

ARE. Well miss?

ROSE. My husband didn't kill her.

BOB. (*quietly*). Bless you Rose. Yoo're the brave one here.

ARE. Bob –

BOB. She were bleedin' when I come in.

ARE. Let me consider. (*Goes to one side.*) The sun rose on the horizon – and fell back, and all the world is darkness. Courage good heart. If the sun goes from its course, why – bring it back. The oaf will hang and the truth with him. But it must be done quietly, and now the hussy will drag me in. Lester will scrawl me up on the wall of every jakes as a jack-in-the-box with a sword in its hand! 'Tis intolerable.

ROSE (*to* BOB). Does his lordship always eat breakfast with a sword?

ARE (*goes back to them*). Bob I must tell thee plainly thou art a trouble and deserve thy wife: yet I wish ye the same happy deliverance I had. What you or I say is no matter. Truth is what the lawyers say it is. You have none, whilst I ...

(*Gesture*.) If Bob confesses, the killing is an accident. If he accuses me – well, have ye ever listened dumbfounded while ye contradicted yourself ten times in a minute? My lawyers will torment him till he runs to the scaffold – many an innocent man has willingly hanged to be rid of a lawyer. What if I go into the dock? 'Tis still an accident. But what a fool I must seem! Marrying the coalman's daughter blemished my name, but this – 'tis a scene from a farce. I cannot say why I did not know she was my wife. Had a kinder providence set the scene in a London salon, under two chandeliers, I'd have recognised her even with one of her father's buckets over her head. Would ye give evidence against me Bob. A lord dragged down by a working man? 'Tis against all civil order. Ye see the enormity of the thing? We are at the heart of the matter. In my person I am society, the symbol of authority, the figurehead of law and order. Make me a fool or a villain and the mob will dance in the street. If ye will be innocent, Bob, anarchy must triumph, your windows be broken, your mother's head cracked and your wife stoned for a blackamoor (He *takes* BOB *aside. His chain rattles*.) Come, we are Englishmen and may talk freely together. Ye have this chance to serve your country. Robert the Hero, hail! The nation asks it of ye. Stand trial. Be acquitted. I'll buy the jury. I withdraw while ye consider your reply.

The Gentleman (BOB *and* ROSE)
He steps out of the way to let her pass
On one arm she carries a child
In the other a battered case
With the hinges broken
Tied with a strap
He takes the child and holds it on his shoulder
He opens the gate to let the woman pass

He has not seen her till now
What politeness he shows the stranger!
In his hand there's a rifle
At the door to the gas chamber
He hands the child back to her arms

> Who would raise a whip when an order is obeyed?
> Why lift up your fist when a pointing finger will lead?
> Who would raise their voice when soft words will do my
>   friend?
> Why use a knife when a smile makes cuts that bleed?
> When you have the mind why bother to chop off the
>   head?
> When white hands will do the work why make your hands
>   red?

THE PARSON *returns with the* GAOLER. *The* GAOLER *lets the* PARSON *into the cell upstage. The* GAOLER *lounges beside the open door and waits.*

ROSE. The judge is staying at the Tabard. I'll go into –

BOB. Wait, we can't afford to make an enemy of him.

ROSE. He's guilty and you're innocent.

BOB. Yes but that ont seem t' matter. We accuse him we'll starve gal. Never git another job's long's we live. We jist hev to go along for the sake of appearance – like he say.

ROSE. Yer said yer always obey the law.

BOB. But he is the law – so I must obey him.

ROSE. But he's guilty and you're –

BOB (*head in hands*). Ont know what I ought t' do! Less think woman!

FRANK (*off*). Sold the silver and lived like a lord. Whored in the mornin', whored in the afternoon, whored in the evenin' when I weren't pissed!

ARE (*calls*). Confound it parson, pray to some effect!

FRANK (*off*). He's on his knees doin' his best, aren't yer old cock?

THE PARSON *comes in.*

PARSON. Patience sir. When they're to hang there's nothing to threaten them with. Not even hell. In this atheistical age they don't believe in it.

THE PARSON *goes back into the cell*

FRANK (*off*). Swillin' and screwin' till the landlord stopped me. Bastard knew me silver was runnin' out, just waitin' till the reward was bigger than what I had left. Slipped off in time. Lived in the fields. Robbed the churches.

PARSON (*off*). 'Tis not a confession, 'tis boasting.

FRANK (*off*). Jumped out the hedges onto the women and screwed 'em in the ditch! The last wild beast in England! I almost made London!

ARE (*to* ROSE). By the by, I brought the rapier in for Bob to polish.

FRANK (*off*). Open winder in Barnet. Put me hand in. Son of the house crep' up behind. Knock me out. Thick country lout. Drag back here. But it was worth it!

ARE (*calls*). Parson muzzle him with your cassock. – Robert my business presses.

BOB. A minute longer.

FRANK (*off*). Oi! is that Lord Arse?

PARSON (*off*). Purge his heart and still his tongue.

PARSON *runs out of the cell.* GAOLER *slams the door and locks it.*

FRANK. (*appears at the grill in the door*). Is that you Arsehole?

BOB (*to* ROSE): Least this way we got a chance.

ROSE. I won't keep quiet.

FRANK (*at grill*). Arsehole! I can smell yer! I thought it was the prison sewer! God rot yer, yer'll hang one day yer pox ridden rat!

BOB (*to* ROSE): I've said I did it, said sorry! They'd laugh in me face if I towd the truth now –

ROSE. If we don't it'll be too late.

FRANK (*at grill*). Arsehole!

ARE (*rattling his cane through the grill*). Fellow if your insults had any wit I'd stay to applaud. (*To* BOB:) Tis a great sadness but I see ye will stand on your own.

> ARE *goes to the door and is about to leave.* BOB *gestures to him to wait.*

FRANK (*at grill*). Arsehole! I thought my life had no more pleasure! It's worth hanging to call you cur to your face! I watched you lie in your vomit! Fool! I deserve to hang for not throttling you then!

BOB. It's according as your lordship wishes.

ARE. Good – you choose your protector well.

FRANK (*falls down*). Rot yer!

> *Sounds of raving.* GAOLER *opens the door of* FRANK'*s cell.* PARSON *goes in and almost immediately comes out to shout at* ARE.

PARSON. Beware! Your lordship's adjacency brings on convulsions. He crawls upon his stomach on the floor. He'll die before scaffolding day!

> ARE *goes.*

BOB (*to* ROSE): I played the sheep, now I'll play the man. I'll git us through. Ont fret Rose. I'd rather hev yoor smile.

PARSON (*peers through the open door of the cell at* FRANK). A serpent or a great newt!

FRANK (*off*). Rot! Rot! Rot him!

PARSON (*running down stage*). Gaoler! Tis from Revelations!

FRANK lurches into the cell. His hands are manacled. His leg chain pulls him short and he crashes to the floor.

Song of Talking (BOB *and* FRANK)

My mate was a hard case
Worked beside me on the bench for years
Hardly said a word
Talking isn't easy
When the machines run
One day he dropped a coin
He unscrewed the safety rail to get it back
The press-hammer struck his head
He looked up at the roof and said
   The green hills by the sea
   Where the light shines
   Through tall dark pines
A minute later he was dead

Didn't speak even on the street
Once I saw him shopping with his wife
He only nodded
He was decent to me
But I'd heard rumours
He'd done time in chokey
And his fist could hit you like a steel-capped boot
Then he unscrewed the safety-rail
I nursed him on the concrete floor
He looked up at the roof and said
   The green hills by the sea
   In the dark grove
   I first made love
A minute later he was dead

You didn't pick a row with him
Once I bumped him on the parking lot

No real damage
He stared through his windscreen
Then drove off fast
A frown made him handsome
I never knew what team he supported
Then he unscrewed the safety-rail
I nursed him on the concrete floor
He looked up at the roof and said
   The green hills by the sea
   Where the gulls cry
   In the white sky
A minute later he was dead

My mates ran to fetch the nurse
The foreman wouldn't stop the machines
I bent to listen
He looked like an apprentice
He was gently crying
And babbling to himself
I touched his hand – no response
The hammer was still beating
I nursed him on the concrete floor
He looked up at the roof and said
   The green hills by the sea
   Through the tall dark trees
   The sea weaves
   A shining thread
A minute later he was dead

Scene Seven

Hilgay.
Copse.
Off, from time to time pig bells and pig grunts.
ROSE *and* GABRIEL, *the blind swineherd.*

ROSE. They found him guilty.

GABRIEL. He'll hang. Never seen my boy's face.

ROSE. Are killed her.

GABRIEL. Hev he·any witness?

ROSE. No.

GABRIEL. Best howd yoor row . . . People allus fuss over what they can't mend. The whole world tip up an' everyone slid off – thass jist a saucer of spilt milk. Tell yoo what: know a sow's carryin' be the way her bell waddle. Another hev a great fat sound, thass time for the butcher. This job's all Sundays, like sit listenin' to bacon in the pan. Wife, roof, dry sty, eat an' sleep like an old boar.

ROSE. You talk Gabriel. Yer'd see if yer could. Even if it were jist ten minutes an' yer had to watch Bobby hang.

GABRIEL. Wrong gal. Ont hev it, ont want it. Sight's a curse laid on them who lead me, feed me, thatch the roof an' hang the door – life a sweat an' grind an' small pittance in the end. Better off sat in the sun, an' in the copse when it's hot. Ont bother no one. Break me cane, I git home feelin' 'long the trees. Whass the use of talkin' to neighbours? – could be winkin' in me face all I know. Got blind fightin' in France. Ont see the chap that took my sight – lookin' the other way at the time. After, they're all rejoicin' 'cause we won the war, an' I say: now what, can't work like this? – end up on street corner collectin' rain in me hat. Happen lucky, the old swineherd took it in his head to die an' I got took on at his job. Now where's the chap that hit me? Could a bin dead next day, fell off a ship, tree struck him. Who's to say what luck is? I hev the fruit of the world without its pains. Bar one. Mornin's – jist afore I wake – dream I hev me sight. Run up the hill, wave me arms an' holler at the sun. Then I wake up an' say: thass jist the boy left over in me. So I ont sneer at it – an' I ont weep. Yoo see before yoo a happy man.

MOTHER *comes in. She is out of breath.*

GABRIEL. What yoo all hot an' cross for mother?

MOTHER. She ont supposed to interfere with yoor work. Lose a pig there's all hell to pay. Whass she bin sayin'?

GABRIEL. Nothin'.

MOTHER. Hardache's up at the cottage. Push the door open with his stick an' say yoo wrote him. Sent him round the long way an' cut cross the fields. You let on whass gooin' on here, I'll cuss the day you wed my boy.

ROSE. He'll help Bob.

MOTHER. Ont need help.

ROSE. They'll hang him.

MOTHER. Ont talk such rot. No sense of proportion. This is his big chance. Doo his lordship a favour like this an' he's set up for life. Poor people can't afford to waste a chance like this, god know it ont come often. Time our luck change. Yoo start trouble, who pay? Us. Yoo're off to London, we git chuck out. End up at the workhouse. Work like a slave, workhouse disease – ont last six months, seen it afore. Too old to hev my life mess up. Look at him: come back from France an' got took on 's if he had twenty eyes. Could a cost his lordship no end of pig. He stood by him – like he doo Bob. So ont meddle Rose.

ROSE. Bob's in prison waitin' to –

MOTHER. Worse places outside. Ont expect his lordship to

goo in the dock for the like of her. Jist drag his family name through the mire. Whatever next! Ont know where to look next time I went to the village, they knew I work for someone like that. 'S'n accident *who* it was. Silly woman deserve to git killed. She come into my kitchen dress' up I give her a whack of my fryin' pan she ont git up from.

ROSE. He's hanged but the roof's over yer head.

MOTHER. You think I'm that sort of woman, my dear, thass yoor privilege.

ROSE. O I don't understand you people!

MOTHER. Jist ont stand in my boy's way when he hev his chance to goo up in the world. Lie on oath doo it help him, say I saw him run to fetch the sword.

ROSE. Why should Arseface help him? Bob's a labourer, no better than –

GABRIEL. Howd both yoor rows, yoo upset my pigs. The same thing if he kill her or not. (*Calls.*) Sibby! – If thass between him an' his boss, stand to reason who win. Drat pig! After them acorns at Pallin's End.

ROSE. It's not between Are and Bob. It's between two bosses.

MOTHER. Now whass she on about?

ROSE. When yer black, it pays t' know the law. You're not allowed t' benefit from your own crime. Are killed his wife – so he loses her money. It goes back to the next of kin: her father.

> HARDACHE *steps in. He fans his face, neck and inside his jacket with his hat.*

HARDACHE. Pretty place. Sorry I had to miss the funeral. A neighbour had to sell up and I couldn't miss the opportunity. Then the trial: had to arrange a little shares shenanigans. Rose, you married a villain but no one's perfect. All the bitterness was squeezed out of me long ago when my first warehouse went up on fire. Tell Bob I haven't wept since.

MOTHER. It was accidental Mr Hardache.

HARDACHE. Ay lass but some have accidents and some don't. Lads keep falling into my furnaces all the time. You'd think they did it on purpose. I see a furnace I go round it not in it. And if I saw a ghost I'd leave the room like any sensible man – unless it were me late wife.

MOTHER. That wicked gal's got it into her head my Bob didn't do it.

HARDACHE. Not do it? Is that right Rose? Then who did?

ROSE. Are.

HARDACHE. His lordship. Nay I've never heard the like. Happy young couple like that? Why ever should he be so rash? No, she were struck down by your overhasty young man, I can't believe otherwise – his lordship you say?

MOTHER. Yoo talk sense into her sir.

HARDACHE. Well I'm struck both ways sideways. What a predicament to fall into our laps – (*quickly correcting himself*) land on our heads. A real taramadiddle and no mistake. Did he strike her Rose?

ROSE. Yes sir and talked Bob into taking the blame.

HARDACHE. I shan't take kindly to bein' deceived Mrs Hedges. Now's the time to speak out. You know what's at stake: my daughter's memory. D'you know owt?

MOTHER. Well – I doo an' I don't. What should I say?

HARDACHE. The truth woman! It's a christian country, i'n't it?

MOTHER. Well – if his lordship kill her – what's the good of what I say?

HARDACHE. What good? Does justice count for nothing in these parts? When I think of that innocent young man – you did say he was innocent, Rose? – alone in his cell, my withers weren't more wrung for me own daughter. Well Mrs Hedges?

MOTHER. I suppose – if thass how it is – I hev to tell Mr
Hardache that my son towd me he ont do it.

HARDACHE. And also testified that Are cajoled him into
covering up his own crime. What a dastardly villain!

MOTHER (*finishing repeating his words*).... his own crime
what a dastardly villain.

HARDACHE. Well. Now we know. I'm right glad I came to
pay respects to my daughter's grave: you run into business
anywhere.

ROSE. Mr Hardache you're our only friend.

HARDACHE. And you'll never have a better. Leave all to me
lass. Mind, no speakin' out of turn. We must go careful if
his lordship's acquired the habit of murder. Good day.

ROSE. Will yer go straight to the judges?

HARDACHE. Tch tch didn't I say leave all to me?

ROSE. I'll show you the quick way to the house.

     HARDACHE *and* ROSE *go*.

GABRIEL. Gad woman! – if yoo was out a' doors yoo'd still
let the roof fall on yoor hid!

MOTHER. Caught me between.

GABRIEL (*calls*). Sibby! Yoo git fat yoo jist make work for the
butcher. – Gad woman them pigs talk more sense'n yoo.

Legend of Good Fortune (MOTHER)

Men lived in peace and plenty
When the world was as young as the day
But a god came down from heaven
And took the good things away

He put them all in a basket
And slowly climbed up to his cave
He put the basket under his head
And slept like a weary slave

There passed on earth ten ages of war
Men groaned and lived as the dead
When the dreaming god stirred in his sleep
And the basket fell out of his bed

Then from the heavens there rained on man
The gifts of plenty and peace
Bread and honey and fruit and wine
And the new golden age began

Slowly the god woke up from his sleep
And came down to rob again
This time men said what we have we shall keep!
And they fought till the god was slain

Send for the wise to share your bread
Take the beautiful into your bed
And if ever that god is seen in your land
Take all he's got – and break his head!

Scene Eight

Peterborough.
Holme Cottage.
Table. Chairs.
BOB *and* PARSON.
BOB's *legs are fettered. He scratches a pen on paper*

BOB. Hev a skill for learnin. Jist lack the opportunity afore.
Hev a terrible struggle with my S. Drat squiggle of a letter.
Letters is a miracle parson. Dance afoor yoor eyes an goo
t'gither like a candle flarin up afore it die. Are say I'll be
put in charge of clerkin. Scribe his bills. Chap born in a
cottage ont hope t' rise so high.

PARSON. Bob do not set thy heart on a pardon. Seek salvation.

BOB. Ont be so glum parson. For the moment us hev t' make the best of a bad way.

MRS WILSON *comes in.*

WILSON. Dont splash your ink on my ceiling. Your mother's here, (*Gives* BOB *a duster.*) Wipe your manacles. Dont want visitors saying I dont keep you in a proper state. Look at my floor!

MRS WILSON *goes out.*

BOB (*annoyed as he puts down his pen and takes up the duster. He polishes his chains*). Drat! I was jist at grips with my S.

PARSON (*exasperated*). You are under sentence of death! Try to reap the benefit of that!

BOB (*polishing his chains*). 'S'natural yoo fret. Us understand how yoo feel, but it ont help. Come now ol' friend, ont like t' see you so depress. Cheer up an smile, doo us'll git cross.

PARSON (*aside*). The child's a simpleton. Lord Are promises a pardon to comfort him – and heaps coals of fire on his head!

BOB (*throws down duster*). Done! – In t' battle! (*Takes up pen.*) S's like a snake havin a tussle with itself which end's its hid an which its arse!

PARSON. Hedges put down that pen and listen! Our battle is with Satan. Bob – have you heard?

BOB. Ay parson, our battle with Satan. (*Aside as he puts down the pen.*) Us'll hev a sermon now. Rather hear the judge tell me he's booked me for hangin.

PARSON. What befell his lordship on that tragic morning – before breakfast, as he told the court – is not our business. I thought the London footman might don the halter. His lordship is adamant tis to be you. That is the situation we

must live with. As god made water clear, you are innocent.
But it is your duty to be hanged.

    MRS WILSON *comes in with a broom and sweeps round the feet of* BOB *and the* PARSON.

PARSON. Lord Are is the guardian of our laws and orderer of our ways. Topple him from his mighty seat and Beelzebub will walk the lanes of Hilgay. Already the methodists rant at his lordship's hats!

BOB (*trying to concentrate*). . . . rant at his lordship's hats.

PARSON. There has been a murder and so there must be a hanging.

WILSON (*to* BOB). Up.

    BOB *raises his feet and* MRS WILSON *sweeps under them.*

PARSON. Then the village will return to its ancient peace and Satan be shut in that darkness which – authority tells us – even his abominable fires cannot illuminate.

WILSON (*sweeping*). Winter coming but authority doesnt help me with the fuel bills.

PARSON. Bob thou art chosen *because* thou art innocent! Have ye not seen? – god always punishes the innocent and not the guilty! – that those in greatest need may be saved! For surely the bowels of the most hardened sinner will be moved by thy fate! In truth we are all sinners. Tis hard to follow in the footsteps of One who walks on water – there are no footprints to guide us.

BOB. . . . footprints to guide us.

PARSON. Be of good cheer! You are not the first man asked to die for his country – nor will you be the last. If you had seen the suffering of the wicked you would rejoice at your fate! Their rooms are little but they hold the empire of hell. For them I would gladly take your place on the scaffold. But I must protect the cloth, d'ye see? To desecrate this sober serge would be as impolitic as to loose his lordship's gaudy ribbons. You – though humble – are chosen in our stead! Bob! – pay attention. (BOB *starts*.) For now I must enter into theology.

BOB (*aside to* MRS WILSON). Take the kettle off Mrs Wilson. If he's in t' *that* us'll hev tea late.

PARSON. Your summary demise will atone for Adam's sin in Hilgay.

BOB (*aside to* MRS WILSON). An late supper by the sound on it.

PARSON. But Bob, the atonement you make for others does not weigh in the balance of your own sins. You see the theological quiddity of the thing! The lamb must be shriven before it's shorn. Repent! You cannot confess to murdering your mistress – not even *after* breakfast – but you lived long enough in London to assemble your own goodly collection of flaws! Purify thy heart! Soon you will enter the bosom of your lord. To enter that hallowed place you must be spotless! – Mrs Wilson cannot follow after you with her broom.

WILSON. I need a new one. The authorities dont provide that either.

MRS WILSON *goes out*.

PARSON. Repent! Christ would forgive you if you'd murdered a hundred Lady Ares!

BOB (*writing*). If I'd done that I shouldnt settle for salvation – I'd expect a reward!

PARSON. Bob have you followed what I've said?

BOB. Nope. I give up listenin weeks back. Jist cause a bloke's told he's t' hang everybody think they hev the right t' sermonize him. All that ol' quatch sound like the devil talkin backward – beggin yoor pardon parson. Jist leave me t' my book. Then I can read my pardon. (*Reads*) M-a-n-i-s-w-h-a-t-h-e-k-n-o-s-e. Kernosey?

PARSON. Knows! The k is silent and the e modulates! – how many more times? Those who dont pay attention in class come to a bad end! I should make you write it a hundred times. *Man is what he knows.*

BOB. Ask me the chap who invented writin ont know how t' spell.

PARSON (*aside*). Let us leave him to his book. If he go to heaven with a mind able to read god will see that I hath laboured in the vineyard to put some light into its natural darkness – though indeed this place is more like a tavern. (*Sigh.*) Alas we who help to carry the cross cannot be spared the spectacle of the crucifixion. I will call in at the church and comfort my knees on the cold chancel floor. His martyrdom will strike a blow against the methodists! I season my tears with gladness. (*To* BOB.) The silent k! (*Reads* BOB'S *book to him.*) 'Socrates: "He who loves wisdom obeys his country's laws with a gladsome heart!" and so saying he supped poison. Likewise "Man is what he knows".'

BOB. Was Socrates a writin man?

PARSON. His words were written down.

BOB. Us'll look him up when us git home.

PARSON (*sighs*). The Bible will meet thy needs. God spake the word and there was light. Man and woman to cleave unto him. And the birds and beasts of that ineffable garden. The stars in their firmament and the greater and lesser light. And the water that rolls on the bed of the sea. And the law of life. Look therefore that ye speak and teach wisely: for man is what he . . . (*Reflectively.*) kernosey.

MOTHER *comes in.*

BOB. Mother. Bear up old gal.

MOTHER. Bob.

They don't embrace because she must put down her shopping.

WILSON. Kettle's on.

    MRS WILSON goes out.

BOB. Where's Rose?

MOTHER. Ont allowed in.

BOB. Why not?

MOTHER. Ont make the law.

BOB (*to* PARSON). Why not?

PARSON. Perhaps a regulation.

MOTHER. She's outside. (*Shrugs.*) Would come.

BOB (*goes to the door. Calls*). Rose! Rose!

PARSON. I'll go to her. Remember your promise: the best behaviour.

BOB. I want her here!

    PARSON goes.

MOTHER. Well if thass all the welcome I git I'll goo home. Thought it'd blow over by now. Hev yoo back at yoor job.

    Knocking on the ceiling.

BOB. Sod.

    BOB goes. MOTHER looks round in bewilderment and fatigue. MRS WILSON comes in with the tea things.

WILSON. Where's Bob?

MOTHER (*looks at ceiling. Vaguely*). Knockin'.

WILSON. Mr Wilson, my husband. Sit down. You look worn out. (*Lays the table.*) I make him wash and brush his hair. Some of them lose interest towards the end. No trouble with his appetite. I can't begrudge what I put on the plate. I'll be out of pocket. I was surprised how little Lord Are was willing to pay. It's so much nicer here than in the cells next door. (*Pours one cup of tea.*) If he gets off (O I'm sure he will) Mr Wilson loses his hanging money. This was supposed to make up the loss – which means it'll add to it.

MOTHER. Thankyoo.

WILSON. Mr Wilson's poorly. They say it's nothing but I know better. Those two are like father and son. Bob's propped his stick by the bed. Soon's he hears the rap he's up those stairs, rattling away. I don't say. D'you eat turf cakes? I made these little ones. There. I'm not the sort of person to count what they put on the plate. Five.

MOTHER. Thankyoo.

WILSON. His turns get worse. Passed the age for outside work. It's a holiday for them, but that's what it is for him.

    BOB *comes in.*

Try not to clank dear. My head's been arguing with me all morning. We're down to three. I don't suppose we'll eat them all. Why didn't you offer your mother a chair you rude boy? I don't mind who uses them.

    BOB *writes on a corner of the table.*

Mr Wilson says his assistant couldn't take a sweet out of a bag if you opened it first. We daren't give the job up, even I can't manage on what he makes next door. I like to have things round me, otherwise what is there to show? A change of curtains. Proper tea things but that lid's cracked. A carpet upstairs. A few pairs of Sunday gloves. They stick out a mile when everyone puts their hands up to pray. You feel a pauper if you haven't got a change of colour.

MOTHER. Thankyoo.

WILSON. I'll put the tin beside the plate. Then what we don't eat can jump back. Help yourself. (*She pushes the plate further away.*) They ought to bring it indoors. There's always talk but it comes to nothing. Out all weathers. Once the ice was so thick on the rope they had to take turns in breathing on it. Now Mr Wilson ties it under the horse's belly to keep it warm. He's come home with the buttons frozen to his coat. Had a dead cat thrown at him once. No wonder he has turns. And the abuse if they fancy someone! You'd think it was all done for his benefit. I tell him 'They'd know if they let them all off'. He said 'I think they will next'. That was after the cat. Mind, there's two sides isn't there? The better class tip. But you can't even rely on them. One day they might just shake your hand. Even if I know he's got a busy week ahead I can't say 'I'll go out and buy that new teapot'. (*To* BOB.) What was it this time?

BOB (*writing*). Hand shook an' splash his shirt. Had to howd his cup.

WILSON. O don't tell me he's having one of those. Eat your turf cake.

BOB. Ont hungry.

WILSON. O a mood is it?

BOB. No.

WILSON. Don't have moods in my house. We set the cat on them. Well when you ask it'll be gone. (*She eats his cake.*)

    Knock on ceiling.

BOB. Drat! Forgot his Bible.

WILSON. What are our young people coming to? Fancy forgetting a Bible! Under that chair. (*Calls.*) Bible's on its way. – You are a funny lad at times. (*To* MOTHER.) It occupies his mind when he's like this. He writes all the births and baptisms and weddings in the front –

    BOB *goes out with the Bible.*

– and his work in the back. Glues in extra pages. Goes through them to soothe his mind. Reminds him of all sorts of things he's forgotten. Memory plays funny tricks. I'll clear away, there are light-fingered gentlemen around. I'll wrap that cake with the bite in the side. I believe that was you. It'll do for the way back.

MOTHER (*gently tugs* MRS WILSON's *sleeve*). His wife's outside. It preys on his mind.

MR HARDACHE *comes in*.

HARDACHE. Mrs Hedges. Ma'am. His lordship's here.

BOB *comes in*.

Say nothing Bob. I can read your face. A harmless prank and you were the engine of fate. Here's half a guinea.

WILSON. Half a guinea.

BOB. Thanks. (*Gives it to* MOTHER.) Rose have that.

WILSON. Mr Hedges you're as thoughtless as my guests next door. Now what have you got for tips?

LORD ARE *and* PARSON *come in*.

ARE. Bob, these are better –

BOB. Rose ont allowed in.

ARE. You'll see her soon.

BOB. Rather see her now. Goo back to the cell if thass necessary.

ARE. Surly Bob, do not abuse my trust.

BOB. Ont hev her stood in the street.

ARE (*aside*). Well, move how he may it only tightens the rope.
  – Ye make it deuced awkward for your friends Bob. I broke regulations when I took you from your cell as a pledge of your release. Let the blame fall on me again. Fetch her parson. She was on the corner as we passed.

PARSON *goes*.

BOB. Hev yoo my pardon sir? Let me see it.

ARE. I have it not on me, but 'tis safe. There's a style to these things Bob. The terror of the law, majesty of office and so forth. 'Tis not unknown for it to be held back till the man comes to the scaffold. Never lose hope. When you think the hangman is reaching for your neck he may be handing you your pardon.

HARDACHE (*taking* ARE *to one side*). We have a little business to settle.

ARE. What Mr Hardache?

HARDACHE. Your murder of my daughter.

ARE. Bob show your mother your letters. I'm having him taught his letters Mrs Hedges.

MOTHER. There! I shall hev a readin' an' writin' son. (MOTHER *and* BOB *sit at the table.*)

ARE (*to* HARDACHE). The Black Slut? – Father-in-law you did not build your empire by listening to trash.

HARDACHE. Wrong lad I listened to it very well. I call you lad because I notice you've started to call me father. I dont like interfering – but she was my daughter and she'd want the right man to hang.

BOB. I writ Rose. Parson can mix the letters up to spell eros – an' that, he say, is the lower form of love.

ARE (*calm and precise*). Why here at such a time?

HARDACHE. Where better? All parties to hand. If questions have to be asked they can answer them directly. And if you have to take lodgings in the prison next door – you're spared the extra journey.

ARE. Sir. My drinking companion the lord lieutenant – in whose bosom my hand lies deeper than ever the dearly beloved disciple's lay in christ's – will not let you clap me into gaol. Tomorrow I am promised for the races and twould quite spoil his party.

HARDACHE. Son-in-law. Your title gives you acquaintance, money gives me mine. I pay for the coach that takes your mighty friend to the races. Here's a riddle: why does a sensible man like me let his daughter marry a fop like you?

ARE. Fop? A fella don't boast but –

HARDACHE. Coal.

ARE. I misheard.

HARDACHE. No. Under your land.

ARE. I have been rooked.

HARDACHE. Your title cost me a packet but I meant to pay for it with your coal. The marriage made it mine. Or my grandson's – I think ahead for the good of the firm. The firm'ld do very nicely out of thee and me. Now this mishap upsets my grand scheme.

ARE. Why didn't my steward tell me I had coal?

HARDACHE. I paid him not to. But you can't have disloyal retainers round you, lad, so I sacked him on my way here and put my man in his place.

ARE. Father-in-law you are Father Satan.

HARDACHE. Ay well you meant that as flattery but happen when you know me better you'll think it's deserved. (*Document.*) Here's a simple agreement of intent. Our lawyers will work out the details later. All what's over your land is yours: that goes for the late Lady Are's money. What's under is mine: barrin' your ancestors' bones. Sign, and my daughter can sleep in peace for a very long time.

ARE. Bob lend me thy pen.

BOB. Expect a pardon look like that.

HARDACHE. Happen it does for some.

ARE (*signs*). This day I sign an alliance with the devil.

ROSE *comes in.* BOB *embraces her.*

BOB. Ont mind if the people see our joy, all's friends here.

MOTHER. Can't stay long Rose. Miss the cart back.

ROSE. Mr Hardache did you go to the court?

HARDACHE. Lass I considered it but it won't wear.

(ARE *leaves.* MOTHER *collects her things and goes to the door.*) You offer no evidence. Take my advice, keep mum. Bob can show me his pardon when it comes. I'll see he's set up in a good way.

Hurrah! *(All those on stage)*

When Englishmen owned half the world
All Englishmen were brave
And every Englishman was free
And cursed the foreign knave
Who meekly bowed to tyranny
When England ruled the mighty sea
All Englishmen learned at their mother's knee
That England was the home of liberty

Her prisons were houses for the dead
And on her gallows tree
The people hanged for stealing bread
Why steal when you are free?
They let him walk the streets in rags
Or dressed him up in soldier red
And taught him the service of the dead
Hurrah! for every Englishman is free
Old England is the home of liberty

They drove him to the factory like a slave
Or chained him like a beast
To crawl in darkness to his grave
His torments never cease
Till butchered in the wars of kings
His mutilated body sings
Hurrah! for every Englishman is free
Old England is the home of liberty

And so the generations go
Into the fire and into the woe

Into the trenches and into the blood
Bellowing shouts of brotherhood!
They break their brothers' bones when they are told
They think they walk in freedom? – they are sold
To the butcher!
They run to fetch the tackle and hook
They write their names in his invoice book
They whet the blade and hand the knife
They stretch their neck and give their life
Hurrah! for every Englishman is free
Old England is the home of Liberty

HARDACHE. Let's leave the youngsters to their peace.

All go except BOB *and* ROSE.

ROSE. Dog don't eat dog when they can fight over a bone.
I'm going outside, climb on the wall of the gaol and shout
'Are is a murderer'.
BOB. Rose he promise –
ROSE. He promised they wouldn't find you guilty.
BOB. He explained. Can't buy a whole jury. Look, old Lady
Are was the king's whore or summat. Anyroad, she's got
the pardon in the bag.
ROSE. Then why ain't you got it?
BOB. Can't jist hand em out. Hev to do things proper
way.
ROSE. I've got money. We could get that chain off –
BOB (*removes fetter from leg*). Thass only for show.
ROSE. God! Then we can go! There's a fast coach to Lynn!
We'll be on the boat tonight!
BOB. Thass madness! I git caught I git hang!
ROSE. You are caught!
BOB. What boat? Where to?
ROSE. Africa! Liberia!

BOB. What I do in the jungle?

ROSE. What I do here!

BOB. 'S different for men. Liberia! That where food grow on trees? Break a stone an' milk come out?

ROSE. Bob the door is open. The window's open. Step through it. If it was shut yer could kick it down. Yer could push the wall down. You're strong. You're a giant. But yer sit and wait to be hanged.

BOB. How I do love thee Rose. All ont lost yet. When I ont git a pardon, then I'll speak out!

ROSE. Too late.

BOB. I am an Englishman, a freeborn Englishman. I hev a right to speak – to shout for all to hear! Thass in our law. Stand up – in court, the street corner, top of the roof – an' shout the truth. It must be so!

ROSE. You're a slave but don't know it. My mother *saw* her chains, she's had marks on her wrists all her life. There are no signs on *you* till you're dead. How can yer fight for freedom when yer think you've got it? What happens to people like you? It's a circus! The clown kicks the mongrel and it licks his boots. He kicks it harder and it rolls on its back an' wags its tail – an' all the dogs laugh. Yer won't go, if there was a chance he'd put yer a mile underground an' chain yer to the wall. Then yer'd be free: yer'd know what you are.

ROSE *goes out*.

BOB. All my life I struggled. Bob the joker. Bob the sport. Walk down the road, the sun shines, eat, work – struggle to keep body and soul together. Yoo got yoor strength Bob, yoo can do anythin'. Where did I goo wrong? I know well enough. I know what yoo tell me now. Long ago I should hev put my boot in their teeth every time the bastards smiled at me. But I've left it late. Now it's dark. Black.

Black. Black. I must goo steady, or make a terrible blunder. I must trust the clown an' hope for my reward.

Song of the Conjuror (ROSE *and* BOB)

The conjuror tied his hands with an invisible rope
He bound his feet with a chain no one could see
He shut himself in a sack that was not there
And locked it with an invisible key
He hung from a hook over a deep dark lake
The people laughed as he struggled in the air
They stood in crowds to watch him twist and shake
With a fanfare he is free!

The conjuror was the idol of the people
He appeared at every festival in the land
He hung far over the top of every steeple
Turning and twisting and bobbing upside down
He struggled to get the invisible key
The people roared and laughed at his clever tricks
With a fanfare he is free!

One day when he turned in his invisible sack
He could not get free
He screamed like a man stretched on the rack
Which no one could see
His mouth was gagged with invisible rags
More more! roared the crowd and waved their flags
As he writhed in the air
And fought for his life in an unseen snare

They gasped as he fell – the splash
Turned the water white
They screamed as they watched him struggle and thrash
With horror they saw him sinking down
And stood on the bank to watch him drown

Scene Nine

London.
Old Lady Are's house.
Drawing Room.
ROSE *and* OLD LADY ARE.

OLD LADY ARE *in a chair. On the floor, across the room, a decanter.*

ROSE. They say my husband murdered your daughter-in-law.

LADY ARE. I shall send him a guinea. I never saw the slut. Her father hawked coals in Manchester and she trotted beside him calling his wares. A suitable training for one destined to converse with my son.

ROSE. My husband didn't kill her.

LADY ARE. D'you like fish? It lures me with the passion that drives youth to its follies. I ate too much at dinner. (*Points.*) My glass child. My maid Dorothea, the vixen, puts it out of my reach.

ROSE (*hands her the glass*). Your son killed her.

LADY ARE. My son? O I've slopped the glass! (*Chokes.*) Dear me. Thump my back child. (ROSE *pats her back.*) Thump I say! Lay on! O 'tis good! The seizure will take me. (*Wipes her eyes.*) Swear 'tis true! I must have my coach at dawn to tell the town.

ROSE. Thank you ma'am. I was afraid you wouldn't believe me.

LADY ARE. Believe ye? 'Tis the easiest thing to believe since the bishop of London's wife gave birth to a child with his chaplain's nose. I can't pay your husband – but you shall have the guinea.

ROSE. Lord Are says you've got us a pardon.

LADY ARE. Pox on the rogue! I haven't seen him since the day his father died. He snatched the pillow from under his head, bounded downstairs (one at a time, he had heels on), threw it at me, yowlped Hurrah! and hounded me from the house. (*Drinks.*) Come, see. (*Takes a huge pile of papers from her bosom.*) Shares, letters, promissory notes. All his. (*Wheezes as she fondles the papers.*) Look, forty thousand pounds. (*Paper.*) A half share in Jamaica. (*Paper.*) That would pay his pox pills. (*Paper.*) A castle in Scotland. (*Kisses papers and puts them back in her dress.*) Home to my heart, darlings. (*Paper.*) A letter from the Prime Minister to the Primate of England. You could blackmail him with this till he had to raise the income tax to pay you – and still have the Primate's reply. (*Paper.*) And this – a charge on his old foe Lester. (*Laughs and stuffs papers away.*) Back to the bosom that gave him suck (one Wednesday when the wet nurse was late) but now makes amends by making him starve. (*Smoothes her dress.*) They go with me to the grave and angels do not lie on softer down.

ROSE. He says the pardon's already –

LADY ARE. Pardon, pardon – cease with your pardons! My glass. There are no pardons.

ROSE. But you can get one?

LADY ARE. 'Tis true my figure sets a fashion few could follow – but the prince always liked a lady of carriage. He'd bed me still but his flesh is wore out with paint. His servants daub it on when they're drunk and he's too blind to wipe it off. Last week his whiskers were plastered to his cheeks with cold cream. They carry him round the palace in a sedan chair. He looks out of the window like a monkey sticking out of its jungle. A pardon? – nothing would be easier. 'Twould be as if the monkey reached up, plucked a banana from a tree and threw it into my lap. But I shall not ask.

ROSE. But Lady Are my husband's innocent!

LADY ARE. True, but he hath put out that he is not. Let him hang for a boaster. Child, who would be safe? Charles my footman would strangle me at table for the sake of a titbit on my plate, Dorothea would crack me over the head with my bottle and drink it, and Trevor my valet would kick me downstairs. Pardon? Ye might as well ask me to lead a riot or open a revolution.

ROSE. My husband is innocent.

LADY ARE. Then let him go to heaven. If he stays in this world he will go to hell with the rest of the footmen. If Society protest every time the law is an ass no one will respect it. I've watched lambs as innocent as driven snow go to the gallows and my head was not one hair the whiter. Console yourself. My son will hang. Stab Lester at cards or step on his toe at a hop. They'll brawl and one will be stabbed and the other hanged.

ROSE. My husband is good and kind and –

LADY ARE. I like him more and more.

ROSE (kneels). I beg you.

LADY ARE. Get up child. A thing is not made more impressive by being said by a dwarf. The ground is what we have risen from. Up! Ye made an old lady merry with a farce and now ye mar it with a wailing play!

ROSE. You bitch! I hope you fall downstairs! Choke! Die of gin! Have your head cracked with a bottle! And get pox from yer monkey!

ROSE goes.

LADY ARE. The wretch hath a tongue on her like Dorothea, but she would have stayed for the guinea. I forgot to get the details! (Calls.) Dorothea! – Coupling with the kitchen boy again? Trevor! – The wretch is drunk! Hush, I'll invent the details. The papers said 'twas at table. She empties his plate on his head, peas and potatoes stream down his face and French coat and he runs her through and slips on a pudding and turns cartwheels while she – O! Ho! Ha! (*Laughs and wheezes*.) her – her – O! I shall be in bed for a week! Peace think of something else! – her last breath blows bubbles in the soup! (*She laughs*.) O! Hoo! Ha! (*Stops*.) The cold wind round my heart ... The turbot. The doctor forbade it. (*Wipes her mouth*.) The cream sauce ... I am an old woman with an empty glass and there is nothing to think of that does not wring me with regret for the past, convulse me at the follies of the present, or make me tremble before what is to come. I have not always lived after the precepts. 'Twould do no harm to prepare for heaven. Pah! a morbid thought. 'Twould drive my son to distraction – that is heaven, and I shall be the *dea ex machina* in it. As in the old romances, he shall be reprieved at the tree. I shall send a copy direct to that scoundrel my son and give him the misery of reading it.

The Fair Tree of Liberty (ROSE *and* FRANK)

On the fair tree of liberty
The fruit weighs the branches to the ground
And look! the fruit are eyes
At the stealthy tread they open to see
The robber who comes to rob the tree
He turns around and runs
The eyes are brighter than a hundred suns

On the fair tree of liberty
The fruit weighs the branches to the ground
And look! the fruit are eyes
At the marching tread they open to see
The axeman who comes to fell the tree
He turns around and runs
The eyes are brighter than a hundred suns

On the fair tree of liberty
The fruit weighs the branches to the ground
And look! the fruit are eyes
At the heavy tread they open to see
The headsman who comes to burn the tree
He turns around and runs
The eyes are brighter than a thousand suns

Deep in the trunk bees murmur like thunder
High in the crown birds call
Telling the names of the passers-by
The eyes watch them as they come
And sometimes the branches rise and strike them down like
    bolts of thunder

And so the fair tree grows
As tall as the pine and strong as the oak
Wreathed with the climbing honeysuckle
The wild rose and the hanging vine
As our forefathers spoke

Scene Ten

Hilgay.
The Hall.
Breakfast Room.
ARE. *For the first time he is seen in a shirt and breeches and
without a wig.*

ARE. Let a man have a fine day for his hanging. 'Tis morose to
    say otherwise. An empty house, all gone for the best
    places. How pleasantly the sun shines in at my windows to
    bless me. This morning I asked after a noise. 'Twas a lark.

I would have sung too but I lacked an orchestra. Flowers nodded, lambs bleated. Peter Sigh the poet would have –

MOTHER *comes in.*

MOTHER. Gentleman.

ARE. Not so downcast Hedges. I tried. The law is a heavy stone for one man to move.

MOTHER. Say it's urgent.

ARE. Tell him no.

MOTHER. Hev a letter.

ARE. O let him deliver. 'Tis a small cloud, 'twill pass.

MOTHER *goes.*

Now to the business of the day: clothes. (*Sighs.*) A suit so sober it seems I shop at a monastery. I tell the truth: I shall be glad when the day is past, when those who are to suffer have suffered and the rest may enjoy themselves as the world desires, without the mournful countenance a christian must spoil his hat with on these occasions.

MOTHER *comes in with the* MESSENGER. *She goes.*

MESSENGER. My lord, your mother's compliments.

ARE. Damme the she-goat repents! The hag's at death's door!

MESSENGER. My lord, my commission is urgent.

The MESSENGER *hands* ARE *a document.* ARE *reads it.*

ARE. Handsome. So Bob has his good news at last. To think he lieth in his pains and I hold in my hand his absolute and perfect liberty. 'Tis feathers to a bird. How the affairs of men stand on their heads!

MESSENGER. I must go to the prison.

ARE. Prison?

MESSENGER. That is a copy. I am commissioned to hand the original to the governor.

ARE. So you are – or it would go badly with Bob. Lookee
there is a great crowd about the roads. I'll take thee in my
coach.

MESSENGER. 'Tis kind my lord, but I am commissioned to –

ARE. Commission the pox! Would ye deny me my pleasure?

MESSENGER. Yes sir. I am commissioned to take –

ARE. But now I think on't I cannot take ye. I have my Lady
Oxy to sit beside me and her mother the Duchess of Blare
to sit opposite and the Duchess will have Lucille her maid.
Now Lucille is an absolute termagant, an hysteric who
rules the Duchess with a rod of iron and will have no man
near her. The Duchess was on the point of saying I must
run behind and hang onto the strap. The maid compro-
mised only because 'twas a hanging. A wedding or thanksgiving and I should have wore out my shoe-leather pounding the rear. So ye see sir ye cannot come in my coach even
if there was room. (*He has poured two cups of coffee. He
hands one to the* MESSENGER *and drinks the other*.) No sir
do not ask: ye may *not* sit on the roof. That's booked by
Lady Oxy's boys and their chums – for the boys will go to
the hangings. We shall have such a hallooing and hurrah-
ing as we fly through the lanes, such a stamping of feet on
the roof, such a throwing of the coachman's hat into the
duckponds ('tis only a matter of lettin' 'em grow up before
we go to *their* hangin') (MESSENGER *laughs*) – that
Lucille will have hysterics, sniff two bottles of smelling
salts dry and must lie down, miss the hangings and have
the Duchess fan her (the poor lady is tyrannised, 'tis a
scandal – and blackmail is rumoured) so that we hear
nothing but the maid's complaints all the way back, when
the rest of the company (in the natural circle of friendship)
wish to discuss the drop and each give his version of the last
confession, in one of which he will protest he is as innocent
as the unborn lamb and in another claim to have been a

highwayman from the age of ten. No sir I will not take ye in the coach for the journey there will be so like the journey to hell ye'd change places with Bob sooner than enter it for the journey back.

MESSENGER (*putting the cup on the table*). No matter sir. My commission demands that I –

ARE. Yet my conscience fears ye will not get through the mob.

MESSENGER. As to that sir, I'll shout 'Clear in the King's name'!

ARE. Never do that! Nay if ye shout that I cannot let ye through the door.

MESSENGER. Is the king not honoured here sir?

ARE. They will suspect ye bring a pardon and pull ye from your horse. 'Twould spoil their day. They have travelled the country since dawn, bought their pennorth of pies and tuppence of beer and practised their song sheets. When a man's hanged the rest of the day's theirs, for riot or sober reflection. When he is not, they work.

MESSENGER. I'm grateful for the warning sir. I'll ride hard with my mouth shut. Now my commission must –

ARE. Wait! (*Aside.*) Must I kill another before breakfast in this room? I shall run out of Bobs.

MESSENGER. Good day sir –

ARE. I have it! I have it! It would go hard with thee to fail in thy commission – I would not see thee and thine suffer it. I cannot take you in my coach – but I may take the pardon.

MESSENGER. But sir my commission says –

ARE. Sir you surprise me! Thou hast dawdled long enough. More delay and I must complain to thy officer. Here are thirty guineas in gold. The bringer of good news is rewarded.

MESSENGER. Thirty guineas!

ARE. 'Tis naught. Fly to the tavern and drink my health. 'Tis a commission. God bless thee. I must dress and jump about.

MESSENGER. I thank your lordship.

The MESSENGER *gives* ARE *the pardon and goes.*

ARE. Now sure I am looked on by a guardian angel – though from whence I know not! I hold in my hand his pardon. I shall not deliver it. What, no lightning stroke? No thunder? The sun does not stop in its course! Lookee Are: thou art a strange soul. I begin to like thee, and I might worship thee. Ye have talents, nay powers I knew not of! Why d'ye live in poverty and marry an ash-raker's daughter? Ye neglect the proper care of thyself. Why have ye not twenty houses? An army? A hundred women? Ye fear Lord this and fawn on Lady that, ye hack your way down the street with your cane – when ye might be carried along it on the backs of the mob! All shall change. There shall be a new world. (*Calls.*) Hedges! Lay out my blue coat and yellow hat. Nay, my pink with the purple plumes. Let us not add to Bob's woes: he shall see a good hat at his hanging. Faith 'tis so spectacular 'twill take his mind off the rope. I shall doff it to the hangman – but Bob may take it as a courtesy to himself. Let the Great Boob hang to prove the world's in its senses. Besides, 'tis heartless to deny a mob. *Noblesse oblige:* Hang him.

Yet I grow fond! Think, I cannot ride up with the pardon! I must forgo the hanging! I take not the coach. I say I go horse-back to go faster. On the way I fall. Racing and hollooing with the joy of glad tidings, over I go tippity-top – knocked out. When I get to my feet the jade hath run. (I shall whip her off. 'Tis a faithful beast and will cling – but I'll break my whip on her, and if that don't serve throw stones.) Then I have my limp. (*Practises.*) Nay severer. (*Practises as he talks.*) I hobble (I have cut a stick from the hedge) to a nearby farm. Deserted. All at the hanging. We have not seen such desolation since the black death. On I crawl. Till time hath run out and poor Bob the Boob is led under the tree. He looks up at heaven – in the direction of the parson's finger – to the welcoming face of god: and all he sees is the black beam above him. I sit in the hedge and weep. Yea, I uncover my head and kneel in the nettles and pray: for the rope to break.

O thou great blazing sun! Great fire of ever-lasting day! My life! My ministering star! Blaze! Blaze! Blaze! Blaze! Hail great sun! Light of the world that I shall stride in! . . . O my friends –

MOTHER *comes in.*

MOTHER. Blue an' pink's laid out.

ARE. Hedges. Rest in thy chamber.

MOTHER. Keep busy. Cry for him last night, cry later.

ARE. Mothers know best. Lookee, light a fire against my return. The day might yet be cold. Warm thy old hands at the blaze. Here is a paper to start it. (*He gives her the pardons.*)

ARE *goes.*

MOTHER. Kind on him. Save me fetch the kindlin'. Official. Pretty crown on top. Cut them out for Christmas decoration. (*Shakes her head.*) Best do what yoo're towd. Bob was learnin' to read. (*Tears the papers.*) Ont start that doo yoo ont git the work out the way.

MOTHER *starts the fire.*

ARE (*off*). Hedges!

MOTHER (*sighing to herself as she stoops – she has become much older*). Now what?

ARE *comes in shouting.*

ARE. 'Tis too much! Hedges will ye make me a fool! Dress me in motley? Set me up as a clown?

MOTHER (*calm, flat*). Sir whatever is the —

ARE. Damned impertinence! Can a man trust nothing! I kept your man when I might have celebrated my title by sacking him! Are you as blind as he?

MOTHER (*calm, flat*). Now sir I'm sure there's no call to —

ARE. No ye did it on purpose! Petty revenge! (*Holds out his blue coat.*) Where is the button! D'ye see it? No! 'Tis off! (*Throws his blue coat on the floor.*) Here, here (*Thumps his chest.*) where every fool can see it! You ancient hag must I sew it myself? I give ye the roof over your head, the ground under your feet, the food on your plate — for a gaping hole with two black spots and a white thread like the lower-anatomy of a mouse! An idiot's badge!

MOTHER. Give it here, I'll see to —

ARE. Now? When it lies in the filth? (*The floor must be filthy since I have not swept it today.*) I must dress like a tramp! O she will sew the button now the coat can't be worn! (*Kicks the coat.*) Madam sew it on and throw the coat in the kennels for my bitch to whelp on. Let her at least have the respect of a full set of buttons. (*Suddenly becomes his old self again.*) Now I must wear my green. So I cannot wear my pink. Twould look like a maypole. I must wear my yellow — which I wore twice at the races. (*Aside.*) 'Tis true I can't go to the hanging. But now the whole county will say 'twas because I could not afford a new hat!

ARE *goes.* MOTHER *mutters to herself as she goes back to the fire.*

MOTHER. Can't sew it on. Ont give me the button.

Suddenly (BOB)

It came suddenly like a bomb
They didn't die with the gestures of dying
They didn't cover their heads in fear
They didn't lift their hands in supplication
They died with the gestures of living

It came suddenly like a bomb
Mouths were open but the words were not spoken
The salt was lifted but wasn't shaken
They died with the gestures of living
Fingers beckoned and hands stretched out to feel
Heads leaned forward in concentration
On words they would never hear

So sudden was the disaster
So swift the moment of fate
It fell at the time of the midday meal
When the fork was halfway between
The mouth and the plate

Scene Eleven

Peterborough.
Holme Cottage. A beer barrel.
MRS WILSON *and* BOB.

BOB *is in shirt sleeves and without fetters. He drinks at the table.*

BOB. When woman? (MRS WILSON *fills his glass. He grabs her arm.*) She's a sly one.

WILSON. Behave or I'll tell Mr Wilson.

BOB (*lets her arm go*). His nibs is quiet. He'll hev to come down for my pardon.

WILSON. Let him sleep. I pulled his door to so he shan't be disturbed.

BOB (*shouts at the ceiling*). Who's in the land of nod? Shh!

WILSON. I'll confiscate your glass.

BOB. Phew. Had enough. Powerful stuff.

WILSON. On your feet. Put your jacket on. Sit there in your shirt sleeves.

BOB (*stands, staggers slightly, steadies himself with one hand on the table*). Oops.

WILSON (*buttons*). Fasten you in.

BOB. Us'll shake hands. Thankyoo sir. Hope yoo hev the same one day. (*Giggles.*) Think when they see how posh I am they most likely give me two pardons.

WILSON. I'll top you up.

BOB (*flat palm over the glass*). Nope. Ont drink 'n'more.

PARSON *and* ROSE *come in.*

Rose! My gal. How I hev miss you. (*Kiss.*) There – thass better now. All's turn out well. The terrible times are over. (*Whispers to* ROSE.) Mrs Wilson say it's come today. Sh! – Parson yoo let your faith wobble but yoo'll git a surprise. Mrs Wilson do the man the honours an' pour his drink. (*Wipes the glass clean on his sleeve.*) Drat spoil me coat. (*Hands the glass to* MRS WILSON.) The letters swim in my head like thass a shipwreck.

PARSON (*low*). Mrs Wilson a drink for his spirits is one thing. But to do this at such an hour is cruel. Wrong. A needless adding to his burdens.

WILSON. I don't need a sermon on how to run a gaol. The profit I make on this it's not worth buying in. (*Gives him the glass.*) No doubt you'll take your glass parson?

PARSON (*slight embarrassment*). Yes yes, thank you. His and my way go differently today.

MRS WILSON keeps a tally of the beer that is drunk. She marks it on a slate with chalk.

BOB. Rose is ought wrong? (*She has her back to him. He turns her. Her face is showered in tears. He steps back. A moment's bewildered fear.*) That . . . ont tears of joy . . . (*Vaguely.*) Why'm I wearin' my best jacket? My pardon come today . . .

PARSON (*hands him an open prayer book*). Read your prayers to me.

BOB. Ont want a lesson!

WILSON (*to* ROSE). Hand me his glass.

BOB. Ay! Less drink! Sorry parson. Why's this gloom fall all around? Rose, ont make my heart sick to see yoo cry. Rose I only lent his lordship my name.

The PARSON *has three prayer-books open at The Burial of the Dead. He reads and recites Psalm 39 continuously (interrupting himself only once) and the rest of the scene goes on round him. He finally stops reading when he says 'At last. Better. He comes to thee'. After that he prays silently. As the* PARSON *reads from his own book he offers* BOB *the second book open at the place.* BOB *snatches this and throws it on the ground.*

Ont pray at me! Ont be hanged!

The PARSON *picks up the book while he reads his own.*

Drunk! (*Empties his drink on the floor but does not throw the mug.*)

WILSON. O I see we're going to have one of those days. – He should have been told properly. Not decent treating him like this. – Bobby sit down. Crying won't help.

BOB (*stares at* MRS WILSON). Woman what yoo done? . . . Yoo towd me my pardon was . . . (*Sudden idea.*) Ah!

BOB *lurches out.* MRS WILSON *goes on her knees and mops up the beer.*

WILSON. Mrs Hedges stand by him or go outside.
ROSE. He's innocent.
WILSON. They all are if you listen long enough.

Crash upstairs.

There goes the door. That'll cost someone. All this fuss! You come here and behave as if I had nothing better to do.

Crash upstairs.

WILSON (*shouting up*). You wicked boy! (*To the others.*) It's my husband's job. He'll expect his dinner when he gets home. I wish you'd stop cluttering up my kitchen.
BOB (*off*). Ah!
WILSON. There'll be the dickens to pay.
BOB (*off*). Bed made. Cold.

GAOLER *comes in with* FRANK.
FRANK *is drunk.*

GAOLER. Cart's outside ma'am. Jist git the horse in.
FRANK (*morose, almost inaudible*).
Old Samson had a daughter, her name was Isabelle
The lily of the valley and the primrose of the dell

When she went a-walking she choosed me for her guide
Down by the Arun river to watch the fishes glide
FRANK (*Sees* BOB *through the door*). Two of Bob. Have to hang twice.

BOB *comes in.*

BOB. So I'm to hang. Skinned alive. Rose what'll us do? (*Tries to think. Turns to* PARSON.) Howd his row or I crack his head! (PARSON *prays uninterruptedly.*)

GAOLER. Goo quiet or goo shackled, you hev the choice. (*Pours drinks and raises glass.*) Drink to both gents. Wish I could drink to better times. (*Drinks.*)

BOB. Curses! That a man dies so! Git Are here! That blackguard! Why doo he doo this? When was I angry at him? When did I raise my fist? Touch cap – work quiet – bow – ont that enough? Now he want my head!

FRANK.
The first three months were scarcely o'er,
The young gal lost her bloom
The red fell from her bonny cheeks
And her eyes began to swoon

PARSON (*to* BOB). O do not deny yourself the comfort of his word.

BOB. Yes Frank sing! Kiss me Rose! Yoo ont ashamed of me. How I doo love thee! Ont miss the world: miss thee. (*Jumps onto the table. Poses like the hero of a penny dreadful print.*) Shall we hang? Then hang so high! (*Points up.* FRANK *tries to climb onto the table with him.*)

BOB *and* FRANK.
The next nine months was passed and gone
She brought forth to me a son
And I was quickly sent for
To see what could be done

FRANK (*continues alone*).
I said I should marry her
But o! that would not be

PARSON (*tapping* FRANK *on the back*). My friend open your heart –

FRANK. Git off me yer sinful old bugger! I'll open you!

FRANK *snatches the prayer-books and throws them away.*

The GAOLER moves in. The PARSON motions him back.
He closes his eyes and goes on reciting the prayers aloud by
heart. BOB notices nothing of this but comes down from the
table.

WILSON (*pouring beer*). Four. I keep count so no one's over-
charged. (*To ROSE.*) They're allowed one in the cart. I'd
offer, but now there's the door to pay . . . (*Pours drinks for*
everyone.)

Drum Song (BOB)

A drummer beat upon a drum
And no sound came
He hit the skin
He struck the skin
And no sound came
Wild in his frenzy
A madman sweating blood
He beat he struck he hammered blows
And no sound came
He thrashed and lashed
All through the night
And on into the light
Till his hands bled
Till his eyes bled
Till blood ran from his ears
Till the teeth shook in his head
Till the bones rattled in his body like dice
And still he made no sound
He struck with sticks of iron
With sticks of bone
With sticks of steel
He staggered
He began to reel
In pain

He hammered on
Again! Again!
He crawled upon the ground
He flailed the drum lashed to his side
And no sound came
From the beaten hide
He did not stop till he was dead
    And other men are silent
    When they labour them
    About the head

BOB. The pardon'll come on the square. I can't be so lied to.
Rose I'm scared to die. (*Holds her.*)

PARSON. At last. Better. He comes to thee. (*Kneels and prays
silently.*)

FRANK. God rot yer Bobby Hedges! I'll pay to go second an'
see yer swing. There's justice in this! Yer dragged me to
the gallows, yer rantin' hypocrite! Remember the mornin'? If I'd gone with the knife an' fork an' spoon I
wouldn't have took the rest! Twelve knives. Ten spoons.
Eighteen forks. I'd have been careful then. No drinkin' an'
whorin'. Made me way to London like a sane man. Gone
round a corner for ever. Safe. Home. The rope don't
stretch that far. I hope yer hanging's a cruel one. Yer live to
cry mercy on the rope an' don't get it!

    He falls down.

GAOLER (*calling to outside*). She playin' yoo up?

ROSE. Drink. (*Gets glass.*) Bobby.

    BOB *takes the glass and gulps it down.* MRS WILSON
    refills BOB's *glass and holds him as* ROSE *pours it into his
    mouth.*

PARSON. Mrs Wilson I'll lodge a complaint.

    GAOLER *picks* FRANK *up and lays him over the barrel.*

ROSE (*tilts* BOB's *head back and pours drink down his throat*). Drink. Drink. Drink.

PARSON. No! Let him feel the pain or god's anger is not slaked!

WILSON (*to* BOB). Mr Wilson will help you. You were kind to him. He won't hurt you. It doesn't take long.

GAOLER (*calling to the outside*). Ready?

BOB (*pushing the glass away*). No. Ont. Clear head. Speak. In square. Innocent. Englishman. Are's murderer. Murder me. English.

PARSON. Nay! Who can believe a man who speaks so harshly? I forbid you to name his lordship. Have you no gratitude?

BOB. Ay? Ay? Gratitude they want? . . . What can I say? . . . Who'll hear all I can say?

GAOLER. Pay no heed parson. They say all sorts – (*To* BOB.) and out there no one listen. They'll shortly give yoo cause to wish yoo'd saved yoor breath.

VOICE (*off*). She's in.

BOB (*shakes his head to clear it. Then, aside to audience*). I ont believe this.

> GAOLER *takes* BOB *and* FRANK *out.* FRANK *sings. The* PARSON *picks up the three prayer-books and puts on his last vestments as he follows the others out.*

WILSON (*to* ROSE). You can lie down upstairs. Bed's made. Clear this mess away. Wish Mr Wilson didn't have to go out today. When he's had a turn he's nervous. The young man's waiting for something to go wrong. Then he'll step in. Some of them would push you in the river to get your job.

> ROSE *has followed the others out.* MRS WILSON *checks the amount she has sold.*

Scene Twelve

London Bridge.
ROSE.

ROSE. I stand on London Bridge. Bodies float in the sky and
sink towards the horizon. Crocodiles drift in the Thames.
On the embankment the plane trees rattle their fingers.
Men walk the streets with chains hanging from their
mouths. Pillars of black smoke rise between the towers and
the temples. The stars will come out like scabs on the sky.
There is a gentle breeze.

What have I learned? If nothing, then *I* was hanged.

Man is What He Knows (ROSE)

Does the judge say
I send your arms to prison today
But your feet are free
To walk away?

Does the boss buy
The apple core from the market stall
And leave the skin?
He buys it all

Do the troops shoot
To kill your stomach but not your head?
They shoot to kill
You drop down dead

Once Satan roamed the earth to find
Souls that money could buy
Now he comes to steal your mind
He doesn't wait till you die

Man is what he knows – or doesn't know
The empty men reap death and sow
Famine wherever they march
But they do not own the earth
Sooner believe I could strike it a blow
With my fist and miss!

Geese fly over the moon and do not know
  That for a moment they fill the world with
    beauty
    Flakes do not know where they fall in
      the snow
      Wind and rain cannot tell where
        they blow
        But we may know who we
          are and where we go

  I say these things for me and Bob Hedges. There is a gentle
breeze from the city. I cross the bridge and go into the
streets.

End

Notes

1) This is the PARSON's prayer for Scene Eleven:
I said, I will take heed to my ways: that I offend not in my
tongue. I will keep my mouth as it were with a bridle:
while the ungodly is in my sight. I held my tongue, and
spake nothing! I kept silence, yea, even from good words;
but it was pain and grief to me. My heart was hot within
me, and while I was thus musing the fire kindled: and at
last I spake with my tongue; Lord, let me know mine end,
and the number of my days: that I may be certified how
long I have to live. Behold, thou hast made my days as it
were a span long: and mine age is even as nothing in

respect of thee; and verily every man living is altogether vanity. For man walketh in a vain shadow, and disquieteth himself in vain: he heapeth up riches, and cannot tell who shall gather them. And now, Lord, what is my hope: truly my hope is even in thee. Deliver me from all mine offences: and make me not a rebuke unto the foolish. I became dumb, and opened not my mouth: for it was thy doing. Take thy plague away from me: I am even consumed by means of the heavy hand. When thou with rebukes dost chasten man for sin, thou makest his beauty to consume away, like as it were a moth fretting a garment: every man therefore is but vanity. Hear my prayer, O Lord, and with thine ears consider my calling: hold not thy peace at my tears. For I am a stranger with thee: and a sojourner, as all my fathers were. O spare me a little, that I may recover my strength: before I go hence, and be no more seen. Glory be to the Father, and to the Son: and to the Holy Ghost; as it was in the beginning, is now, and ever shall be: world without end. Amen.

2) Songs.

In the play's first production 'Hurrah' was cut from Scene Eight. In the Royal Shakespeare Company's production in 1988 'Legend of Good Fortune' was cut from Scene Seven. In its place Mrs Hedges sang 'Falkland Song'. The text of this song is printed on page 283.

'Dream Song' could be taken from its place in Scene Eleven and sung between Scenes Ten and Eleven. 'Suddenly' would then have to be cut.

The music for Frank's song in Scene Eleven is the traditional 'Bogie's Bonnie Belle'.

3) An alternative, shorter version of Scene Seven is printed beginning on page 279. If it is used Gabriel does not appear in the play.

4) Comments on directing and acting the play, and especially on Scene eleven, are given in 'Commentary on the War Plays' in *The War Plays* (Methuen Drama, 1991).

Alternative version of Part Two, Scene Seven:

Part Two

[Scene Seven]

Hilgay.
The Hall.
Workroom.
MRS HEDGES *peels potatoes.* ROSE *comes in.*

ROSE. They found 'im guilty.

MOTHER (*continues to peel potatoes*). Only t'be anticipated.
'Is lordship'll take care of it.

ROSE. Are killed 'er. Bob's coverin' up.

MOTHER (*stops peeling in alarm*). Howd yoor row, gal.
Yoo'll git us all threw out on us necks. I know what
you're up to. Hardache's come. Waitin' outside. Say
yoo wrote 'im. Yoo let on what's gooin' on 'ere, I'll
cuss the day you wed my Bob.

ROSE. Hardache'll 'elp 'im.

MOTHER. Ont need help.

ROSE. They'll 'ang 'im.

MOTHER. Ont talk so far back! No sense of proportion.
This is 'is big chance. Doo 'is lordship a favour like this
'e's set up for life. (*Starts peeling potatoes again.*) Poor
people can't afford t' waste a chance like this. God know
it ont come often. Time our luck change. Yoo start
trouble, 'oo pay? Us. *Yoo're* back t'London, *we* git
chuck out. End up in the work'ouse: work like a slave,
work'ouse disease – ont last six month. See it afore. Too
old t' 'ave my life mess up. So ont meddle, Rose.

ROSE. Bob's in prison waitin' t' be –

MOTHER. Worse places outside. Ont expect 'is lordship t'goo in the dock for the like of 'er. Jist drag the family name through the mire. Whatever next! Ont know where t'look next time I goo t' the village, they know I work for someone like that. 'S'n accident *who* it was. Silly woman deserved t'git killed. She come into my kitchen dress up, I give 'er a whack a my fryin' pan she ont git up from.

ROSE. 'E's 'anged but the roof's over your 'ead.

MOTHER. Yoo think I'm that sort of a woman, my dear, thass yoor privilege.

ROSE. I don't understand you people! Why should Arse-face 'elp 'im? Bob's a labourer, no better than a –

MOTHER. Jist ont stand in my boy's way when 'e hev 'is chance t'goo up in the world. Lie on oath doo it 'elp 'im, say I saw 'im stick the sword in her gut. 'Sides, even if what yoo say's true – which it ont – if my Bob stood up in court an' spoke *rashness* 'bout 'is lordship, 'ood believe 'im? Ont yoo know nothin', gal? If there's a row between man an' boss, stand t'reason 'oo win.

ROSE. It ain' between man and boss. It's between two bosses.

MOTHER (*still peeling potatoes*). Now whass she on about?

ROSE. It pays t'know the law when you're black. You're not allowed t'benefit from your own crime. (MOTHER *snorts in derision.*) If Are killed 'is wife, 'e loses 'er money. (MOTHER *stops peeling.*) It goes back to the next of kin: 'er father.

> HARDACHE *steps in. He carries a walking stick and with his hat fans his face, neck and inside his jacket.*

HARDACHE (*gesturing behind him*). Pretty place. (*To* ROSE.) Saw you crossin' the fields so I followed you in. Sorry I missed the funeral. Carry on, Mrs – Hedges in't it? (MOTHER *starts to peel potatoes again.*) A neighbour had to sell up and I couldn't miss the opportunity. Then the trial: I had to arrange a little shares shenanigans. Rose, you married a villain but no one's perfect. All the bitterness was squeezed out of me long ago when my first warehouse went up on fire. Tell Bob I haven't wept since.

MOTHER (*stops peeling potatoes*). That wicked gal's got it in 'er 'ead my Bob ont do it.

HARDACHE. Not do it? Is that right, Rose? Then who did?

ROSE. Are.

HARDACHE. His lordship? Nay, I've never 'eard the like. Happy young couple like that? Why ever should he be so rash? No no, she were struck down by your over-hasty young man. I can't believe otherwise – his lordship, you say?

MOTHER (*peeling*). Yoo talk sense into 'er, sir.

HARDACHE. Well, I'm struck both ways sideways. (MOTHER *goes on peeling but watches* HARDACHE *intently*.) What a predicament to fall into our laps – (*Quickly correcting himself.*) land on our heads. A real taremadiddle and no mistake. Did he strike her, Rose?

ROSE. Yes sir and talked Bob into taking the blame.

HARDACHE. I shan't take kindly to bein' deceived, Mrs Hedges. Now's the time to speak out. You know what's at stake: my daughter's memory. D'you know owt?

MOTHER (*carefully peeling*). Well – I doo an' I don't. What should I say?

HARDACHE. The truth woman! It's a Christian country in't it?

MOTHER (*as before*). Well – if 'is lordship kill 'er – what's the good of what I say?

HARDACHE. What good? Does justice count for nothin' in these parts? When I think of that innocent young man – you did say he was innocent, Rose? – alone in his cell,

my withers weren't more wrung for me own daughter.
Well Mrs Hedges?

MOTHER. I suppose – if that's 'ow it is – (*She stops peeling.*)
I hev t'tell Mr Hardache my son towd me 'e ont do it.

HARDACHE. And also testified Are cajoled him into
covering up his own crime. What a dastardly villain!

MOTHER (*finishing repeating his words in her attempt to
memorize them. The peeling knife and a potato are held up in
the air over the bowl*). . . . coverin' up 'is own crimes
what a dastardly villain.

HARDACHE. Well. Now we know. I'm right glad I came
to pay respects to my daughter's grave: you run into
business anywhere. (*To* ROSE.) Leave all to me lass.
Mind, no speakin' out of turn. The fish still has to be
landed by an expert tickler. Good day.

ROSE. Will you go straight to the judge?

HARDACHE. Tch, tch, didn't I say leave all to me?

ROSE. I'll show you the stairs to the –

HARDACHE. Nay, I can't be seen ascendin' from the
servants' quarters. Best slip out the way I came and go
round to the front. Don't want to put suspicion into his
lordship's mind if 'e's acquired the habit of murder.
(HARDACHE *goes out the way he came.*)

MOTHER. Ont stand there, gal! Take these out an' git 'em
on the stove. Dinner'll come 'round t'day jist as it did
yesterday. (ROSE *goes out with the bowl of peeled potatoes.*)

This song can be sung in Scene Seven in place of 'Legend of Good Fortune'.

Falkland Song (MOTHER)

My son why have you broken my leg?
My son why have you crushed my arm?
My son why did you tear the hair from my head?
My son when did I do you any harm?
My son you don't hear what I say

You lie in a hole with your broken leg
Your arms are crushed and hold emptiness
Your skinhead is cracked like a helmet of steel
You're dead and you don't feel any pain
My son you don't hear what I say

My leg is broken – my arms are crushed
My breast was torn by the bayonet thrust
I bear all the pains a soldier bore
But you're dead and you don't feel your pain anymore
And you don't hear what I say

I don't know what the Spanish for suffering is
Or the Spanish for mother or son or war
Or the Spanish for winter or summer or pain
Or for waste or for wounds or for wind or for rain

My son it isn't for you that I mourn
And I don't feel the pain of your flesh being torn
I weep for the enemy you shot at Bluff Bay
When the sun stood high on a cold winter day
For the enemy you butchered on Tumbledown Height
In the bayonet charge of the army of night
But you don't hear what I say

What is the Spanish for gun and for bomb?
What is the Spanish for SAS and hell?

What is the Spanish for night?
What is the Spanish for innocence?
What is the Spanish for fight?
What is the Spanish for hooligan?
What is the Spanish for pain?
What is the Spanish for government?
What is the Spanish for wind and for cold and for rain?

My son they told you you died for me
You killed to set your countrymen free
But I mourn for the soldier you killed by the sea
I curse you with each blast of wind from the shore

You sleep in peace – don't feel pain anymore
I curse you with the shout of each breaking wave
You murdered your brother – you murdered your brother
For he was my son – he was my son
Though he spoke only Spanish and never knew me
You murdered my son by the cold winter sea
For I was his mother – I was his mother
And you made my womb a grave

What is Spanish for money?
What is Spanish for shares?
What is Spanish for he is the loser who dares?
What is Spanish for loss?
What is Spanish for gain?
What is Spanish for dividends?
What is Spanish for pain?
What is Spanish for wind and for cold and for rain?
My son you are dead and I ask in vain

Restoration

The music

Given here are the melodies composed by Nick Bicât for the play. Full orchestration can be obtained from London Management & Representation Ltd, 235 Regent Street, London W1R 7AG.

ROSES (BOB)

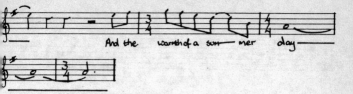

And the warmth of a summer day

SONG OF LEARNING (FRANK)

1. For fif-ty thous-and years I ⎧ lived in a shack I
⎨ harrowed and toiled
⎩ followed the plough the

learned a shack is not a place to live in ——— For
⎧ All I made was ta-ken a-way ——— from my hands
⎩ food I ate was left by the beasts—— of the field

fif-ty thou-sand years I ⎧ built man-sions for men of wealth
⎨ ran fac-tries for men of wealth
⎩ dug gar-dens for men of wealth

That's how I learned to ⎧ build a man-sion for my- self
⎨ run a fac-try for my- self
⎩ dig a gar-den for my- self

fif-ty thou-sand years I waited at ta-ble——— I
fought in their wars———

learned to cook and how to un - bottle the wine   For
died so of-ten I learned— how to sur-vive   For

fif-ty thou-sand years I watched rich men tuck in like swine
fought battles to save their wealth

From now on the grub is gon-na be all——— mine———
that's how I learned to loathe the en - e-my my—self

5. } For fif-ty thou-sand years I printed their books   I
6. }   gave them my life   But in

learned to read by look-ing ov-er their shoul-der   For
all that time they ne-ver learned how to live —   For

fif-ty thou-sand years I { built   li-braries for men of   wealth —
                         { was go-verned by men of   wealth —

That's how I learned to write the books I   need my-self —
Now I have learned to make the laws up for my-self —

I have known pain and bowed be-fore beau-ty shared in joy and died —

— in du-ty   Fif-ty thou-sand years I lived well —

learned how to blow up your   hell.

DREAM (ROSE)

At night I pass through the land un-seen Though you lie a-wake   To coda

My smile is as sharp as the blade in my hand

But when the fire is spent the ground is not scorched the trees are not charred The land is fresh in the mor-ning dew

The ca-ttle went through the flames yet are not dead

On-ly the white-man's bones are black   ly-ing by his burned out banks   Now cat-tle graze by the ri-ver banks

Men and wo-men work in the fields

All they grow they own   To be shared by young and old

In the eve-ning they rest And the song of free-dom is sung

I am

CODA

I am

The ven-om does not kill the snake.

THE WOOD SONG (MOTHER)

SONG OF THE CALF (BOB)

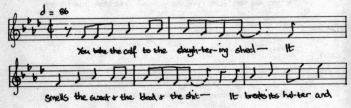

runs thrugh the lanes The haltering men run af—ter it — 2. It

snorts in the fresh clean morning air — It bell-ows and laws and

toss-es its head — And af—ter it — with sticks or ropes come the

halter-ing men from the slaughtering shed. 3. It reaches the town and

runs thrugh the streets It tries to hide but the chil-dren shout It

burns at bay and throttles & groans The halter-ing chil-dren have

found it out —   4. It scat-ters the mob and

flees the town — It stops to rest in a qui—et lane — Then

peace-ful-ly strolls back home — to its field — And pass-es the woo-den gate —

— a-gain —   5. There stand the men from the

slaugh-ter-ing shed — In a cir-cle with sticks & a halter or chain — They

seize the calf and fet-ter it fast — And lead it back to the but-cher a—gain   6. For though it will run and

bell-ow and rear— The calf will be tied to the slaughter house door The

but-cher will cut its throat with his knife It will sink to its knees and

lose   its   life   7. The morning is o———ver—

the work is done   You eat and drink

and have your fun   The but-cher is—

sharp-en-ing— his knife to——day   Do you know, do you

care,   who will get a—way?

A MAN GROANS (ROSE AND MOTHER)

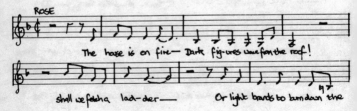

ROSE

The house is on fire— Dark fig-ures wave from the roof!

shall we fetch a lad-der——   Or light brands to burn down the rest of the street? You to whom the an—swer is eas—y

Do not live in our—time You have not vi—si—ted our city You

weep be—fore you know who to pi—ty Here a good deed may be a crime

—and a wrong be right To you who go in dark—

—ness we say it's not ea—sy to know the light

MOTHER (8ve lower than written)

A man sits huddled in a cell People dance in the streets—

Shall we stretch our hands thru the bars — Or run to the street and

dance in tri—umph? You to whom the an—swer is ea—sy

Do not live in our time You have not vi—si—ted our ci—ty You

weep be—fore you know who to pi—ty Here a good

deed may be a crime —and a wrong be right

ROSE + MOTHER (8ve lower)

To you who go in dark—ness we say it's not

THE GENTLEMAN (BOB AND ROSE)

He steps out of the way to let her pass

On one arm — she carries a child —

In the oth-er a bat-tered case with the hinges bro-ken

Tied with a strap   He takes the child and

holds it on his shoul-der —   He o-pens the gate to

let the wo-man pass —   He has not seen her till

now What pol-ite-ness he shows to the stran-ger —   In his

hand   there's a ri-fle   At the door — to the

gas   cham-ber —   He hands the child back — to her

arms — who would raise a whip when an or-der is — o-beyed?

why lift up your fist when a   point-ing fing-er will   lead?

Who would raise their voice when soft words will do — my friend?

Why use a knife — when a smile makes — cuts that bleed? — When you have the mind — why — bother to chop off the head? When white hands will — — do the work why make your hands — red?

SONG OF TALKING (FRANK AND BOB)

♩ = 92

FRANK + BOB (unison)

1. My mate was a hard case. Worked beside him on the bench for years. Hardly said a word. Talking isn't easy when the machines run. One day he dropped a coin. He un-screwed the safety rail to get it back. The press hammer smashed his head. I nursed him on the concrete floor. He looked up at the roof and

said   The green hills by the sea Where the light shines Thragh tall dark

pines ——————————— A min-ute lat-er he was

dead   2. Did-n't speak ev-en on the street   Once I

saw him shop-ping with his wife   He on-ly nod-ded He was de-cent to

me   But I'd heard ru-mours   He'd done time in

cho-key   And his fist   could hit you like a steel-capped boot

Then he un-screwed the safe-ty rail   I nursed him on the con-crete

floor   He looked up at the roof and said   The green hills by the

sea   in the dark grove I first made love ——————

A min-ute lat-er he was   dead

3. You did-n't pick a row with him   Once I bumped him on the park-ing

lot   No real da-mage   He starred thru' the wind-screen Then drove off

BOB

FRANK

FRANK + BOB (unison)

FRANK

FRANK + BOB (unison)

fast   A foreman made him handsome I

never knew what team he supported   Then he unscrewed the

safety rail   I nursed him on the concrete floor   He looked

BOB

up at the roof and said   The green hills by the

sea Where the gulls cry In the white sky —

FRANK

A minute later he was dead

FRANK + BOB (unison)

4. My mates ran to fetch the nurse   The foreman wouldn't stop the ma-

-chines I bent to listen   He looked like an ap—

-pren-tice   He was gently crying   And

babbling to himself   I touched his hand No response   The

hammer was still beating   I nursed him on the concrete floor He looked

up at the roof and said   The green— hills — by the

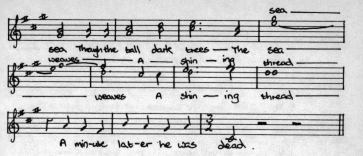

sea — Though the ball dark trees — The sea —

weaves — A shin — ing thread —

weaves A shin — ing thread —

A min-ute lat-er he was dead.

LEGEND OF GOOD FORTUNE (MOTHER)

Men lived in peace and plen-ty When the world was as young as the

day But a god came down from heav—en And

took the good things a—way He put them all in a

bas-ket And slow-ly climbed up to his cave He

put the bas-ket un-der his head and slept like a wea—ry

slave There — passed on earth ten

a—ges of war Men groaned and lived as the dead then this

god stirred in his dreaming And the bas-ket fell out of his
bed   Then from the hea-vens there rained on men The
gifts of plen-ty and peace   The bread and hon-ey
fruit and— wine And the new gol-den age be-gan —
slow-ly the god woke up from his sleep & came down to rob them a-
-gain   This time men said what we have we shall keep and they
fought till the god was slain   Send for the wise to
share your bread take the beau-ti-ful in—to your bed   And if
ev-er that god is seen in your land Take all he's got & break his
head.

SONG OF THE CONJUROR (ROSE AND BOB)

Turn-ing and twisting & robb-ing up-side
down
He struggled to get free in-vis-i-ble-
— key
The peo-ple roared & laughed at his clev-er
tricks
They clapped the an-tics of their brill-iant
clown
With a fan-fare he is free

ROSE & BOB
One day when he turned in his in-vis-i-ble sack
He could not get free
He screamed like a mad
stretched on a rock
That no-one could see—

BOB
His mouth was gagged with in-vis-i-ble rags
BOTH
More

BOB
More! roared the crowd & waved their flags as he writhed in the air—
BOTH

BOB
And fought for his life in an un-seen snare—

BOTH
They gasped as he fell the splash turned the wa-ter

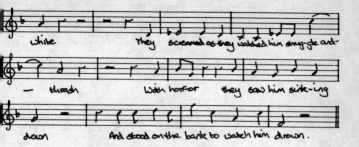

white   They screamed as they watched him dangle and

— thresh   With horror they saw him sink-ing

down   And stood on the bank to watch him drown.

TREE OF LIBERTY (ROSE AND FRANK)

ROSE: 1st x   on the fair tree of li-ber-ty — the

FRANK: 2nd x   On the fair tree of li-ber-ty — The

fruit weighs the bran-ches to the ground And look! the fruit are eyes—

fruit weighs the bran-ches to the ground And look! the fruit are eyes—

— At the steal-thy tread they o-pen— to see— The

— At the march-ing tread they o-pen— to see— The

rob-ber who comes to rob — the tree — He

axe-man who comes to fell — the tree — He

turns a-round and runs — The eyes are bright —

ROSE
— ter than a hun-dred suns — On the

fair tree of li-ber-ty The fruit weighs the branches to the

ground And lo! the fruit are eyes — At the

clank-ing tread they o — pen to see the headsman who comes to burn

— the tree He turns a-round and runs They eyes are bright

FRANK + ROSE
— ter than a thou-sand sons Deep in the trunk bees

murmer like thun — der High in the crown birds call

UNISON
Tell-ing the names of each pas-ser by As the eyes watch them come

For some the branches rise to-ge — ther and

strike   like thun—der bolts   The rest are re—freshed in its cool

— green— shade   And

so the fair tree grows—   FRANK + ROSE   As tall as the pine and as strong

— as the oak—   Wreathed with the wild rose— & the hanging vine

As our fore—fa—thers spoke and so the fair tree grows—

— As   tall   as the pine and as strong—

— as the oak—   Wreathed with the wild rose r the hanging vine

— As our fore—fa—thers spoke.

SUDDENLY (BOB)

♩ = 196

It came sud—den—ly like— a bomb— They didn't die with the

ges—tures of dy——ing   They didn't cov—er their heads in   fear—

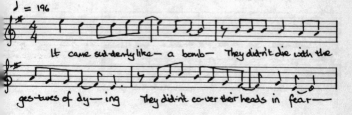

They did-nt lift their hands in sup-pli-ca-tion They died with the ges-tures of li-ving It came sud-den-ly like a bomb

Mouths were o-pened but the words were not spo-ken The salt was lif-ted but was-nt sha-ken They died with the ges-ture of li-ving Fin-gers beck-oned + hands stretched out to feel Heads leaned for-ward in con-cen-tra-tion Heads leaned for-ward in con-cen-tra-tion On words they would ne-ver hear

So sud-den was the di-sas-ter So swift was the mo-ment of fate It came at the time of the mid-day meal When the fork had reached

TO CODA

Da Capo

half-way be-tween the mouth + the plate

half-way be-tween the mouth and the plate.

THE DRUM SONG (BOB)

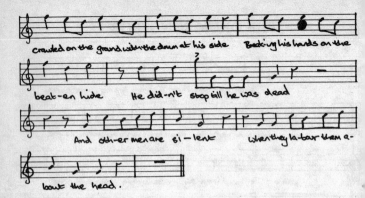

crawled on the ground with the drum at his side Beating his hands on the

beat-en hide   He did-n't stop till he was dead

And oth-er men are si—lent   when they la-bour them a-

bout the head.

MAN IS WHAT HE KNOWS (ROSE)

Does the judge say I send your arms to pri-son to-day But your

feet are free— To walk a-way? Does the boss buy the a-pple

core from the mar-ket stall and leave the skin ?   He

buys it all— Do the troops shoot to kill your sto-mach but not your head? They

shoot to kill— You drop down dead Once   sa-tan roamed the earth

— to find— souls that he could buy — Now he comes to steal

— your mind He doesn't wait till you die — The

hous-es burn on the edge of town It's on-ly the dawn we can tell

when it rea-ches your house you will fight like the

men locked in their cell — Man is what he

knows or doesn't know — Some men reap

on-ly death and sow fam-ine where-e-ver they march But

they do not own the earth — Soon-er be-lieve I could strike

— it a blow with my fist And

miss Geese fly — over the moon + ne-ver

know — that for a mo — ment they fill the world with beau-ty —

Flakes fall — in the snow Not knowing where they fall But

each flake falls to the world be-low — And in the

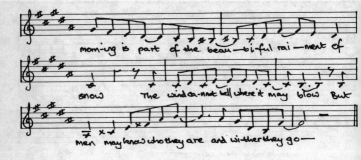

morn-ing is part of the beau—ti-ful rai—ment of snow The wind can-not tell where it may blow But men may know who they are and whither they go—

Restoration

Poems and Stories

Poets
A Hand
The Falklands Quotations and Poems
The Lord of the Beasts
A Story
Sports Ground Inferno
Water
I Could Not Say
The Window
You Are the First Generation
The Swallows

Poets

On the radio the poets said
Poets should not speak of happiness but joy
As if on the floor of the salt ocean
There rose a spring of pure water
And death tasted better to those who drowned
Once to explain evil to a seminarist
I told him of the guard who helped old people
Into the gas chamber as gently as if
He helped his mother to cross the street
The seminarist said christ is in everyone
And took joy in his god who visited death camps
Since then I have avoided seminarists
Prisoners praise the sun at cell windows
The poor hop like sparrows over crumbs
And slaves clean their chains in love of brightness
Joy lives with pain and so outlasts happiness
And evil is its own reward
The evil act out of love and goodness of heart
The state of evil is terrible: it is joyful
The guard will die for the fatherland with the joy
That makes him bear the misery of service
If poets would be joyful
Let them eat with the hungry and work with the slaves
But because when they write they must be free
It is the job of poets to build prisons

A Hand

A man passed his neighbour's house. Through the window he saw something on the table. He wanted it.

That evening he sat at home after his meal and watched television. Suddenly the thing came into his head. He thought about it for a minute. Then he shook himself and concentrated on television. Next morning he woke with the thing in his head. He thought about it on and off through the day. As he came home in the evening he looked in his neighbour's window. The thing was still on the table. He stopped. Suddenly the curtain was jerked across the window. He saw his neighbour's fingers clutching the edge of the curtain as he jerked it. Once or twice he had quarrelled with his neighbour.

Next day the man thought he might offer to buy the thing. But he knew his neighbour would not sell it for what he had to offer.

That night the man could not sleep. He thought of ways to get the thing. His neighbour was usually at home. He would wait till he went out. Then he would break in at the back of the house. He would walk through to the kitchen and . . . but the thing wouldn't be on the table. His neighbour would have hidden it. He had seen him looking at it. The man was just about to scratch the back of his neck when he felt a large hand placed on his head. He started and turned round to see who had stolen into his room. His work supervisor? His neighbour? There was no one.

But a moment ago a hand had touched his head. As a threat? Or was it a pat? He couldn't be sure because his startled movement had pushed the hand away. Deeply perplexed he was just going to scratch his brow – as his and reached the level of his eyes he saw it had grown. It was half as large again as its normal size. He turned it over. The knuckles were white and knotted. The nails made him think of the doors of dollshouses. It was his own hand he'd felt on his head.

He must go to the doctor in the morning. When he woke the thing was in his head. The hand had grown. He was afraid to go to the doctor. He would send him to a specialist hospital – an institute for freaks. By mid-day his hand was four times its natural size. He didn't feel shocked. He felt numb. It might have been someone else's hand growing.

In the afternoon he dozed off in exhaustion. He dreamed of the thing. He woke with the idea in his head that the hand was growing to help him. It must be so. It was already five or six times its proper size. He wouldn't have to go into his neighbour's house. He would reach in from outside. Open doors, rummage in cupboards, turn out drawers. He trusted his hand. He stared with respect at the great strange shape. It was as cumbersome as a bull's carcass. The lifeline was as deep as a ditch. The fingerprints were like furrows on a forehead. Why should he be afraid? When he'd got the thing the hand would shrink. There wouldn't be any need for it to be big. Of course he couldn't explain *everything* – but only the ignorant thought you had to do that. He kissed the hand.

By now it was so big he couldn't tell how quickly it was growing. He couldn't hold a tape-measure to measure . Its size made him awkward. It was as if he was one-handed. He fed and dressed himself with his other hand. He carried the big hand round as a dead weight. Sometimes he forgot – he tried to use it and broke things. He looked forward to the day when the hand would stop growing. Then he would know it was time to ransack his neighbour's house. After all, it would be silly to come away with just one thing when his hand was making such an effort to help him.

Next morning he didn't wake up. The heaviness of his hand had tired him. He slept for three days. This was a pity. When he woke the hand was bigger than the rest of his body.

The man felt that at last the time had come to go to his neighbour's house. If his neighbour was in he would hide behind his hand. Or use it to push his neighbour into the yard. No one would believe his crazy story about a giant hand. The man giggled with excitement.

He dressed. He couldn't put on his shirt in the usual way. He put his left arm into the left sleeve. He wrapped the right sleeve round his neck. He crept from his bedroom. He had to be careful to hold the hand up off the ground. But then it blocked his view. It seemed to take him half an hour to reach the bottom of the stairs. He crept along the hall to the front door. Fortunately this was locked with a bolt. He slid the bolt and awkwardly fumbled the door open by squeezing along the edge of it with his hand. He stepped back. He felt cold air from the street. There was a crash. As he'd stepped forward to leave his house his hand had slammed the door in his face. He couldn't find the bolt. Perhaps his hand had knocked it off.

The man was worried. The hand was meant to help him get into his neighbour's house. Now it had made him prisoner in his own. It began to grow much faster. He turned round in the hall. He would still be able to squeeze himself up the stairs to his bedroom. He wanted to lie down. Then he thought it would be better to get to the kitchen. He tried to push the hand before him. It was like trying to push an elephant. Suddenly he saw it was foolish to try to push it. Instead he used the fingers as legs – as children do when they play hand-puppets.

The great five-legged carcass soon set the rest of him in motion. His feet couldn't reach the ground. He was attached to the hand like a little tail on a pig's rump. As the hand moved he seemed to be wriggling with pleasure.

The hand stuck in the kitchen doorway. With the fingers he tore off the doorposts and made a bigger hole. The hand bundled into the kitchen with a slurping, unblocking sound. The man could still use his will on the fingers. If only the room were bigger he could even enjoy himself! Dance with five legs! He tried to twist the hand round – or make the hand twist him round. He wanted to get to the sink. He wanted to drink some water. He couldn't get to the sink. The hand was pressing him to the wall. If he could get to the kitchen table . . . to the knives in the drawer. He could take out a knife with his other hand. He'd cut himself free. Or stab the hand. There would be a lot of blood but that wouldn't matter.

By now the hand grew so fast he heard the great tendons and muscles creaking and groaning and snapping. His arm and shoulder were being sucked into a wall of flesh. If he could he would have bitten through his wrist but it was buried deep in the flesh.

Even now he could control his fingers – but awkwardly. The kitchen walls were squeezing them in a vice. If he could manoeuvre them he'd tear down the kitchen and prise himself free. Float on this swamp of flesh. Breathe. Make a plan. For the first time for many hours he thought of the thing he'd seen on his neighbour's table. Not angrily or covetously. He just saw it as a mirror might reflect it. It's said that when someone drowns they see their whole life. As his hand engulfed him he saw the thing. He felt he was being trodden down by a voiceless crowd. He seemed to hear their feet. It was the blood pounding in the great hand. His struggles to free himself became the pressure that crushed him. He was squeezed to death by his own fist.

The kitchen walls cracked. The ceiling twisted and rose. The gas main exploded. The house went up in the air. The house next door lost its windows.

Only fragments of the man were found. There seemed to be a lot of them. The ambulance men said it always seemed to be like that.

The Falklands Quotations and Poems

I Press

'Skinhead Ian "Walter" Mitty would put the frighters on anyone. With his close-shaved head, tattoo-covered body and heavy bovver boots, he looks every inch what he is – a hard man. But Walter, 20, from Richmond, Yorkshire, was near to tears yesterday when he learnt that his dearest wish – to get at the Argies with his bare hands – had been denied.' – *Reporter*[1]

Precision technology invented by scientists and built
    by skilled engineers
Was used in the state-of-the-art comms room
On HMS Invincible
To send this report
From the task force
To a newspaper

And later violent denunciations of football louts
Were published by the same press
That complains of the impurity of the water
While it swims in its own cess

II High Opinions

'I have a high opinion of 3 Para; they were very hard men. Some of them said they had only joined because they could kill legally.' – *Falkland Islander*[2]

Only the very wise know what they do
They know they may not ask too much
And that their questions should not lead
To questions of greater ignorance

Not that we should be patient with fools
Or sit with torturers or work for the sellers of lies
But that the mother tongue we speak and hear each day
Is the language which must be translated to us
Before we understand what we say and hear

If anyone has a high opinion of those who wish to kill
We should ask what *they* wished who made the killing
    legal
The orator is responsible for what the mob says
And politicians for crimes their acts make legal
Where torture is legal many have high opinions of those
    hard enough to torture
If gutters could think they'd have high opinions of
    sewage
But gutters keep their innocence: they only seem to
    gurgle with glee as they devour filth

Once conquerors boasted of the numbers they'd killed
After Hiroshima they claimed the number was less
We need not believe every lout's posturings
But the bones of dead patriots murmur and corrupt the
    mother land in which they're buried
It would be better to cast their bones in the gutter and let
    the rain babble harmlessly over them
And when we're told to Rejoice! Just rejoice!
    It would be wiser to shudder

III Titus 9

A newspaper ran a daily competition for 'Argy-Bargie'
jokes. Nine-year-old Titus won £5 for a joke about two
British soldiers killing hundreds of 'Argy' soldiers.[3]

Five pounds for a little boy's story
Of a few hundred Argies dead
What sort of tales do they tell you

As they tuck you into bed?
With luck you'll have a nightmare
Full of bleeding Argie wops
And wake in the night and scream
Then write and tell us how many you saw
And your number might come up tops
In our 'Bingo-War-Game Dream'
If you claim thousands of bodies
And thousands and thousands more
And are careful how you spell
We'll send you a ton of ice cream
For helping our paper win
The Great Circulation War
But Titus 9 of Brighton
Hear this and remember well
The laughter of devils is louder
Than the groans of the damned in hell
And the colour of black-and-white is red
When papers have blood to sell
In the language of Shakespeare say it
While jackals howl in the pit
We should speak and write only that
Which is seemly and decent and fit
For many millions have perished
By bombs and bullets and swords
But beyond all counting are those who were
Sent to their death by words

IV An Armchair

He sat in a heavy armchair
Many summers had faded the cloth and time had become
    its pattern as if it could be bought from a superior
       sales catalogue
His brown shoes were cleaned with three brushes

One dubbed cream – one gave the first polish – one the
    gentleman's finish
Two brushes scraped and flattened his yellow-grey hair
Where his flannels stretched tight over his thighs the
    creases were two rigid lines
His sportsjacket and waistcoat were cut from the same
    check
And there was a tartan tie
With the marks of old knots crushed into the cloth like a
    wizened Lilliputian throat hanging under the knot
When he went into the world he tied his tie in rage
His mouth rarely closed and over it like a wraith of
    smoke from a pit there was a small moustache
His eyes were intense but dead like eyes cut from a
    photograph – upturned bottles askew in a standing
      ocean
His stomach bulged – it might have been cut from an
    animal and awkwardly strapped onto him with a
      truss
In one hand he held a tumbler of gin and tonic and ice
And said
The wisp of smoke moved heavily as if the pit gave off
    swamp gas
And the creases in the tie were as grey as the encrustations
    and scourings left by years of rain under a drain
      spout
And I saw his fingernails were flat as if they'd been
    trodden on
And the ice in his tumbler was still
        We must turf 'em out
          Know our local lads are keen for a crack at 'em
          Die for our liberties like in my young day
In the room there was silence
The armchair aged in the sun
Authority had handed me a form with a box to fill in

He rattled his ice – it clinked like a toy sabre
He was an elderly man – older than the armchair and the
    elm that would coffin him had long been old
The friends of his youth lay at Arnheim and their fathers
    at Flanders
And the horrors I thought I would be spared because so
    many had suffered them
Were there
Time had gone and nothing is learned and no one is
    spared
Cruelty drinks gin from a tumbler and evil talks as if it
    read a cartoon
And we are killed by the horror in the armchair

V Change

'On the way down [to the Falklands], this chap had been
saying that he would never be able to press the button
when the time came; he could never kill someone like that.
Later, after his first Sea Dart firing, someone asked him
how he felt. "Bloody marvellous".'[4]

The weapon has not changed
Your uniform has not changed
The enemy's uniform has not changed
The buttons and buckles and zips ripped open on gaping
    camouflage combat-jackets have not changed
Rain soaks the blood dried into camouflage combat-
    jackets and it runs
Rain and blood do not change
The water through which missiles travel has not changed
The water in dead men's boots does not change
The sky through which missiles travel does not change
The albatross and gull hear men's curses and warning
    cries as they hear one sheep call to another

Their business is land to nest and shore to pillage: they
     scream and are not changed
The earth which is torn open by missiles does not change
Earth corrupts the body and neither is changed
The dead in camouflage combat-jackets seemed dressed in
     crumbled maps of the land they died for and are not
        changed
Give the dead maps and they do not march
Set them up in motley and they do not dance
The soldier falls back from the bayonet and writhes on his
     trench floor like a corpse gnashing its teeth in the
        grave and the worms wake in their clay walls and
        are not changed
It is the same with dust as with sand: unchanging
And it is the same with rock
Fire begets smoke but it drifts away – and if the fire is
     ardent it drives the smoke from it
This lesson is taught on battlefields and in hallways and
     other places
Your children will grow but you will not know it because
     you will not see whether their eyes are changed
When they run to greet you the dead enemy will place his
     hands over their eyes
If they stumble he will catch them and laugh
And when you call to them in anger or loneliness – after
     your kind – he will weep for you
The dead cannot take away their hands
The enemy you killed has not changed
He is merely dead
You are changed
And now you must return to your children and city

VI Ajax Bay

'When the first one went down, right in front of us, straight into the water off Ajax Bay, it seemed as though the whole Commando Brigade stood up and cheered and clapped and jumped for joy.' – *Marine*[5]

The false camaraderie of ranks divided by class
When leaders cannot let down their lads
And the led must respect the officer gentlemen
So that sentimentality corrupts violence
Making it mawkish sustained and bloodier
And the jeering and monkey-dancing as men are killed
    and burned and mutilated
And the officers' brutal efficiency and nabob-clumsiness
And the rank-pique that kills the led
Yet putting all this aside
Men went bare-handed into fires to bring out wounded
And set down helicopters on white cliff-faces shrouded in
    blizzard snow
Certainly there was good here
And we regret that persistence is turned to stubbornness
And great skill into a wizard's tricks
At home many are left to rot in sickness
And many innocent shut in prisons of paper stone panic
    and listless despair.
This waste! – for the lease on a millstone
And a bogland for sheep and geese and graves

VII Crosses

To tighten its grip on power a reactionary government
    invaded the islands
To tighten its grip on power a reactionary government
    invaded the islands that had been invaded

A reactionary government lost
A reactionary government won
A reactionary government fell
A reactionary government tightened its grip on power
A reactionary government stood trial
A reactionary government held elections
A reactionary government was condemned by the people
A reactionary government was re-elected by the people
 The ballot papers could have been marked with
   upright crosses

The Lord of the Beasts

How inefficient is the Lord of the Beasts!
The jaguar brings down the doe in seconds
The fish darts from the rock and quickly devours the
    meal speared on its snout
The hawk hovers but is swift in the drop
If it flies off to nestlings the little mouse gripped in its
    talons as if gift-wrapped by Lucifer is already dead
The cat couldn't fall on its prey faster if it were a pencil
    that drew it
And it doesn't play with it because it can't work out how
    to kill it but to sharpen its skills
It's true snakes engorge a rabbit as slowly as if they
      gave birth to it backwards: but that's not because
        they're condemned forever to choke on the apple
          but because they wolf their food whole like
            Man the Lord of the Beasts!
Man obliterates thousands in a flash (praise where it's due)
    as if they had never been
But the rest?
Some of the gassed took years to die
Children he's attacked – and not with the furtive efforts
    of a lonely street-lurker but assisted by pals and
      encouraged by bonuses and every token of
        honour – linger for days
Some even hang on for years and die at a great age when
    a bug (of which he claims to be lord) brings them
      down in an hour
After a battle he leaves the field littered with wounded
    muttering scorn or bellowing taunts at his
      incompetence
And after an air raid people only half dead skulk under
    the rubble and jeer 'can't catch me!'

The world is full of his failures

Those in the jungle he can ignore – but at home he must
build houses to hide people so fit they lie on their
back in bed for years

And many are left to parade the streets and taunt him
with their crutches and plastic limbs – their
wheelchairs and faces like joke masks

Out of respect for his feelings you contrive not to see
them but who could deny them their right to mock?

If the lamb gets away it's because the lion is old or
dyspeptic

But men go out killing in their prime – and they're not
restricted to natural weapons like the other poor
beasts – they have the most modern equipment

And it's his favourite occupation – yet even jackals and
hyenas could give him some tips!

The Lord of the Beasts is an inefficient killer

You'd think he'd be ashamed to kneel at his thanksgiving
services

Or is he kneeling in shame at how many got away?

A Story

There was once a rich man
To get rich he did many bad things
He stole a dustbin from an old woman and sold it back to
     her with an anti-theft device
He lent money and made the borrowers repay twice as
     much
He made the poor work for him and took half of what
     they earned so that they paid him to keep them poor
But he didn't mind: he was rich
Only one thing worried him
Down the road lived another rich man
Now our man knew how he'd got his own money and he
     said to himself
This other man must be as wicked as me
So he didn't trust him: he slept with a pistol under his
     head
That should've made him feel safe
But it didn't
Did the pistol still work?
Were the bullets dud?
Perhaps his neighbour could creep like a cat and come
     with his gun to rob him
So he sat up all night trying to keep awake and nodding
     off over his pistol
Sometimes he woke with a start
Sometimes the pistol fell from his hands and he snatched
     at it
Once he saw a shadow creeping towards his bed
He fired
The safety catch was on
After that he tried to stay awake with the safety catch off
You could see him bent over the muzzle

Gaunt and tired
Grizzled stubble on his chin
Nodding and muttering and cursing his neighbour
The man who knew what thieves were because he was a
    thief and who put a pistol under his head so that he
        could sleep in peace
Lived in terror
And one day he nodded off and shot himself

Sports Ground Inferno

Ranks of spectators in the wooden stand

Excitement! Sensation! – the match swings this way and
     that

Sudden heat – spectators look round – they watch the
     clothes of others near them smoulder and burst into
     flames

The floor crackles – in an instant the roof is a rolling sea
     of fire

Those who escape to the pitch look back

In the bright furnace they see dark blemishes like lumps
     of coal – bodies

A man in blazing clothes and with an expressionless face
     comes from the flames

And strolls – that is the word witnesses will use later –
     over the pitch

Others sit upright in their seats as flames run between
     them along the handrails

They do not seem to know what is happening to them or
     what they might do to save themselves

Later that day survivors will stand by the charred corpses
     and tell how they had felt they were in a dream

And in this way one Saturday afternoon as women
     worked or drank tea with their neighbours and
     children played or fed their pets

The little holocaust fell on the busy city where many
     dreamed and did not know what they might do to
     save themselves

Water

In a certain city there had been for many hundreds of years a shortage of water. This caused disease and other suffering to the citizens. Each spring there was a heavy rainfall and the silent people watched the precious life-stream running in gutters that would soon be as dry as bone. In time modern machines were constructed. There were new spinning factories and iron foundries in the city. These places needed more water and so did the new workers. The city's rulers were practical and philanthropic men. They used their new machines to build a dam in the hills over the city. The dam collected all the water the city needed. Unfortunately when the spring rains fell the lake behind the dam became too full. There was a danger that the pressure of water would explode and engulf the city in sudden destruction. The dam wall shook like the hand of a sick man. This terrified the workers and some of them ran away from the factories and lived in the hills. In the general panic there was rioting and looting. Priests held special services. Factory owners called on the government to enforce law and order.

As the rulers of the city had been clever enough to build the dam they ought to have been clever enough to make it safe. They might have built aqueducts to take the water safely round the city or through the parks and squares to make them beautiful with lakes and fountains. But understand that there was panic and fear of collapse. In such times rulers don't blame the machinery of society but its people. Indeed they look on disaster as a test of national spirit. So instead of reconstructing the dam the rulers called on the citizens to serve their city with greater efforts: they were to drink more water.

Water drinking festivals were organized. Drinking

squads patrolled the streets. The good citizen was seen at all times sipping from a glass of water in his hand. Medals were given to those who consumed large quantities. It's surprising what well-intentioned and public-spirited individuals can do on such occasions. One man drank fifty gallons of water each week for three weeks running before he drowned internally. He asked to be buried in a bath. There was much washing of the person and of possessions. People whose curtains were not constantly dripping could expect to have their windows broken by groups of young pioneers who were called The Water Babies. As the whole city was damp and as people went about in clothes that had been laundered to shreds and slept in damp beds, there was a lot of influenza about. Newspapers published daily casualty lists. These showed great increases in the number of cases of pneumonia. People also suffered from water on the knee and on the brain. Because the doorsteps and streets were washed so often many people slipped and the casualty service had to deal with sprained ankles and broken legs and backs. Of course the wounded – who had already made the sacrifice – could no longer drink very much or wash very often. The burden fell more heavily on the rest.

About this time patriotic people began to set fire to their houses so that firemen could hose them down. Loyalists also burned public buildings such as galleries, museums and schools. Nothing could be allowed to impede the city's efforts. National security was at stake. We can confidently say that the people's morale was never higher. And it worked. The level of water behind the dam fell. This overwhelming argument was used against those few disruptive elements who asked whether there might not be an easier way to control the dam. The dam wall no longer trembled. Dissenters were taken to their cell windows and made to stare up at it and declare that it stood as firm as a rock. Every day the media reminded the people of the days when the dam had been called Old Palsied and they had lived in fear of The Burst. Things were going well. All the more reason, then, for the massive outbreak of dropsy to come as such a severe blow to the regime. This blow was followed by another: people began to burst. The rulers even wondered if the people could hold out. As the Governor looked from his window he saw passers by fall over in the street and roll to the side of houses and lie there for minutes at a time without drinking. Perhaps there were inherent weaknesses in the national character. How could such a nation survive?

The Governor himself felt worn out by the struggle against water. He decided to address the people – perhaps, he told himself, for the last time. The Water Police rounded up the survivors and assembled them on the main square. The Governor was surprised at the smallness of the crowd. If the people had not been so bloated he would have seen that it was even smaller than he thought. As the Governor spoke one or two exploded. A new illness had broken out: a fever which heated the blood and so caused the water to boil. Sufferers emitted large amounts of steam and a high whistling scream from their ears, mouth, nose and anus till their bodies burst. The Governor spoke with great dignity, raising his voice over the screaming, blurping, plopping, pissing and exploding. 'Fellow citizens! This morning the figures were delivered to my desk. The level of water in the dam is now so low that – should any of you survive – you will be assured of three whole years without danger of a dam burst. What the future holds beyond then we cannot tell, but these three years are safe – no matter how much rain falls! Citizens I salute your great victory! God bless us!' He then became over-heated with patriotic fervour and began to boil. He screamed and emitted a cloud of steam. The crowd had counted up to five before he exploded. As spring rainclouds gathered on the hills Water Police went among the crowd using the new-fangled hose-and-pump contraptions that had recently been introduced to enable them to pump water down the gullet of those who, however willing, were unable to swallow any more.

I Could Not Say

I could not say to those gathered in ghettoes to be gassed
Or to the El Salvadorean woman whose son was scalped
    and blinded
By soldiers looking for info before they butchered him
It is wrong to fight
When the problem is simple why make the solution hard?
But when the problem is hard we need a simple solution

Soldiers who fought the SS in Europe were sent to Africa
    to fight freedom fighters
The freedom fighters called the soldiers murderers
Soon the freedom fighters were honoured and entered
    into the councils of nations
So the soldiers were murderers?
No the regimental histories were not rewritten or medals
    taken from showcases
The soldiers were not murderers but merely instruments
Those who are instruments turn into beasts as the history
    of great follies makes clear

Too many are willing to squeeze triggers – pull levers –
    press buttons
And be instruments
That is why the rest of us are at the mercy of beasts
When enemies go to war it is too late to say it is wrong to
    fight
It must be said in peace
If you arm for war you make yourselves instruments and
    soon you will commit the great follies of beasts
You will murder the whimpering child – the dazed old –
    and the generations between
They are all as innocent as you
To spare you this hard fate there is a simple solution

It is better to kill your parents and wipe the blood from
    your hands on their grey heads than kill old people
        you have not seen
It is better to kill your child and wander the streets with
    its blood on your hands than kill children you have
        never heard cry
In this way you will keep your innocence

And there are even simpler ways to keep it
Bows and arrows are beyond human understanding –
    riddles set by devils to astound gods
But nuclear weapons are simple and may easily be
    understood

The Window

The bombardment and flushing-out had ended some days ago. The bombardiers were walking in the ruined town. Broken bits of buildings stuck up from the piles of rubble. The town looked like the fossilized graveyard of a herd of giant prehistoric reptiles.

They went into one of the ruined houses. One wall still stood. It was three storeys high. It was covered with the wallpapers and paints of several rooms. The joist holes for the floors and staircases were as neat as rows of bullet holes. Fireplaces still clung to it. The other walls, the floors and the roof were heaped on the ground to one side where the blast had blown them. The doors were gone from the hinges. There was a smell of damp dust and of acrid smoke from fires survivors had lit in some of the other ruins.

In the wall one window was left. It wasn't even cracked. A woman stood on a box in front of it and cleaned the glass. She had a rag and she'd filled an old plastic basin – the rim was badly chipped – at the emergency watertank on the square.

She wore bottle-green ankle-socks over her stockings, a dark mauve skirt, a grey jumper and a dark overcoat with large flat ugly buttons and a skimpy mottled bit of velveteen at the collar. Under the overcoat she wore an apron – pale green with blue zigzags. Round her neck there was a tooth-check scarf.

The woman saw the bombardiers. She stopped cleaning the window. As there were only three bombardiers she thought they were marauders. They would harm her. She raised her hands. One of them held the sopping rag. It dripped. The box didn't wobble.

The bombardiers stared at her. One of them gave a

quick reassuring wave. His hand rose no higher than his shoulder. The woman took the wave as an order to go on working. She thanked the bombardiers with two sharp syllables in her own language and gave an awkward but courtly little bow.

She turned her back on the bombardiers and went on cleaning the window. She began to jabber. Her voice was rather loud – as if she were talking to someone over her shoulder. That's how she'd shouted to her daughter or a neighbour before the house was ruined.

One bombardier asked the others 'Why clean a window in a ruin?'

Another asked 'What's she saying?'

Their voices were low. The first bombardier said 'She's saying it wasn't me. Had nothing to do with it. Didn't know what was going on.'

The bombardiers had a few hours off while the battery was rested. They walked on like tourists inspecting the ruins. They came to a low wall and sat on it. They'd drunk beer at the canteen tent. The day was sunny and still.

'Why?'

In the far distance an army lorry's wheels began to churn in mud.

'Mad. Thinks she's still at home with the family.'

'It was her house. She's getting on with minding the home.'

'It's where she worked. Thinks she's got to get it clean or the missuss'll sack her. Fall behind with the rent. Get chuck out.'

'The day our mum was bombed she swep the floor, hung the mat out to dry – the firehoses'd soaked it – boarded up the wall and cooked tea on our primus. My brother had to sit at the kitchen table and do his homework. Wiped the brick-dust off his exercise book. His teacher rowed him out for being mucky.'

'When a cathedral's bombed there's always one window left standing.'

'A cathedral's got lots of windows. One of 'em's bound to survive. Same with towns. You send so many shells in you think only the worms are happy. Then some bastard crawls out of the ground. Same with soldiers and dugouts. There's so many people some survive.'

During the following days the incident was talked of a few times in the battery. The medical orderly said the woman was mad. But even if the shells and bombs had driven her mad, wasn't she doing something sane when she cleaned the window? The padre took it up in a sermon.

Some time later the three bombardiers walked through the ruins again.

'Let's look at the window.'

They couldn't find the house. Perhaps the wall had fallen down. They gave up looking and came on it by chance on their way back. One of them recognised the wallpaper in the top bedroom. They walked into the ground floor. There was the window. It was clean. Did the woman clean it every day? There was only one stain on it. Near the bottom some fluid had splashed across the glass. It had left a mark like the tongue of a cartoon fox.

The three bombardiers stared at the window for a minute.

'The old bird not here.'

'Should leave a tin of coffee on the ledge.'

'Too late. No time to come back. Battery moves tomorrow. All this'll be knock down when they rebuild. I hope the old crow –'

He stopped as the arm swung and the stone hit the glass. It shattered. The window had two panes. The bottom pane was shattered. A bombardier bent. He picked up a second stone – really a corner of a brick. He threw it at the top pane. It broke. Part of it shattered into the street. Part of it fell down and got hooked up on the jagged bits of the pane below — as if it was cutting the throat that ate it.

There was silence. There were no little fires burning in the ruins. The people had been moved out. A booby trap had blown off a soldier's foot.

None of the bombardiers spoke. War had turned them into expert watchers. They'd spied for targets and their eyes had wandered over the ruins they and others had made. Now perhaps they were waiting for the woman to come in screaming. Or to wander in with her chipped basin of water, see the broken window, kneel down and cry. Or shout. After the first shout she wouldn't risk cursing them. She'd curse the ruins. Or pray. Or mutter to herself as if she was telling the rubble how she'd lost her children. Or just say over and over in her strange language the word for hunger.

The woman didn't come. The bombardiers stood in silence for five minutes — a long time in a break in a war. Then they went away.

To them for a few days war seemed a little more decent.

You Are the First Generation

Each generation before us had a heaven
The miserable of the earth would be fed and clothed and
	the mighty stripped naked of power
So misery was borne on earth and scant happiness
	sacrificed
For joy in a place which did not exist in eternity on a
	calendar that began with an event that did not take
		place
But if the superstitious had not hoped for heaven the
	rulers would not have feared hell
They would have fallen on the people like wild beasts
Without illusions all would have perished
From illusions came understanding and truth – as always
In the flames heretics howled the ugly imprecations
That Newton refracted in prisms and found five laws
There was no god but he walked among us

Now we have made the machines and a thousand suns
	stand over the night and the darkness of day
Illusions no longer bring happiness or make us do good
If we believe we do not believe as the old believers
	believed
If we believe in their god we turn into devils
All gods are destroyed by their worshippers' miracles
We have killed god: he is possessed with devils
The calendar has fallen into its own emptiness
And what is true of religion is true of politics – as always
We are the first generation without a heaven
We howl because we're in heaven
We are armageddon
Satan presides at our judgement

Already there are signs
The rich richer – the poor poorer
Children mortgaged for generations with the debts of
    their fathers
Aristocratic skeletons resurrected with bone grafts
Frenzy at little wars
Confusion and slippery management
More prisoners – calls for capital punishment
In an age of technology these things are among the first
    signs of fascism
Then there are nuclear weapons: we arm the figure in the
    mirror and fear it
There is no devil but he walks among us

To understand our state consider a simple creature
The startled hare in the torchlight
Erect ears as tall as the rest of its body
Each strand of fur as rigid as a rifle barrel
Each whisker as tense as a trigger-finger
The eyes as concentrated as two nails in a coffin
For a moment it eavesdrops on death
And chews
Then bolts over the grass in every direction between
    cradle and grave
And chews
The jaws move at their own pace as if they did not belong
    to the leaping body
They work as fast as bobbins knitting a shroud
It is the delirious gossip of one who sleeps
Or the ticks in a clockwork mask on a corpse
Before the hunter came it learned: eat or die
It repeats its lesson to the gun that knocks it in the air
It chews
And somersaults into the grave with a mouthful of grass

Can you survive your strengths?

Illusions have given you armies and crafts – factories
farms hovels and citadels – injustice from which
you made noble laws and errors which served
you as the highest truth

You were idols of clay with feet of marble and danced on
water

It was all god would allow you to do – he coveted the
earth and its fruits

God was devious and the oracles spoke riddles

So heretics were confused and foolish: but they could not
lie

You are the first generation able to lie

The machines have told you the truth: they do not covet
or riddle

Illusions will not save you from the death lies bring

Learn to be human

Only humans can live with machines

Only devils can live with god

Machines are not devious and they cannot forgive

Nor can they change but you are not made in their image

To justify your crimes you boast you stand in the ranks
of angels

To excuse your brutalities you claim the birthright of
beasts

Now you must learn to be human

Or you will somersault into the grave with a mouthful of
grass

The Swallows

At five in the morning the flock of swallows flew down
    to perch on the little boat
In rows on the railing and ropes preening and shrilly
    chittering
Their heads turn with a series of quick little jerks as if
    they worked on ratchets
Some burrow their beaks into their backs – some
    suddenly shoot out a wing – a fan hit open or razor
        slash – and run the edge through their beaks
The edge is marked like a samurai pennant with little
    white squares and their eyes are set in a black band
They preen as insistently as if they gnawed their own
    flesh
When they stop their faces are blank
The pin-thin beaks jut from the downy round heads like
    pivots on top of globes
For ten minutes the mob chivvies and squeaks and vies
    for places though no place is more sheltered than
        another or gives a better view
They jerk as awkwardly as puppets tangled in their
    strings
The noise! – madmen let loose in a belfry or condemned
    fighting their executioners
And suddenly they are silent – all at the same instant
Not one sound or movement
Not even a feather ruffles
They are not asleep
After five minutes one slightly cocks its head – one looks
    down at its feet – one opens and shuts its silent beak
Then they are still
No wind or wave or traffic

They look before them as if each gazed at the same thing
    though many perch back to back
And minutes pass
There is a photograph taken inside a room that's said to
    show the last man being shot in the second world
      war: he falls back from a sunny window
        dropping his gun
In every war someone is the last to be killed
In time someone will be the last to be killed by any
    weapon
Then there will be silence – a great peace will grow and
    we can imagine how it will change as time passes
Already memorials to that man or woman stand in our
    streets and birds come to rest on them
Suddenly the swallows rise in a fast sweep and swirl
    down the wind tunnel over the river
There is one fading screech
And I am left with the bare rail and the ropes

[Notes]

1 *Gotcha!* (The Media, the Government and the Falklands
Crisis) by Robert Harris. Faber & Faber, 1983. p. 36.
(Reprinted by permission of the Peters, Fraser and
Dunlop Group.)
2 *Task Force: The Falklands War, 1982* by Martin
Middlebrook. Penguin Books, 1985. p. 282. (Reprinted
by permission of Penguin Books.)
3 *Gotcha!* p. 46.
4 *Task Force*, p. 165.
5 *Task Force*, p. 231.

Summer

For Hans Werner Henze

Summer was first presented in the Cottesloe (National Theatre), on 27 January 1982, with the following cast:

DAVID	David Yelland
XENIA	Anna Massey
ANN	Eleanor David
MARTHE	Yvonne Bryceland
GERMAN	David Ryall

Directed by Edward Bond
Designed by Hayden Griffin
Lighting by Rory Dempster
Sound by Rick Clarke

Scenes
1. House. Night.
2. House. Morning.
3. House. Afternoon.
4. Island. Late afternoon.
5. House. Night.
6. House. Morning.
7. House. Late morning. (The Agreement)

In the first production there was an interval after Scene 5. The author would have preferred an interval after Scene 6. The last scene could be played slowly, lasting quite a number of minutes. The lines could be separated into their natural groups.

The present.
Eastern Europe.

The terrace of a cliff house facing the sea. Down right a door leads downstairs to the street. Up right a door leads upstairs to other parts of the house. In the wall at the back, left, a door leads to a room. Left, railings face the sea.

ONE

The house. Night.
DAVID *comes in with* XENIA *and* ANN. *He carries cases.*
XENIA *and* ANN *carry hand luggage.*

DAVID: You're in your old room. I'm sorry I couldn't meet you at the airport.

XENIA: It doesn't matter.

DAVID (*smiles*): I'd swapped with a colleague to have the morning off.

XENIA: It wasn't your fault our plane was late. We sat at Heathrow all day.

DAVID: I'll take these things up and fetch the rest from below.

ANN: I'll help you.

DAVID: No no I can manage. You must be tired.

DAVID goes.

XENIA (*calling after him*): Where's Marthe?

ANN (*glances round*): Nothing's changed.

XENIA: You don't know it as well as I do. That hideous new hotel. A dreadful holiday camp stood on end. I shouldn't complain. People must have holidays. I'll be all right tomorrow. Waiting at airports always depresses me. It's so inefficient. At least they've left the sea where it was. Thank God you don't see the hotel from here. You'll see it from below.

DAVID comes in with two cases. He nods at a case already there.

DAVID: I'll come back for that.

XENIA: Where's your mother?

DAVID: Resting.

XENIA: I suppose your new hotel has a discotheque?

DAVID: Wednesdays and Saturdays.

> DAVID *goes upstairs.* XENIA *follows him out. She takes her hand luggage.* ANN *is alone. She goes to the railing and looks at the sea.* DAVID *comes back.*

DAVID (*points to the case*): Shall I put that in your room?

ANN: Yes.

DAVID: I'm glad you're back.

ANN: Thank you.

DAVID: Are you tired?

ANN: A little.

DAVID: I have to work in the morning. I have the afternoon off. I'll take you swimming.

ANN: Thank you.

DAVID: I've arranged to have most of my time off while you're here. I have to go in some mornings to see a sick child.

XENIA (*off, calls*): Ann.

ANN (*calls*): Coming. (*To* DAVID:) You mustn't inconvenience your colleagues because of me.

DAVID: It's part of my holidays.

> ANN *goes.* DAVID *is alone. He taps on the rear door.*

(*Low:*) She's gone upstairs.

> DAVID *sits. He stretches his legs in front of him and broods. After a few moments the door opens and* MARTHE *comes out.*

MARTHE: When I hear her voice it's as if I'm back in the past.

DAVID: Why let her come?

MARTHE: I can't stop her. Anyone can book the guest rooms.

DAVID: Say they're already booked.

MARTHE: Don't be a child. I don't mind her.

DAVID: She upsets you. Let me send her away.

MARTHE: It would be cruel to do it now. Let things go on as before.

DAVID: As you please. But don't see her tonight. That can wait till the morning.

MARTHE: Yes that would be best.

ANN *comes in.*

ANN: Hello.

MARTHE: My dear. (*She kisses* ANN.) Was it a dreadful journey?

ANN: The plane took off late. We had to wait at the airport. We couldn't leave because our flight could have been called at any time.

XENIA (*off, calls*): Ann darling.

ANN: Excuse me. (*Calls:*) Yes?

XENIA (*off, calls*): Bring my keys. I want to undo my cases.

ANN (*calls*): I haven't got them.

XENIA (*off, calls*): I gave them to you when we left the house.

ANN (*calls*): They're in your handbag.

XENIA (*off, calls*): O no you've left them behind! It's too much.

ANN (*calls*): Look in your handbag.

MARTHE (*moving towards her room*): Will you want anything to eat?

ANN: No, we've been eating all day.

MARTHE: You look well.

ANN: Thank you.

MARTHE: A little pale. You'll soon catch the sun. Till the morning. We'll breakfast together.

MARTHE *goes into her room and shuts the door.*

DAVID: Has she lost her keys?

ANN: I don't know. Anyway a lot of her things are in my cases.

DAVID: How's your father?

ANN: Always the same. He's on a diet. He's been on it for years. He enjoys having the house to himself while we're away.

DAVID: I thought you were a happy family.

ANN: We are. We never quarrel. I meant it must be nice when there's no one to bump into.

DAVID: Shall I come to your room tonight?

ANN: No, if you don't mind. The journey's tired me.

DAVID: It's all right. You'll feel better after you've slept. Would your mother like a drink?

ANN: I'll ask when I go up.

DAVID: Is anything wrong?

ANN: O please. I've been travelling with strangers all day. Surely it's natural for me to want to be quiet? It doesn't mean I'm ill, does it? Why must you – intrude all the time?

DAVID: You've grown very beautiful this year.

XENIA *comes in.*

XENIA: I was in the hallway at the foot of the stairs. Just before we left the house. Daddy had brought the car to the front. I gave them to you to mind and went back to make sure Timmy was shut in the kitchen. You remember?

ANN: No.

XENIA: It's too much. On top of everything. Sometimes one can't rely on you at all. Have you looked for them?

ANN: I haven't got them.

XENIA: Give me your bag. (*She looks in* ANN's *travelling bag. She finds keys.*) These are yours.

ANN: Yes.

XENIA: How absurd. I'll have to break the locks. The three cases will be ruined. Shops won't replace locks on cases anymore. David, have you got any case keys?

DAVID: Yes, in my room.

XENIA: Did you buy your cases in the West?

DAVID: No.

XENIA: Then your keys won't fit my locks. Please bring me a hammer and a robust screwdriver.

DAVID: No. It's silly to break them. I'll get some keys for you to try in the morning. Ann or my mother will lend you what you need till then.

XENIA: I like to feel at home in this house – unpack my things and hang them in their place. Now there's all this muddle. I might as well be in a hotel.

DAVID: You've had a bad day.

XENIA: Well at least Ann brought her own keys. We must be grateful she didn't leave them behind with mine. It will do me good to put up with the inconvenience. I'm not a good traveller. I don't know why Ann travels with me. If we had the same luggage your keys would have fitted mine. Have you looked in your pockets?

ANN: You didn't give me your keys.

XENIA: Well if you did put them in your pocket they'll have dropped out in the plane or the airport, so I hope you didn't.

DAVID: Would you like a drink?

XENIA: I'm surprised they didn't build the hotel on one of the islands. Yes I know the islands are a national monument. That wouldn't stop them. Can you still bathe from these rocks?

DAVID: Why not?

XENIA: Doesn't the hotel litter float by?

DAVID: The odd ice cream carton.

XENIA: I shall telephone Daddy in the morning and ask him

to look for my keys on the hall table. I hope he doesn't find them before I telephone.

DAVID: A military man would survive the shock.

XENIA: It isn't a question of shock. It would distress him to know I had been unable to open my cases after a tiring journey. That's why I want to reassure him I'm not upset. It's a question of two people caring for one another.

ANN: I don't see the point of knowing they're on the hall table.

XENIA: If I know they're there I won't spend the whole of the holiday worrying about them. Are the telephones working?

DAVID: Yes.

XENIA: They didn't two years ago.

DAVID: That was after the hurricane.

XENIA: So it was. Where's Marthe?

DAVID: In her room.

XENIA: Is she unwell?

DAVID: She lives down here now.

XENIA: Why?

DAVID: To be next to the terrace. She sits there during the day.

XENIA:: What's the matter? She's ill.

DAVID: Yes.

XENIA: Seriously? I must go to her.

DAVID: You'll see her in the morning. She needs rest.

XENIA: But what's the matter with her? Why didn't you tell me before?

DAVID: I didn't have a chance.

XENIA: Nonsense. You could have told me down in the street.

DAVID: She has a reticulosis.

XENIA: What's that? Please don't confuse me with medical jargon.

DAVID: It's a disease of the lymphatic glands.

XENIA: Is it serious?

DAVID: Yes it's terminal.

XENIA: But she'll get better?

DAVID: No.

XENIA: You think she ...?

DAVID: Yes.

XENIA: David what are you telling me? Surely there's a cure?
   (*Panic whisper:*) Dear god can she hear us? Really David I
   think you might have told me sooner. That ridiculous fuss
   about my keys.

DAVID: It doesn't matter. Please don't upset yourself.

XENIA: Of course I'm upset. It's a terrible shock.

DAVID: Yes.

XENIA: Is there no cure?

DAVID: No.

XENIA: O god. Is she in pain? Our holiday is off. You
   should have written and told me.

DAVID: She wouldn't let me write. You'd have come anyway.

XENIA: Certainly, to nurse her – or help in some other way.
   You must tell me what to do.

DAVID: Don't strain her. Just behave as you normally would.

XENIA: Of course, of course. How long will it take? You
   can't possibly know. Tell me the worst so I'm prepared. Is
   she in pain? Can she walk?

DAVID: You won't see much change so far. She has no pain.
   We've known for six weeks she was dying. I don't know
   how much longer she'll live. It doesn't shock her now. She
   knows it's true.

XENIA: Are you treating her?

DAVID: Yes.

XENIA: David I'm so sorry.

DAVID: Yes it's very sad.

XENIA: She's lucky to have you. You will tell me what I can
   do? Nursing, washing, anything.

DAVID: Thank you but there is nothing.

XENIA: And you, if we can help you in any way. It's terrible for you. You are so close. We mustn't stay here gossiping. She must have rest and quiet.

DAVID: You've forgotten what else I said. Please behave as you normally would. Otherwise you'll frighten her and aggravate her condition.

XENIA: Yes of course. David goodnight. Ann come with me.

DAVID: Goodnight.

> XENIA *goes.* ANN *looks at* DAVID *and then follows her mother out. He sits hunched in the chair and empties his mind.*

TWO

> *The house. Morning.*
> MARTHE *sits in her chair up left.*
> XENIA *comes in.*

XENIA: Marthe.

MARTHE: Hello. How are you? (XENIA *kisses her.*)

XENIA: Oughtn't you to lie down? I'm surprised David lets you sit out here.

MARTHE: Did you sleep well?

XENIA: Would you expect me to? I was so tired when I arrived. We'd spent all day at Heathrow. After David told me you were ill I hardly slept at all. He seems very pessimistic about this lymphatic-thing. Sometimes doctors almost sound proud of the diseases they're treating. They like to look on the dark side so that they can claim a miracle cure. It's good for their reputation even if it's bad for their patients. Let me get you a shawl.

MARTHE: I'd be far too hot.

XENIA: My mother moved into that room whenever she was ill.

MARTHE: So she did. I'd forgotten.

XENIA: Fortunately I can stay on this year till you're better. Ann will look after the boutique. It's time she learned to stand on her own feet. I can keep in touch by telephone. I'll have to go back for the spring buy but that won't –

MARTHE: I can't disrupt your life like that.

XENIA: Well I've offered. I hope you change your mind.

MARTHE: Thank you. We'll see.

XENIA: What d'you do all day?

MARTHE: I can still do a little work. Mostly I sit and look at the sea.

XENIA: I don't like to see you resigned like this. You seem to have given in. You're still young, your life is worth saving. How can you be sure nothing can be done? Because David's your son I suppose you find it hard to believe he's wrong. Doctors do make mistakes – more than the rest of us. Who made the diagnosis? Have you taken a second opinion? Has David discussed your treatment with a specialist?

MARTHE: Everything was done as it should be.

XENIA: Modern medicine moves so fast. They do things now that would have been miracles a few years ago. If you'd telephoned I'd have brought drugs from England. I don't know how up-to-date David's clinic is or if they have any equipment. He'd be cross if I asked.

MARTHE: He does all that can be done for me. Which isn't hard – there's very little. Did you find your keys?

XENIA: I knew my shouting woke you last night.

MARTHE: I wasn't asleep.

XENIA: David said he would get me some keys this morning. O let's not worry about the wretched things. Do you have pain?

MARTHE: No. I get tired, but that's more mental than physical. The strain.

XENIA: Come to England. David has money. And Bertie and I would help. A gift – or a loan if you wished. You could go to a private clinic for a check-up. Surely David wouldn't stop you. I've seen other people in your situation. You'll leave it and make up your mind when it's late. Then they'd have to bring you in a wheelchair. Another excuse for them to do nothing: the journey would be too tiring.

MARTHE: David says nothing can be done.

XENIA: He can't know that. I've been told not to tire you so I'll be careful. But at least I can ask you to take a fresh look at yourself. That can't do any harm! Fight. Don't sit in a chair and wait. I'm glad I didn't know you were ill before I came. I can see what's happening with a fresh mind. You're all so apathetic. You've resigned yourself as if you were meeting fate. It's not like you. A doctor's word isn't law.

MARTHE: I don't want to die.

XENIA: At least you can still talk sense. I'm sorry, but you're irresponsible. It's criminal to stay here. If you went you'd have a chance.

ANN *comes in.*

ANN (*showing two large hoops of keys*): Look. (*She kisses* XENIA.)

XENIA (*half-attention*): Good heavens there must be hundreds.

ANN (*kisses* MARTHE): Hello. I borrowed them from the hotel.

XENIA: Obviously they hadn't heard of your way with keys.

ANN: David came with me. I'll go and try them. Cross your fingers.

XENIA: Don't force the locks.

ANN *goes.*

All this fuss. If they're broken they're broken. I'll get some cheap ones in town to last till I get home. You can have the old ones. Perhaps you can still get locks fitted here. If not they'll be useful for something. She slept with David last year. Obviously he'll be thinking about other things now. Has he a steady girl? Most young doctors seem to have several unsteady ones. Ann would never live here.

MARTHE: Has she said?

XENIA: O she knows too much about the past. It would be a terrible wrong to a child to force it to fight its parents' battles. We do them enough harm without that. I've never forced my views on her. I've simply told her the truth. Children have a right to know the world they're in. I showed her the spot that used to be the library where her grandfather was arrested. I showed her the walls of the prison where he died. I showed her where his pictures hung in this house. You can still see the marks if you know where to look. Even when they paint the walls they come through again in a few months. She knows the history of every stone in this house.

MARTHE: Why do you come here every year? There are other places where you could find the sun. You're married, you have money, your own shop. You have a new life.

XENIA: It's natural to want to come back to the place where you were born. Even if it's another world. This house was my home for twenty years. I have friends who've lived on in the town. I like to speak my own language.

MARTHE: Wipe our dust from your feet. That's good advice. This isn't your home anymore. You're a stranger here. Some of the flats have changed hands eight or nine times since you left. Most of the people in them have never heard your family name.

XENIA: The trees in the garden are the same. The lizards must be distant offspring of the ones who were my pets when I was a child. It's the same sea even if it's dirtier. There are still two islands. Some of the cacti I planted on my visits have survived. I come to water them. People put out their cigarette butts in the soil. Lean from the side of their canvas chairs and grind out their cigarettes in it. That's such an ugly thing to do. It desecrates the earth. There's nothing you can say.

ANN *comes in.*

ANN: The third one. I've hung your things in the wardrobe.

XENIA: Bless you. Make a note of the key numbers. I'll telephone Daddy this evening and ask him to send duplicates. We must hope the post delivers them before we go. Don't lose those before you get them back to the hotel.

ANN: Marthe would you like us to go away?

MARTHE: No. Unless staying depresses you.

ANN: It's just that there's nothing we can do to help.

MARTHE: That's not true. Don't be sorry for me. As David can look after me I can stay here to die. I've lived on the sea since I was a child. I'd be unhappy if it was taken away now. David says he can make sure I'll feel no pain.

ANN: What is it like to be told?

XENIA (*reproof*): Ann.

MARTHE: At first I was sick. Out of fear I suppose. Once when people knew they were dying they prayed and confessed and worried like a dog that had lost its bone. They wasted the little time they had left trying to get a promise they would live for ever. Ridiculous. They could never even know the promise hadn't been given. Death is the most certain of all things yet it's the thing people try to create the most doubt about. When you die you're dead. You don't wake up. There's nothing. This is my last chance of happiness. We all share our lives. If your lives go on in their normal way, so will mine for a little longer. If they don't, I've already started to die. I don't want to do

that till I have to. So let's go on as we did before. That's
how you can help me.

XENIA: I can't. David says you're dying. That changes
everything. I don't know what to do yet – or what to think.

MARTHE: You'll get used to it.

XENIA: You've had six weeks. I'll need more than one day.

ANN: David's taking me out in his boat this afternoon. We'll
go for miles and swim in the deep sea. Far out, so that the
coast keeps bobbing below the waves. I know you like it
there. Come with us.

XENIA: I'd feel as if I were splashing in a puddle.

DAVID *comes in.*

DAVID: Did they fit?

ANN: Yes.

XENIA: Thank you David.

DAVID: Well that problem's solved. I'll borrow them again
for you when you leave. Now you can forget all about it and
enjoy your holiday. You're quiet. Have you rowed?

XENIA: You are supposed to be at work.

DAVID: My mother has reticulosis. To be precise a lymphosarcome. The diagnosis is certain but details of the
prognosis are not. My mother might live for only a few
months from the onset of her illness. A number of new
treatments are available here and abroad. A typical
example is cis-Platinum. It's given in a drip and causes the
patient to vomit for several days. It doesn't appreciably
prolong life. I treat my mother with chlorambucil. Doctors
have used it for twenty years. Lymphocytes are white
blood cells. There's another sort of white blood cell, the
polymorphonuclear neutrophils. In lymphosarcome the
number of lymphocytes increases greatly, from the normal
one to two thousand per cubic millimetre to fifty thousand
or even a hundred thousand. As it were, they take over.
When such a thing happens the cells circulating in the

peripheral blood are no longer mature lymphocytes but immature ones – or even worse, their precursors the lymphoblasts. There's a rush to destruction, as if a nation losing a war had started to put its children into uniform. Then the ravages of death begin. To reduce my mother's WCC – white cell count – I give her each day six milligrammes of chlorambucil. Her total WCC should be between five thousand and fifteen thousand per cubic millimetre. Last week it was twelve thousand five hundred. Now its eleven thousand. Unfortunately chlorambucil also attacks the other white cells, the polymorphonuclear neutrophils, and these are our main protection against infection. That is to say the treatment attacks the body's defences. Yet we must treat. So there is no escape. If necessary death becomes, as it were, an adverse side-effect of the cure. You will have wondered about the manner of my mother's death. Normally cancer patients progressively weaken and waste away. In time they are bedridden. At the end there is coma sometimes complicated with pneumonia. With the reticuloses there is terminally a tendency to exsanguinate. For example from the upper respiratory tract. A nosebleed. As to hope, we might hope that my mother dies sooner and

ANN *leaves the room.*

so more quickly. She has two chances of this: by coronary thrombosis or pulmonary embolism. Both are on her cards. In coronary thrombosis a coronary artery supplying heart muscle is blocked and the portion of heart muscle normally supplied with blood by that artery dies. If a main coronary artery and consequently a large amount of heart muscle is involved the heart stops immediately. There is collapse, a few stertorous respirations – a sound, we said as students, as of feet struggling to free themselves from quicksand – and then death. My mother is sixty-five. At

her age segments of coronary arteries will have been nar-
rowed by plaques of atherome. A tiny haemorrhage in the
depths of such plaque would cause it to swell and occlude
the artery. Coronary thrombosis follows. The other possible alternative is pulmonary embolism. In pulmonary
embolism a clot or thrombus forms in a vein, breaks loose –
after which it's known as an embolus – and begins its long
floating journey to the stage right atrium of the heart. A
few seconds later it blocks a pulmonary artery. If the clot is
gross enough death is virtually instantaneous. Marthe's
mobility is reduced and she's a bit dehydrated. Together
these factors favour the formation of a clot in a leg or the
pelvis. This dvt – deep vein thrombosis – may precede
pulmonary embolism by hours or days. It announces itself
by a swelling of the calf and foot – if a calf vein is involved –
or the whole leg if it occurs in a pelvic, iliofemoral vein. As
with coronary thrombosis, death is immediate. If my
mother were to die in one of these two ways she would to
that extent be fortunate. The body

ANN *comes back with a glass of water.*

has not yet evolved means of terminating its life efficiently
on all occasions when it's desirable from the patient's point
of view for it to do so.

ANN *gives* XENIA *the glass.*

XENIA(*to* ANN): Thank you. (*To* DAVID:) How interesting.
(*She drinks.*)

Off, a drunk sings.

DAVID: A drunk.
XENIA: From the hotel?
DAVID: Clambering over the rocks. So early. On all fours.
Like Father Neptune. Last June one was knocked down in
front of the hotel. All fours met four wheels.

XENIA: Ann told me you've invited us to swim with you this afternoon. Thank you, I look forward to it. Excuse me. My cases are open and I can change my clothes.

> XENIA *goes.* ANN *sits hunched on the floor by the back wall.*

MARTHE: That wasn't necessary.

DAVID: It was necessary for you not her. She will tempt you Marthe. Don't fall. You are going to die. If I hadn't told you you could pretend. But you know. As long as you are alive you must choose how to live – even though the end's inevitable. You must agree to die. Otherwise you can't die in peace. The time will come when you can't fool yourself. But you won't be prepared. When that happens to someone they die in bitterness. I've seen it. I don't want you to die like that.

> DAVID *goes left, leans on the railings and watches the sea.*

MARTHE: Bitterness? I'll be glad to die. I welcome it. But why must I wait? This isn't my body anymore. Some horrible bundle I carry round. It's coming undone. God knows what will fall out. (*Goes to* DAVID.) Give me something David. Don't make me suffer this. David. David. Let me kill myself. My nose is bleeding.

DAVID (*evenly, without turning round*): That woman's undone everything.

MARTHE: Why is my son cruel?

DAVID (*as before*): When Priam came to Achilles and asked for his murdered son's body Achilles said 'That is the fate gods give wretched men to suffer while they are free from care'.

MARTHE (*goes to* ANN *and shows her the blood on her face*): Ann ask him for me. Perhaps he'll do it for you.

> ANN *edges away along the wall.*

DAVID (*as before*): I must go to the garage to buy petrol for the boat. Don't come. There'll be a queue of tourists. The sun and the engines make it as smelly and hot as a furnace.

MARTHE: Shall I wait till you all die? It won't be long before you set fire to yourselves. Your generation will have no memorial. The sound of a whirlwind, the name of a skull: Hiroshima, Nagasaki. People turned into shadows on their doorsteps. Human negatives. The dead living.

DAVID: We'll take a picnic on the boat.

MARTHE (*to herself*): Yak. Human rubbish overflowing from dustbins. Such stench. Dogs mawling it in the gutter. Ha, cry for that!

ANN: I'm not coming.

DAVID (*as before*): We'll leave in an hour. We come back when it's dark. You meet the fishing boats going out and see the men working in the lamp-light on the decks. It would be better if mother took her tablet at the same time each day. I can't always get away from the clinic when I want. You can take charge of her. You'll have to watch her to see she takes them.

> ANN *goes.* DAVID *turns, goes to* MARTHE *and offers her tissues.*

MARTHE: I managed on my own.

> DAVID *tries to help her.*

Don't touch me. I don't need that help.

> DAVID *goes.* MARTHE *goes into her room and shuts the door.*

THREE

The house. Afternoon.
MARTHE *sleeps in her chair.* ANN *reads a book.*
DAVID *comes in.*

DAVID (*quietly, to* MARTHE): I'm off to the clinic.

ANN: She's sleeping.

DAVID: Will you be all right on your own?

ANN: I told you I like to be alone sometimes.

DAVID: Yes. I suppose you're busy at home.

ANN: I suppose so. Work, concerts, cinemas. We have a crowd of friends. Daddy brings officers home from his regiment for mother to entertain. Her cooking is famous. In England it's foreign.

DAVID: Why won't you sleep with me any more?

ANN: What can it lead to? I have to go home soon.

DAVID: We were happy last year. When you left you meant to sleep with me. Why've you changed?

ANN: Last year I was a child.

DAVID: Do you have a man friend in England?

ANN: Yes.

DAVID: Do you sleep with him?

ANN: Yes.

DAVID: Is that why you won't sleep with me?

ANN: No.

DAVID: Will you marry this man?

ANN: I don't know.

DAVID: Has he asked you?

ANN: No.

DAVID: What's his name?

ANN: David there's no point in these questions.

DAVID: Sleep with me tonight.

ANN: No.

VOICE (*off, calls*): Ivan.

DAVID: Why not? Is it because mother's dying? Many towns have natal wards and hospices for the dying in the same grounds. Before you knew my mother was dying did you mean to sleep with me?

ANN: No. I made up my mind on the plane.

DAVID: At least the decision was late.

MARTHE (*wakes startled*): David. (*He goes to her.*) What's the time?

DAVID: Twenty past two. I'm late for the clinic. Are you all right?

MARTHE: Yes.

DAVID (*kisses* MARTHE): Goodbye.

MARTHE: Goodbye.

DAVID *goes.*

MARTHE: Your dress is pretty.

ANN: Mother's boutique. She has good taste.

MARTHE: Is she still in town?

ANN: Yes. She had lunch with a friend.

MARTHE: David looked forward to seeing you. He talked about you a lot – till the last few weeks. Yesterday I remembered something that happened when he was a child. I think of these things because I sit in my chair all day. David can't leave here Ann. He wouldn't be happy away from the clinic. Would you live here?

ANN: He hasn't asked me. If he did I'd say no. This is mother's house – I know we've been turned out. But that's still how I think of it.

MARTHE: You needn't live in this house.

ANN: I feel as if she was born in the middle ages. What was she like when she was my age?

MARTHE: Very kind. All her family were. They owned half the town. That isn't a figure of speech. Factories, a bank, the local paper, the farms in the hills. Your grandparents were almost royalty. They expected to be bowed at in the streets.

ANN: Were they hated?

MARTHE: Sometimes. They were also loved and respected, which was worse.

ANN: Why?

MARTHE: Some people loved them for what they were, others for what they thought they were. But it didn't matter what they were.

ANN: Why?

MARTHE: When you have so much power you might as well be nobody. Necessity takes over. Factories and banks aren't run by kindness. They run on their own laws. The owners and owned must both obey them. The kindness of one person to another can't change that. If it could the world would be a better place. After all, we all mean well. What decides our lives isn't what the owners are like. They must never be the chosen few – even if they're the best. Your family made the people who loved and respected them confuse kindness with justice. That is corrupting. You can live without kindness, you can't live without justice – or fighting to get it. If you try to you're mad. You don't understand yourself or the world. And then nothing works. You and everyone else suffer the consequences of your madness. Whole generations bleed for it. The state of injustice is always a state of madness.

ANN: You're severe.

MARTHE: Some things require such severity.

XENIA *comes in.*

XENIA: How are you?

MARTHE: Fine.

ANN: Did you enjoy your visit?

XENIA *goes out. Almost immediately she returns with a chair and a bottle.*

XENIA: Look, brandy from the duty free shop. Not local fire water. I've already had a tot. Are you allowed to drink some?

MARTHE: Yes please.

XENIA: You're sure? I don't want to be arraigned by the medical authorities.

ANN: I'll get some glasses.

ANN *goes*. XENIA *sits*.

XENIA: My visit wore me out. I sat and listened to three hours of complaints. What can I do? I'm helpless. The neighbours' children are noisy. I shouted at them. They ran away laughing. After fifteen minutes they came back and were even noisier. She has no friends. No one calls. All the people she knew are dead or abroad. Every morning she gets up and brushes her hair into that bun she's worn for fifty years – and it's been grey for twenty.

ANN *comes back with three glasses*.

Then she sits in a chair till the light in its mercy fades and she can creep across her room to bed. You serve. (ANN *pours*.) It upset me. To go on living after the world's been taken away from you. (ANN *gives her a glass*.) Thank you. Cheers. (*She drinks*.) A disgraceful neglect of an old woman.

MARTHE: I'll ask David to call on her.

XENIA: She doesn't need a doctor. She's as tough as a horse or she wouldn't have survived. She needs companionship.

MARTHE: I know. I used to call on her. It became too tiring. She hates so many things. She's thrown her life away.

XENIA: O I did some shopping. (*From a bag*.) There.

MARTHE *unwraps the parcel*.

MARTHE: What is it?

XENIA: A waiter's crumb brush.

MARTHE: For me?

XENIA: The birds. You throw them your crumbs. Now you can do it in comfort and not waste any. I hope they sing louder. My grandmother gave them as Christmas presents.

ANN: Where did you get it?

XENIA: The old ironmongers. They had a box of them in the back of the storeroom. If you make a fuss they'll find anything. (*She sips.*) This is good. When I was a girl we went to the islands almost every day in the summer. Often we camped there. Mother and father would bring their friends for the day. There was always some young man who could play the mandolin. The women sat under silk sunshades and the men rolled up their trouser-legs and stood in the shallows to fish. I expected an old Chinaman to come out of a cave and kneel to pray or draw a map of the sky in the sand. At night we dived from the rocks and floated in the sea and looked at the stars. I'm sorry. Seeing the old woman upset me. She was my father's friend. She came here to our dinners. After the grown-ups had eaten they sat out here on the terrace. If I was a good child I was allowed to sit with them. The family and guests talked quietly as if they were in awe of the moon, it was so high. On this terrace. And down in the garden. It was a garden then. Often a breeze came off the sea and blew the scents of the flowers and shrubs over us. I sat in my father's lap and listened to his heart and the racing of his watch. He bought his cigars in Paris. Then the farmers sang in the hills. I expect my father paid for their songs. We listened in silence. The farmers worked hard and yet they created that beauty. I fell asleep on my father's lap and woke in my bed. In those days my happiness frightened me – it was so great I thought I would die of it. Long ago. I didn't know that men who sang so beautifully could hate so deeply. I still don't believe it. That's how we lived till the fanatics came. Then the crowds cheered and waved and marched as if the town had been taken over by a circus. And after them came the war. Shells. Sea mines. Foreign uniforms. The ugly little huts on the islands. People hounded and tortured and shot. And when the war was over they threw down the gods and goddesses from the terraces. Zeus Hera and Aphrodite lay on the rocks with no arms or heads. Our fault. It has all gone. We were foolish. It will never be given back. I hope those who have it are happy. What's the use of saying all this?

ANN: More?

XENIA: A drop. (ANN *pours*.) Thank you.

MARTHE: I want to tell Ann something.

XENIA: O dear now I've upset Marthe. How silly of me to rake up the past. How stupid.

MARTHE: You know that once I was going to be shot.

ANN: Shot? No! By us?

MARTHE: Haven't you told her?

XENIA (*shrugs*): There seemed no point. (*She sips.*) This is good.

MARTHE: It was the Germans. A German soldier on a motor-bike was shot at. The motor-bike crashed and both the driver and an officer in the sidecar were killed. The Germans took hostages. Two hundred for the officer and a hundred for the driver. In those days when you saw Germans you hid or hurried away. I was trapped in a sidestreet and taken to the islands.

ANN: These islands?

MARTHE: Yes. Your family still owned them then.

XENIA: It was terrible. The Germans commandeered them for a concentration camp. They insisted on paying rent.

MARTHE: Your mother persuaded the German commandant to let me go.

ANN: You saved Marthe's life! Why have you never told me?

XENIA: What was there to tell? We all helped each other under the occupation. I wanted to save them all but I could only ask for Marthe: she was our servant. The commandant probably thought that if his soldiers shot her it would make conversation awkward the next time he came to dinner. He shot the others. We were used to shooting by then. They shot people every day on the islands. For months on end. You could hear it on this terrace. The irony was that father passed information to the partisans through Marthe. That's why we had the Germans to dine. They trusted us and we overheard many things that helped the partisans. You see what a brave grandfather you had. If the Germans had found out they'd have shot him and his family. Not that it helped him after the war.

MARTHE: We were shut in a hut for a day and a half. The barred window had been boarded with planks. Most of us sat on a wooden bench that ran round the inside of the hut. There wasn't room on it for everyone. Some sat on the floor in the middle. We were all women. The men and children were in other huts.

ANN: Children?

MARTHE: The Germans began to shoot the men. We heard bursts of firing. I don't know why we didn't go mad. People seem to be able to bear almost anything. A few prayed. Some cried. Others cursed. No one turned to the wall. We looked at each other. Of course I'd known that I might be shot. But I didn't know how to die. What you did at the end.

XENIA: That's enough. (*She sips.*)

MARTHE (*she seems to forget the others*): When a German was shot everything was taken. Papers, uniform, boots, weapons – everything that could be used. Once – after I'd been released – I found a wallet on one of them. Inside there was a photograph of his father and mother. Then one of his girl. And at the back two of the war. One of these showed six or seven naked women standing in a group in a field. The print was blurred. Wartime chemicals. You couldn't see where they were. There were some trees in the distance and a dark shape that might have been a barn. At one side a grey figure pointed a rifle at them. Very neat and trim. I think his boots were polished. A toy soldier. He must have had other soldiers with him but you couldn't see them. The other photograph also showed women. Two neighbours or a mother and daughter. They were bundled up in clothes and their heads were hidden in scarves. They turned away so that their heads were in shadow. The place was misty or perhaps the film was bad. Wartime quality. The little hill under their feet looked like a cloud. There were no soldiers in this picture. Nothing to show the women were going to be shot. But I knew they were. Immediately. From the gesture of their head and shoulders. It was the gesture of the first photograph. They huddled together and turned away as if it had started to rain. That was how you died. Simply. As if you walked out of life. (*Turns to others.*) I knew by sight some of the women with me in the hut. I'd seen them in town. One woman began to tell us about her life. She'd married an elderly farmer. Her son had been killed in the war. She'd come down to town to sell his clothes and been rounded up. We took turns to say who we were and how we'd lived. We gave our names to pass on if any of us survived. It was as if we were in a schoolroom and were going to die. There was an old woman beside me on the bench. She was so doubled over that if she died facing the soldiers the bullets went in her back. She'd lost everything – her family and her room. When I told them the name of the woman I worked for she said 'If I could live to spit in her face' and spat in the dirt. Later a soldier came in. Most of the women ran to the other end of the hut and wailed. The soldier shouted my name over the noise. I followed him out. While he chained the door he turned to grin at me. He made the thumbs up sign as if I'd won a lottery. He led me along the side of the hut.

You were standing beside an officer. You held the strap of your patent leather handbag in both hands. The soldier saluted. You nodded.

XENIA (*defensively*): To identify you.

MARTHE: The officer clicked and saluted you. I followed you to the landing place and onto the military boat.

XENIA (*confused*): It was windy and choppy. We didn't say anything. If you'd thanked me I'd have laughed.

MARTHE: I spent the next day in my room. I heard the shooting from there. Two hours. I wondered what batch I'd have been in. Several times I thought it was over but it started again.

XENIA: After the war the guards on the island were changed. My father was arrested as an exploiter. Perhaps they put him in Marthe's hut. He was sentenced to ten years hard labour. He escaped by dying in two. My mother had already died during the war. When father was arrested friends took me in. I was smuggled out of the country in an army lorry. That's how I met your father. (*She sips.*) Some of those who arrested him were among those he'd passed information to. What happened as they left the house became a legend in our family. A servant opened the door and my father said 'Thank you'. One of his captors said 'Let him learn to open doors' and another said 'His door will be locked'. They led him away through the garden. There should have been fruit on the trees. A crowd had picked it early. They were too hungry to notice they ate sour fruit. (*She sips.*) I can't understand why you punished him. I understand why you took his house, money, clothes, cattle, land, books, pictures, umbrella – but why punish him? He was an old man who wasn't used to manual work. It was a sentence of death. He had faults. A bad temper. He once hit my mother. But he didn't choose the bed he was born in. He behaved as they all did in his position. Someone must run the world. If you do it better, fine. But why punish him? Nothing was too petty for his trial. Each time he swore at a taxi driver or dismissed someone for bad time-keeping. It was all remembered. They forgave him nothing. Even you gave evidence against him.

MARTHE: I described how he lived. The parties and gambling. Many in the court had starved. It was dangerous to live in your father's world.

ANN: Don't quarrel. Let me think about what you've both told me.

XENIA: Yes think. And learn what people do in this world. Once those islands were one piece of rock. Then the sea tore them in two. I've seen men and women who could have torn them apart with their bare hands their hatred was so great. How can you sit and look at them all day?

MARTHE: I've lived a second life for forty years. Now I've come to my second death. It's a beautiful summer. The very old people say it's the best they remember. I'm lucky but I can't hope to live nine lives. The islands change colour all the time. In the evening they're dark. They're called the eyes of the sea. Why should I mind them? They're not my life. This house is my life. My mother was its first housekeeper and I would have been its second. I came here as a servant. Now I live here by right. I could have died on the island. I was saved – not even by a friend but by an enemy. That's how lucky I was! When the house was made into flats people said I should be caretaker. I went on the town council and served there till this summer. We built a clinic and a school and houses. Now I sit on the terrace and watch the sea. During the day as the shadow moves over the stones I move my chair to stay in the sun. When David was studying he put his table in front of his window where the sun fell on it. As it moved he moved his chair so that he read and made his notes in the sun. When I mind my neighbour's children I put them on the floor and

they crawl to the sun. They cry at the dark but no one cries
at the light. That's what I've learned. I have no memory of
the islands to drive me out of the sun to cry in my cave.

XENIA: You're right. Don't be frightened of bogeymen.
(*Automatically glances at her empty glass.*) No it's too early.
(*To* ANN:) I haven't been on the island for years. Ask
David to take us in his boat.

VOICE (*off, calls*): Ivan.

ANN: Who's Ivan?

XENIA: All the men here are called Ivan.

> XENIA *goes.*

MARTHE: Two girls arm in arm are calling a young man in a
rowing boat.

TWO VOICES (*off, call*): Ivan.

ANN: Has he heard?

MARTHE: Yes. They're waving to each other. (*Stands behind*
ANN *and puts her hands on her shoulders and raises them over
her head in the gesture of lifting the baby.*) When we were
young parents took their new babies down to the rocks on a
sunny day, held them over their heads and shouted their
names to the sea. It was a custom.

FOUR

The island. A sandy floor before a rock wall.
XENIA *sits alone.*
A GERMAN *comes on.*

GERMAN: Speak German?

XENIA: Yes.

GERMAN: Good. Your boat is tied up at the mooring. Please
take me back to the hotel.

XENIA: Is your boat lost?

GERMAN: My son and daughter-in-law dropped me on the island and went for a trip along the coast. They should have been back two hours ago. I can't see their boat on the water. They've made me late for the evening meal. When you take the pension with full board you must come to the restaurant for the evening meal by eight-thirty. It is better to be there at seven-thirty. Then there is time to ask for seconds.

XENIA: Your son and daughter-in-law will come back. They'll worry if you're not here.

GERMAN: That will teach them to make their elders wait. If I'm late I won't be served with the evening meal. The waiters are stern with those who come late. They want to go home.

XENIA: My friend will take you in his boat. Wait at the landing. No, sit in the boat under the awning.

GERMAN: Have they left you on your own? Our young people! I don't complain. Sigi could not be a more dutiful son. His Haidi is like my daughter. Since my wife died I would be lonely without them. They take me on holiday every year. I haven't seen you at the hotel.

XENIA: I stay with friends.

GERMAN: O friends are better than a hotel. The young people are not married?

XENIA: No.

GERMAN: I see them often. The other day I saw them on the rocks. The young man talked to the girl and tried to press himself on her. Our young people!

XENIA: If you care to wait in the boat.

GERMAN: O I said something to shock. You have no reason to complain about the young lady. That is a good daughter. She pushed the young man away.

XENIA: Thank you. I would like to be on my –

GERMAN: You are right. It's wrong for the elders to tell the young people what to do. Sometimes they set us a good example. They remind us we're still young and on holiday! I saw them just now from the mouth of the ammunition cave. They went down the other side of the island. You can't see so far from the cave. If you are concerned for the young lady I shall wander down and pretend to look for something I have lost.

XENIA: You were here in the war.

GERMAN: Ja. I said ammunition cave. That gave me away. You know what happened here in the war?

XENIA: Yes, I lived here.

GERMAN: Ah that war. Terrible. Terrible. Terrible. So much killing. (*He calls:*) Sigi! Haidi! (*To* XENIA:) Haidi is a sensible girl and Sigi has a good underwater watch but they lose all sense of time. They didn't go off to enjoy themselves without me. They think I want to be on my own for a while. It's their way to be kind. It would have been good to come back with comrades and talk of the old days. These islands were a camp. Prisoners were routed on. Terrible times. Tcha. But we must make the best of it. Even in the end – till the very last days – we went to the bars in the evenings to drink a glass of wine and sing the old songs. I carried my accordion all through the war till I got back to Germany. I had to barter it for food. Ruins and blackmarket, that's all that was left. There was no music in my life for years. But we recovered. The spirit inside was not broken. That is what counts. You have a grudge against us?

XENIA: You destroyed our lives.

GERMAN: No no the old days were over. No one was strong enough to save them. Now we must learn to live in a new world. When I got back all my people were dead. The elders, aunts, my brother, even my girl. My family took her in when she was bombed out. They all died together in one house. After the war I married her sister. I have a good job. I sell refrigerators. I can give you a discount. You could bring it over the border.

XENIA: I live in England.

GERMAN: Ah you married an Englander. It is sad not to live in your own country. I'll tell you a secret. Do you know where we are? Guess. This spot. That was the execution wall.

XENIA: O.

GERMAN: In Germany we would put a statue there. We have many artists. When prisoners were shot the lizards jumped into the cracks and stayed there till we left. Then they came to sit in the sun. You have something to eat in your bag?

XENIA: Yes.

GERMAN: There are butter marks on the paper. Today we had lunch early so the children could have full use of the boat. You must hire one for the day. Not cheap. If you don't eat here the sun makes you ill. I learned that from the war.

XENIA (*food*): Please eat this. It's left from our lunch.

GERMAN: Ah sandwich. How English. (*He eats.*) Good. Thank you. It is better to be kind than make terrible wars. But it had to be.

XENIA: Were you here long?

GERMAN: For the duration. There's nothing to hide. We were questioned after the war. By GI Jonny. This wasn't a concentration camp. We were private soldiers: not officers, not Gestapo, not guilty. We garrisoned the town, guarded the roads, kept the prisoners. When we took them to be questioned we handed them over at the door. It had to be. The civvies killed us and our officers. Not in fair play you understand. They crept up on our sentries at night and cut their throats with a knife. People who do these things must be dealt with. Poor bastards. I was sorry for them. I did nothing they wouldn't have done to me. Crumbs fall into your hair when you eat sandwiches naked. (*He laughs and brushes crumbs from his chest.*)

XENIA: You didn't kill anyone.

GERMAN: O yes. Sometimes. When it was urgent. It was forbidden to be questioned or killed on this island. Prisoners were taken to the little island first. To begin with regulations were strictly enforced. But what can you do when prisoners are sitting in the boats and there is no petrol for the engines? You can row them across but it's hard. There are so many prisoners. So organisation broke down and discipline became lax: we knew the end was coming. We started to shoot prisoners here. There was such disorganisation it could even happen that ammunition ran out. Headquarters gave the order: hostages. There is no alternative. It is easy to say hostages, it's not so easy to say ammunition. Many times our CO had to go on the scrounge. He was called a scrounger as if he cadged cigarettes. No he was a generous man. But the officers fell out and swore at each other. Not the behaviour of gentlemen. Bad blood between comrades. The batmen and clerks told us everything. Commander Lauber said: 'If you want to play the hero and get a medal for shooting people use your own ammunition'. That's how things were. How could we win a war like that? They tried to sink them in ships. But we ran out of ships. The fishermen sank theirs before we could get them. We needed ours to patrol the coast. So that was called off. Yes it's good to remember how hard things were. At one time many people were buried on this island. They were killed here so where could we put them? In a war bodies are a problem even to Germans. Take them to the mainland? More work, porters, boats, more lorries to take them from the quay to the hills. Throw them into the sea? No tide. The beaches are fouled. The town can't go about its business. You would think this was the devil's island it was so difficult for our adjutant to run. Now I will tell you about the end. When we had to go home. By then the island was full of bodies. They had been sealed up in caves and pushed down cracks. The soldiers said if the island was a coat the pockets would bulge! The order came: exhume the dead and throw them into the sea. We were angry. It would seem as if we had something to hide. Our enemies were quick to lie about us. We were not criminals. We'd done everything in the open. According to laws of war. Harsh – but war is harsh. Now we must open the graves. Dig the bodies out of the rocks. It is an order. We stood guard while the prisoners dug and carried. Such stench. Can you imagine? For three days. The bodies were thrown into the sea. But there is no tide. The bodies won't go away. The sea will not take them. It is as if it was against us. They floated round the island. Only a few were skeletons. Sand had preserved the skin of the rest. They drifted on the surface or just below it. Some of them held hands – that's how they died. When we went to the land for supplies – O the evenings of songs in the bars were over by then – our boats towed the bodies behind us in our wakes as if they were swimming after us and pointing at us with their outstretched hands – that's how they died. A dead woman clutched a child in the crook of her arm and floated on top of the sea as if she held the child up out of the water to see us. The public address system played dance music to keep spirits high. We came with marches and left with waltzes. (*He walks away.*) Where are those bad children? I was lucky to find someone to speak German. This is my first time in your country since the war. Haidi and Sigi brought me here as a surprise. Other years we went to Majorca. Malta. Spain. Italy twice. Majorca six times. Majorca is best for a holiday. The Crusader Hotel is excellent. Reasonable terms. So is the hotel here. And it's new. It works. Next year nothing will work. Yes I remember those days well. We cut our initials and army numbers in the rock. Now they're gone. The wind erases them with a handful of sand. But it couldn't have done it so soon. It's not so strong. Hooligans did it. And put their initials in our place. You are quiet madam. Is it the sun? Have I eaten your food? I think my stories upset you. This was not one of the bad camps. In the bad camps people were burned. Some of their guards collapsed with fatigue. They were transferred to us here. This was a good posting by the sea. They said that in those places so much fat hung in the air you covered your coffee with your hand and drank from beneath it. It even got into their skin so they didn't smell of themselves anymore. They smelt of other people. Or like the dead. When they were on leave their wives thought they were in bed with a stranger. Ho hoo! That's an army for you! Take the clothes off your back and put you in uniform. Take your name and give you a number. Take your head and stuff it with orders. Then take your skin – and you end up smelling of someone else. (*He points.*) Is that bread? Talking is good for the appetite. I mustn't be greedy. Even if Sigi came now we'd be late for the restaurant. If we go there one minute late they turn us away. The young ones spoil me. I can have what I want at the bar. I say no, such extravagance is a waste. Why pay for food you don't eat? Between us we'd lose three meals. The hotel doesn't lose. Tomorrow the kitchen serves our steaks as casserole.

XENIA (*food*): Please take it.

GERMAN (*eating*): Good. Thank you. Crept up on our sentries with a knife. Slick.

XENIA: We killed as many of you as we could.

GERMAN: Of course, of course. Natural after the rumours that spread about us. People like to believe the worst.

XENIA: I know what happened. (*She points.*) I lived over there.

GERMAN (*laughs*): We were that close? I sailed under those cliffs many times. You see that big house? Our officers dined there. In the war there was a young girl, the daughter of the house. We called her the girl in white. She stood on the terrace and pretended to stare at the sea. Hour after hour for days at a time. We sang to her as we sailed below or swam. We watched her through binoculars. Our comrades' throats were cut. They said it was quieter than shooting – but that's how they liked to do it. We loved her, we were young soldiers. She never smiled or waved. She dared not. The partisans would have shot her. But she was our friend. She stood there as a sign. It was all she could do.

XENIA: I don't understand!

GERMAN: We didn't come here as enemies. We were defenders. Could we have done all we did out of hate? No, our officers said: we acted in honour. To save you from scum.

XENIA: What nonsense!

GERMAN: You see! Our officers were right: all that blood and suffering and nothing is learned. Europe was threatened. Civilization, Beethoven, art. What else is there? Americans and pygmies.

XENIA: She didn't stand there for your sake! I expect she was lonely! So many young men were killed! She wondered how long she had to live.

GERMAN: Men are animals. We can't be trusted with another man's wife or his money. Not even with our own daughters. No one's safe on our streets at night. If we don't get our fodder we whine. What saves us from ourselves? Culture. The standards of our fathers. They struggled for centuries to make them strong. But standards are always as weak as the girl in white. Always. The animal wants to be on top. If that happens we're lost. The apes come out of their jungle. That's why we went to war.

XENIA: You're talking nonsense!

GERMAN: The girl in white could tell you!

XENIA: You invade us, bomb us, rob us – for our good!

GERMAN: That was because you listened to scum. If we'd listened to scum Europe would be a labour camp. If you'd helped us there'd be more hope for the world. Instead you'll see what happens. The jungles are open.

XENIA: Go away.

GERMAN: I can show you the truth. There was a woman who worked for the girl on the balcony. Servant. She was taken hostage: more throats had been cut. The girl asked our commander to let her go. Now parents had begged us for their children on the streets. Tried to climb on the lorries to take their place. We pushed them off. But our commander gave that servant back to the girl. We weren't angry for our dead comrades. Some of us had tears in our eyes. That girl had a right to ask for anything. We were at war for her. What happens to our culture, our way of life, when people like that go? She came from the same class as our officers. She knew that – and what it meant. It was proved when she came and asked for the woman. She needn't have asked, she could have given an order! I wish I could meet her and thank her for all she did for us. It was not to be. When we left her class were shot or chased out. They put some of them in our old huts.

XENIA: How dare you! Who are you? Who told you to say these things to me? Someone paid you!

GERMAN: Ah, you're one of those who benefited from the pickings. You did well out of the end of the war so you see it from that point of view.

XENIA (picks up her bag): Go away!

GERMAN: O madam don't be angry. Thank you for the sandwich. The heat. My empty stomach. I rambled on. Yes, but I will not be humiliated even if I stay on this island all night – at my age that would not be easy. I came here in my prime. I risked my life. The sacrifice of young manhood should be respected. Our young people would have to do all we did if those times come again. It would have to be.

XENIA: Wait here. My daughter's friend will take you in his boat.

GERMAN: It's better if I wait on board. You said under the shade.

XENIA: Don't follow me!

GERMAN: Your friend will leave in a hurry without me.

XENIA: Stop following me! I shall report you to the police!

XENIA goes.

GERMAN (*shouting after her*): My dear lady, I didn't touch you! O dear, Sigi and Haidi are drowned! (*He starts to follow* XENIA.) Haidi wouldn't let him be rash –

XENIA (off): Go away!

GERMAN: – but he doesn't know these waters. The rocks are dangerous. It would be terrible to go home alone.

The GERMAN *goes.* ANN *and* DAVID *come on. They wear swimming clothes. Ann has a light blue wrap.*

DAVID: This island is sacred to us. I won't make love to another girl here. Why am I so happy? From now on we have a secret power: whenever we're angry or sad we'll think of this and it will make us happy. We have fallen in love. You won't stay here. Instead I shall plant a pine in the place where we were today. I'll water it till it grows tall and strong. I'll scatter seed under it so that flocks of birds come there to live. (*Calmly.*) This is the wall where my mother was to be shot. Look at the fossils and veins of quartz and bullet marks in the rock. When they shot simple people – not fighters or hardened politicians but children and old women – they dragged the dead out of sight so that the simple people wouldn't know where they were and run away. There was blood on the ground – but there was blood on all the rocks on the island and on the walls of the rooms. So they thought there was still time for a plane to come out of the sky, or a hand – or a friendly boat to appear on the sea. That was at the start of the war. After a time they made even the simple people climb over the bodies to the wall. If they stumbled they clubbed them. The Assyrian has said I will make him more dead than he was before. The Spaniard has said I will kill the dead twice.

The GERMAN *comes in.*

GERMAN: Speak German?

DAVID: Yes.

GERMAN: Thank god. That is your boat sir. Goodday miss. Please take me to the hotel.

DAVID: Are you stranded?

GERMAN: Sigi hired a boat to surprise Haidi. Now they're lost. I must get back for the evening meal. The door of the restaurant is shut at eight-thirty sharp. If you tap on the glass the waiters look away and the guests hold up the food on their forks and laugh. You can't get the manager, he's cleaning the pool.

DAVID: You can come with us.

GERMAN: Thank you, thank you. I sweat with anxiety. You must not let the lady attack me. I didn't touch her. Sigi and Haidi will be cross. The lady in Ibiza had too much sun oil on her leg. The sand set in the crease. I brushed it off. I don't want any scandal. Because I'm German the older generation – it's natural.

DAVID: I'll take you in my boat.

GERMAN: We work for our holiday. You too. A song in the evening and a glass of wine. I wanted it all to go well today. Three weeks pass so quickly. Tomorrow we go back to Bächelstein. Tonight I wanted to buy a special bottle of wine. Yesterday was Sigi and Haidi's turn. That's how we end our holidays. A toast to the next year.

DAVID: Don't be distressed. Wait in the boat.

GERMAN: The lady is angry. I'll wait on the path. Not to go to the boat till you come? When you pass me on the way down I'll follow you. The lady must not say such things. I don't molest ladies.

The GERMAN *goes out.*

DAVID: Ann. Death creates desire. Lust. The stupid think that's perverse. No. Lust isn't drawn to death. When life sees death it become strong itself, it *will* be strong. While we cry our distorted mouth reaches for one that smiles. You won't stay here – but we'll sleep together every night till you go away. I will plant a great treasure of seed in you to carry abroad to your own country. *There* you will bear a child! The child and that pine are the only things we can give to my mother – or all who die.

ANN: A tense woman sitting upright in a corner of a boat. A hungry old man squatting in the dust halfway down to the landing place. They each have their own thoughts. Angry, offended, waiting for planes, suspecting waiters, staring at their watches. The stranger should be grateful he met us. My mother is angry because we made her wait while we went to the other side of the island. I don't wish to make her angry but it doesn't matter if she is. 'The gods love the widespread races of happy man and willingly lengthen the days of his fleeting life, to share with him the joyful view from their unchanging sky, for a brief span of time.' They're on the edge of the island waiting to leave. We're free and told to be happy. Let's sit here a little longer.

FIVE

The house. Night.
Empty.
XENIA *comes on. She taps on* MARTHE's *door.*

XENIA: Can I speak to you? (*Slight pause.*) You're not asleep.
I looked into your room from the garden.

> XENIA *walks away from the door. After a moment*
> MARTHE *comes out.*

MARTHE: Yes?

XENIA: I must speak to you.

MARTHE: Can't it wait till morning? (*No answer.*) Move my
chair. There's a breeze.

> XENIA *puts* MARTHE's *chair stage centre.* MARTHE *sits*
> *in it.*

XENIA: David and Ann are out.

MARTHE: Dancing at the hotel. Does it shock you?

XENIA: It's not my concern. No doubt he wouldn't dance if
he thought you cared. Shall I come here when you're dead?

MARTHE: That doesn't concern me.

XENIA: I'll do what you want.

MARTHE: Live your own life

XENIA: You might wish me to come. I'd keep your memory
alive: I knew you so well.

MARTHE: Do as you please.

XENIA: Have I ever shown you any resentment?

MARTHE: I'm tired now.

XENIA: I was an only child. When my father died this house
– all he had – would have been mine. It was taken from me
even before he died. Some of the people who took it had
been with us for years. Your son thinks if I was here he'd be

blacking boots. It shows even when he smiles. My father sent clever children to the university whatever their background. Paid their tuition fees, bought their books, clothed some of them, gave them an allowance –

MARTHE: What d'you want to say?

XENIA: – but I've never held a grudge.

MARTHE: No.

XENIA: Then why do you despise me?

MARTHE: I don't.

XENIA: So does your son. Only he's more offensive because he has no excuse. I'm tired of being abused and attacked.

MARTHE: If you have a complaint about David make it to him. I'm sorry if he's been rude to you. He's young and thoughtless.

XENIA: He thinks I want to come back here. I knew that life couldn't go on. I was hated and resented even when I was a child. If I'd had to spend my life like that I'd be old and embittered now. Instead I have a good husband, my daughter and kind friends. There's my shop. I sell the best clothes as cheaply as I can and have the pleasure of seeing young people enjoying life. At their age we could have been shot. Many of our friends were. D'you seriously think I want to go back to all that? Life has been good to me. And there's nothing I need blame myself for. Whatever my family did Marthe I was young when I left – for *those* days little more than a child. Yet you despise me.

MARTHE: No.

XENIA: Don't you know you do? Your condition's worse than I thought. It's a disease you don't even know you've got. That's why you've passed it on to your son. Has he got to live with it after you're dead? D'you want to ruin his life? Can't we get rid of the past even now? Let's sit here quietly till he comes and then the three of us will talk.

MARTHE: What about?

XENIA: O Marthe you wrong yourself! You know. My

daughter told you how much I keep secret. I never tell her things that would shame anyone she knew. But if this is to be your last summer, then at least we two should be honest with each other. I saved your life. Yet you gave evidence against us. Not out of fear. You weren't forced. My father might have been shot. How wrong. Such guilt is almost unforgiveable.

MARTHE: What guilt? Let us talk about ourselves. People in my generation had to depend on your family in order to live. But why should that have been? Your kindness made us beggars. It made some of us grateful, which was worse. There can never be enough kindness to make the world human. If you spent your life being kind people would still die of ignorance and neglect. Much more is needed. Let's leave it till the morning. Years ago your father's bank was robbed and a girl cashier shot. The man who did it hid on the island. Your father saw him through his binoculars and went out in his motor-boat. A group of men were standing beside him at the wheel. The young man saw them and realized he'd been discovered. He jumped into the water and swam for the shore. Your father chased him. He turned and swam towards the open sea. He was that desperate. When your father's men dragged him on board he struggled like a madman to get back in the water. They had to tie him up and lay him on the bottom of the boat as if he was a corpse. Did your father rescue him from drowning or catch a fish for dinner? While that went on your mother and her ladies took tea on the terrace. They weren't a vulgar mob, they didn't line the railings to cheer. They quietly drank their tea. If your father had brought the man here your mother would have given him tea and wrapped him in her stole. Would that have made his punishment easier to bear? The foundations of your world were crooked and so everything in it was crooked. Your kindness, consideration, consistency were meaningless. All the good you did was meaningless. In your world the good did evil. What could be worse? Most of us spent our life swimming out to the open sea. The confusion and competition led to such panic and madness that in the end there was war. The soldiers on the island didn't have much excuse for not seeing the blood they shed. But your state was worse. You had every excuse for what you did: your hands were clean! Your world was a puppet show. You thought the puppets moved because of the little pieces of wood under their bright coats. They were moved by strings: the factories, banks, governments that control our lives. What we do, what we are, depends on the relationship between us and such things. Faced with that kindness is like blowing on a storm to make it go away. But when those relations are just we will live justly. Kindness will have its meaning. Justice and mercy will be one.

XENIA: You remember what you choose! My father was a liberal man. When that thief was sentenced to death he used his newspaper to get him reprieved. The dead girl's family came here to abuse him. I had to be taken out for a walk so I didn't hear the vile things they said. The fascists demonstrated. Their party membership doubled. Father resisted them. We were happy when that man was saved!

MARTHE: I can't say any more. Your father was as kind as you. He could afford his halo. The young man was grateful to him. When the war came he volunteered to fight for your father's world and was shot. It seems to me people like you live backwards. You learn nothing. You spend your life burrowing through the ground to your grave. Well, you have no more power. That's what matters.

XENIA: Now you admit you despise me.

MARTHE (as if XENIA were not there): How do you live through the last moments? The last hour in hospital. Walking out of the cell. Perhaps I should have stayed in the hut when you came. I could have helped the others. Put my arms round the old women or helped the girls who stumbled. I might even have sung. I wanted to fly into the line of light under the door. Then the door opened. I'd secretly begged for life. Not hoped, calculated. (*Smiles at* XENIA.) I knew you'd come. I left them to die alone – as I am now. They're dead, the huts are burned, the island's free. It hasn't changed for me. I saw a photograph of my death. I lived my second life in a new way. I listen to them not you.

XENIA: You shouldn't. They're dead and you're not. When I was a student you were a servant. I envied you. You had more dignity, more intelligence, than the rest of us. Now our roles are reversed. I got away – but you're corrupted by the past.

> XENIA *goes. Music starts in the distance.* MARTHE *doesn't react.* XENIA *returns.*

The discotheque. Now I shan't sleep.

MARTHE: It stops after midnight.

XENIA: I'd better take you to your room.

MARTHE: I'm all right.

XENIA: I shan't come here again. My husband told me not to. This is my grave. They say in prison my father's hair turned white in a week. I didn't see him. I should have drowned myself when they took him away. Gone down the rocks in the dark and slipped into the sea. Now it's too late. They'd say 'A bitter old woman'. I'm not. It's just that you took everything from me – and still want more!

MARTHE: What could I want? Go to your room. It's quieter on your side of the house. (*To herself:*) I spent so much of my life in struggle. Lost so many friends. New clothes become old when I put them on. I'm worn out. I listen to the air going in and out of my body. Like footsteps in a corridor. It's not easy: it's as if a crowd had to die.

XENIA (*to herself*): The world was taken away from me. They threw the furniture out of the house and left me in the

emptiness. I can't begin again. I've spent years pointing at
my dead body – and no one sees it.

MARTHE: Yes, you can't begin. You belong to a family who
die in prisons. The old woman beside me. Gripped the
bench with both hands. Her knuckles shone like a child's.
'If I could live to spit in her face.' (MARTHE *heaves herself
out of her chair, spits in* XENIA's *face and falls back on the
floor.*) It's gone.

XENIA: How dare you! Because you're dying you think you
can be a monster! O you must feel better! You carried a
dead woman's spit round in your mouth for forty years! I
shan't sleep here. I'll go to the hotel. Send my things on in
the morning. I won't trouble you to give a message to my
daughter. I'll write a note.

    XENIA *goes.* MARTHE *doesn't move.* XENIA *returns.*

Are you all right? If you wish I'll help you to your room.

MARTHE: Go away.

XENIA: It's clear you're not well. The drugs you take have
affected you. I don't want to be accused of letting you die of
exposure. No doubt your son would give evidence against
me.

    XENIA *goes to* MARTHE.

MARTHE: Get out.

XENIA: As you wish. I'll leave you to suffer the consequences
of your stubbornness.

    XENIA *goes.* MARTHE *goes to her room and tries the
handle of the door. She can't turn it. For a moment she rests
on the wall. She tries the handle again. The door opens.*
MARTHE *goes into her room and shuts the door behind her.*

SIX

The house. Morning.

MARTHE *comes up from the street with a pot of petunias.*
She puts it on the floor. She goes out and returns with a
folded table. She opens it. She goes out. She returns with a
chair on which there are a cloth and a tray of breakfast
things. She begins to lay the table for breakfast. ANN *comes*
in.

ANN: Good morning.

MARTHE: Good morning. How are you?

ANN: Fine. And you? I have mother's note. You two have
quarrelled.

MARTHE: It's nothing.

ANN: What was it about?

MARTHE: It's finished.

ANN: Really, you behave like children. Mother is difficult
but she wouldn't leave without a reason.

MARTHE: Please ask her.

ANN: O Marthe! (*She sighs.*) I suppose you're upset. Was it
about David and me?

MARTHE: I made this jam. A neighbour gave me some plums
from her tree. The big woman. You've seen her child
playing with her apron while she hangs out her washing.

ANN: I'll lay the table.

MARTHE: I'll do it.

ANN: It's so much nonsense. You make me cross. Are you
quarrelling with me now?

MARTHE: Don't be rude. Laying the table is one of the few
jobs I can still do. I covered the table with a clean cloth and
brought a pot of petunias from the roof. Hand me the
plates. (*They lay the table together.*) Was there a storm last
night?

ANN: No.

MARTHE: I dreamed I went to sleep and in the night a door banged in the wind. I woke up and listened to the sea. I must have been sleeping all the time. This morning everything looks as if it had been in a storm. Dust and bits of paper and rubbish blown away. Boxes and tins blown to the sides of the houses. The leaves are still crooked from the wind. The town looks as battered and new as a child that's cried itself to sleep.

ANN: There wasn't a storm.

MARTHE: No, I dreamed it. Give me the knives.

MARTHE *lays the table.*

I'll set a place for your mother. I don't think she'll come, but she might and it would be better if she found a place set for her. Perhaps she'll come to breakfast tomorrow. Or perhaps she won't. Fetch the coffee and milk from the kitchen. The petunia needs water.

ANN: I'm hungry.

MARTHE: Wait for David.

ANN: He's asleep.

MARTHE: Wake him. Is he a good lover?

ANN: Yes.

MARTHE: The three of us will eat together. I'll cut the bread.

ANN: Marthe. Your ankle's swollen.

MARTHE: It began in the night. I found it like that this morning.

ANN: It must hurt.

MARTHE: No. I stood on it too long. I'll rest it later. Don't tell David. He'll give me more tablets. Pass my wrap. (ANN *gives* MARTHE *her shawl. Looking at the sea:*) The sea is calm and the water's piled up as if it has been in the storm. Everything's open and new. (*Coffee cup.*) There's a stain in this cup. Take it into the kitchen and wash it.

ANN: It's nothing. I'll drink from it.

MARTHE: No. Wash it. Respect things. Use them properly.

> ANN *goes.* MARTHE *wraps herself in her shawl and cuts bread.*

What will you do if your mother asks you to move to the hotel? It's lonely to be on your own. I'd hate it.

ANN (*off*): You weren't *that* horrible to her. The quarrel is between you.

MARTHE (*slightly amused*): She'll say I stole her daughter.

> ANN *comes back with coffee, milk, the cup and water for the petunia.*

ANN: She knows if I stay it's because I want to.

MARTHE: Pour the milk in a jug. (*She pours.*) A jug to make the table beautiful.

ANN: You're making washing-up.

MARTHE: Good. I won't see many more beautiful things. You'll be sad for a few days and then your life will go on again. It will be beautiful. You'll think of me with fondness. Put a chair in front of each place.

ANN: How d'you know it will be beautiful?

> ANN *goes out.*

MARTHE (*working*): What's more useless than death? Life without death would be. How could you find anything beautiful if you looked at it forever? You'd grow tired of it. Why fall in love if it lasted forever? When you'd forgiven yourselves a thousand times you'd tire of forgiveness. You'd grow tired of changing the people you loved. (ANN *returns with three folded chairs, opens them and sets them at the table.*) If you ate for eternity why bother to taste what you're eating? You can taste the next meal. When you've cried for one mistake you wouldn't cry for the next. You'd have eternity to put it right. Soon your eyes would be full of sleep. You'd go deaf. You wouldn't listen to voices because they would give you the trouble of answering. Why listen to them? It would be useless to know which was a sparrow or a waterfall. In eternity there would be no future. You'd sit on the ground and turn to stone. Dust would pile up and bury you. If we didn't die we'd live like the dead. Without death there's no life. No beauty, love or happiness. You can't laugh for more than a few hours or weep more than a few days. No one could bear more than one life. Only hell could be eternal. Sometimes life is cruel and death is sudden – that's the price we pay for not being stones. Don't let the lightning strike you or madmen burn your house. Don't give yourself to your enemies or neglect anyone in need. Fight. But in the end death is a friend who brings a gift: life. Not for you but the others. I die so that you might live. Did you call David? Breakfast's ready.

ANN: I didn't dry the cup.

MARTHE: Let me.

ANN *goes and* MARTHE *dries the cup. She smooths a corner of the table with her hand, goes to a chair at the table, pulls the wrap round her legs and sleeps. The* GERMAN *comes up from the street. He carries a bunch of flowers wrapped in florist's cellophane and tied with yellow ribbon.*

GERMAN: Speak German? . . . Dear Lady. (*He coughs.*) The taxi is taking us to the airport. If we miss the plane . . . It's part of the package. (*He touches* MARTHE's *wrist. No response. He wanders round the terrace. Calls louder, to the house.*) Hello. (*To* MARTHE.) Pst! (*To himself:*) Tch tch. If I wake the lady will she be angry?

VOICE (*off, calls*): Vati!

GERMAN (*calls*): Soon! There's a good girl, Haidi! (*He smacks his hands together as if reprimanding a child and calls:*) Shush! (*He turns to* MARTHE:) The children are cross. I insisted to come up. Now the taxi's ticking over. The driver will charge extra. Sigi will sulk on the plane. (*Slightly tearfully.*) Only to press her hand . . .

Absent-mindedly he goes to the table, spreads jam on bread and eats it. Off, a car horn. He puts the flowers down and goes. DAVID *comes in. He wears a dressing-gown. He goes to the railing and looks at the sea.* ANN *comes in.*

ANN: I thought I heard a call.

DAVID (*grunt*): Who?

ANN (*to* MARTHE): Marthe.

DAVID: Let her sleep.

ANN: She wanted to eat with us.

DAVID (*goes to the table and sits*): She ate some bread. Not taken her tablet.

ANN *sits.* DAVID *pours coffee.*

ANN: She wouldn't tell me what they rowed about.

DAVID (*looks at his watch*): Your mother will.

ANN: Are you late?

DAVID: No.

ANN (*takes coffee*): Thank you.

DAVID: Don't go to the hotel.

ANN: I must see how my –

DAVID: To stay.

ANN: O no, how could I?

DAVID: I don't want to come between you and her. She'll have you all the time when you're gone.

ANN: She's not an ogress. She's kind if you let her.

DAVID: All things under the sun throw a shadow. Your mother throws hers towards the light.

ANN: Flowers. (*She picks up the flowers.*) A delivery man. That's who I heard.

DAVID: Are they for you?

ANN: The envelope's written in German. (*She gives it to* DAVID.)

DAVID (*reads. Looks up*): For you. 'An das schöne Fräulein in weiss.' To the beautiful girl in white.

ANN: How amazing.

DAVID: You wear white.

ANN: Sometimes.

DAVID: Expensive.

> ANN *opens the envelope, takes out a letter and gives it to* DAVID.

DAVID (*reads*): Merciful lady – (*He looks up.*) A common form of address in the German tongue. (*He reads.*) I could not end our holiday in your beautiful homeland without writing this letter. Not till after dinner on that memorable day did I realise I had again met the beautiful girl – (ANN *tries to snatch the letter,* DAVID *runs round the table reading,* ANN *chases him laughing*) – in white we gazed on so long ago. Believe an old but still active man when he speaks from the heart of the great debt he owes you. Merciful lady I understand why you did not speak to me on the boat. Happily you now understand the cause of my disrespect. When I deliver these flowers I shall press your hand in silence and let them speak for me. (DAVID *stops* ANN *with a gesture.*) You will be gratified to learn that Sigi and Haidi are safe. Their boat ran out of petrol. Friendly fishermen took them in tow. Alas there will be no time to present them to you. I have told them of our memorable meeting and will do so again many times in the years ahead. To the beautiful girl in white on the balcony of long ago with the humble respects of her dutiful Heinrich Hemmel. P.S. I am innocent. (*He stops reading.*) With an address.

ANN: They're for my mother. Some old flame. The balcony of long ago. What can it mean?

DAVID: The German we took in the boat. Put them in water.

ANN *goes out.* DAVID *takes a tablet and glass of water to* MARTHE. *He puts the tablet and glass on the floor. He feels her pulse. He kneels in front of her.* XENIA *comes in. She carries a light jacket.*

XENIA: David.

DAVID *presses* MARTHE's *hands against his face, kisses them and covers his hands with them.*

DAVID: She's warm. Her hands are still warm.

ANN *comes back with a large blue vase.* DAVID *begins to cry.*

Still warm. Give me something to cover her hands. Keep her warmth in. Don't let it go! Let me feel her warmth!

XENIA (*to* ANN): Is she – ?

DAVID: Help me! Anything! Anything! Her warmth will go!

ANN *takes* XENIA's *jacket and gives it to* DAVID. *He covers* MARTHE's *hands with it and presses his head against it.*

XENIA: I'm sorry. We had a quarrel. After a dreadful day on the island.

ANN: Go back to the hotel.

XENIA: No no I must stay. There are things to do. You'll need me.

ANN: Wait there. I'll come to you. Your flowers. (*She gives them to* XENIA.)

XENIA: Don't push me like that!

ANN: Please mother!

XENIA: As you wish. I'll send for my things. I won't put you to that trouble. You'll have enough to do.

ANN: Go on. I'll come soon. I won't be long.

XENIA: Stay here. I don't need you. I telephoned Daddy last night to say I'd come home today. Of course I'll stay for the funeral. What are these ugly flowers? (*She gives the flowers back to* ANN.) I'm sorry she's dead. I came to tell her I wasn't angry. My presence filled her with a great rage. It was bad for someone in her condition. If I'd known I'd never have come here.

> XENIA *goes.*
> DAVID *lifts* MARTHE *from the chair. Her feet are off the ground.* ANN *watches for a moment and then goes.* DAVID *presses* MARTHE'S *hands to his head.*

DAVID: Bless me. Bless me. Still warm . . .

> DAVID *lowers* MARTHE *to her knees and kneels before her. He presses her hands to his eyes and cries.*

SEVEN
[The Agreement]

The house. Day.
MARTHE'S *chair has been taken away.*
ANN *sits at the table and mechanically drinks coffee.*
DAVID *comes in.*

ANN: Shouldn't you lie down?
DAVID: No.
ANN: I'll come and hold you.
DAVID: I'm all right.

> *He sits at the table.*

I've seen so many deaths. I cried for them all this morning.

> ANN *pours coffee. He takes it but doesn't drink.*

ANN: I shall go back to England soon. I must find a new job.
DAVID: Perhaps we deceived ourselves. There may be no child.

ANN: I don't know yet.

DAVID: If there is will you keep it?

ANN: Yes.

DAVID: Alone?

ANN: If I have to.

DAVID: You must tell it I'm its father.

ANN: If it grew up I'd bring it to you. Mother must go to the funeral.

DAVID (*drinks coffee*): If you weren't here I'd say no. It's as you please.

ANN: Did she say where her ashes were to be thrown?

DAVID (*smiles*): In the garden.

Summer

Poems

Summer

I wanted to show how ordinary people lived
Married gave birth ate had holidays
And died
But clearly ordinary lives are strange
All who live now are survivors of wars and massacres and
    great dangers
We have witnessed the degeneration of our kind more than
    once
We still arm after the strategy of the insane
The starving queue up to die among us
All this is part of our daily life
To ignore it is as fatal as bearing its blows
But I wondered how we could bear it
The body is frail
The voice can be drowned by an engine
The young are taught folly

> Here is a simple story
> Of war and its aftermath
> Which shows that as we live in history
> We cannot learn to bear the unbearable but seek justice
> And praises those who share the earth

To The Audience

Relations between people can't be described without using
    values
But a play is about the nature of values
How can you know its meaning when you need values to
    find it?
Perhaps your values are being questioned
Certainly a play must question or strengthen them
Well, people are on the move and so doors are open
Communication is possible

The artist admits he may be wrong
He hopes he hasn't attracted your attention unnecessarily
He says only that to write the play he used the values by
    which he lives
And that in judging it you use the values by which you live
And show who you are – it is inescapable

Art can't avoid this effrontery
It describes the relations between people and so the
    spectator is judged
At least this makes criticism democratic
But remember: democracy is a more wrathful tyrant than a
    dictator

What Sort of Morality Is That!

Friends or enemies shake hands
Crowds wave at heroes and murderers
Judas kissed
On the Berlin Station platform the Mädchen gave a bouquet
To the SS chief who returned from inspecting the eastern
    camps
You can smile and smile
You can kneel in reverence or fear
Yet though it's true a workman spits on his hands
And to clean a child's face a mother will spit on her
    handkerchief
When someone spits at another a spit is a spit
Or is it?

Years after supervising the slaughter
Each morning an unnamed soldier drives to his office
How can we know what he is and so judge what he says and
    does
When he reaches his office?

The dead had a number tattooed on their arm
If we tattooed the soldier with all these numbers
He would be known
But he has too little skin
The numbers would run together
It would take many skins to record his crimes

It is hard for us to know ourselves
But at least we could bear our label so that others know us
And then we will bear the consequence of being ourself
Otherwise in the end
(Which isn't far: history sums up at least twice each
   century)
Others must bear it

Avoid hate as an obsession that clouds judgement
But forgiveness is not yours to give if the dead have paid for
   it
The dead are still unburied
(In this century wherever you turn the spade to bury them
You unearth others)
And then there are the living

You want to forgive the crimes that have not yet been
   committed
What sort of morality is that!

If

If Auschwitz had been in Hampshire
There would have been Englishmen to guard it
To administer records
Marshall transports
Work the gas ovens
And keep silent
The smoke would have drifted over these green hills

It's not that all men are evil or creatures of instinct
We – even our subjective self – are products of history
Of political change
In history two things join
Our will and things beyond our will
We change what we are as a means of controlling those
    things
That is: we create a new culture
We remain human only by changing
Each generation must create its own humanity

Our culture makes us barbarians
It does not allow us to live humanely
We must create a new culture
Or cease to be human
And the smoke will drift over these green hills

Always She Meant Well
(How a character is formed)

Always she meant well
But for some time there had been no need
For there to be rich and poor in her world
It was as if the poor were starved
So that she could bring soup to their door

This led to confusion
The poor disliked poverty and were grateful for handouts
But they resented the lady since in the end
They were asked to be grateful for being poor!

As she gave she saw the resentful smiles
She gave more and became harsh in her kindness
The smiles did not change
She meant well but they treated her so badly!

Her goodness seemed to bring out the worst in them!
Soon being good made her anxious
She turned into a misunderstood lady
Who helped the poor though they were undeserving
And supported everything that repressed them
Because she now knew they could not be trusted
And were a threat to civilization

You'd be surprised
How bitter and angry her goodness made her!
Out of kindness she brought forth reaction
Her world was unjust and had no place for kindness
Kindness became just another act of aggression